# BE THE CHANGE

# BE THE CHANGE

*Reinventing School for Student Success*

LINDA DARLING-HAMMOND

NICKY RAMOS-BEBAN

REBECCA PADNOS ALTAMIRANO

MARIA E. HYLER

**TEACHERS COLLEGE PRESS**

**TEACHERS COLLEGE** | COLUMBIA UNIVERSITY

NEW YORK AND LONDON

Published by Teachers College Press, 1234 Amsterdam Avenue, New York, NY 10027

Chapter 8 contains an excerpt from "EPA High prepares first graduating class for college" by N. Neroulias, which originally appeared in the *San Mateo County Times*, December 21, 2004. Used with permission of San Mateo County Times. Copyright © 2015. All rights reserved.

Chapter 8 contains an excerpt from "College may become unaffordable for most in U.S." by T. Lewin, which originally appeared in the *New York Times*, December 3, 2008. Used by permission. Copyright © 2008. All rights reserved.

*Library of Congress Cataloging-in-Publication Data is available at loc.gov*

Names: Darling-Hammond, Linda, 1951– author. | Ramos-Beban, Nicky, author. | Altamirano, Rebecca Padnos, author. | Hyler, Maria E., author.
Title: Be the change : reinventing school for student success / Linda Darling-Hammond, Nicky Ramos-Beban, Rebecca Padnos Altamirano, Maria E. Hyler.
Description: New York, NY : Teachers College Press, 2016. | Includes bibliographical references and index.
Identifiers: LCCN 2015031730| ISBN 9780807757437 (pbk. : alk. paper) | ISBN 9780807774526 (ebook)
Subjects: LCSH: East Palo Alto Academy (East Palo Alto, Calif.) | Low-income high school students—California—East Palo Alto. | Educational change—California—East Palo Alto. | Academic achievement—California—East Palo Alto.
Classification: LCC LC7501.E1385 D37 2016 | DDC 373.794/69—dc23
LC record available at http://lccn.loc.gov/2015031730

ISBN 978-0-8077-5743-7 (paper)
ISBN 978-0-8077-7452-6 (ebook)

Printed on acid-free paper

Manufactured in the United States of America

23  22  21  20  19  18  17  16          8  7  6  5  4  3  2  1

*In memory of Transito Torres, East Palo Alto Academy class of 2005*

# Contents

Contents

# Acknowledgments

Special acknowledgments are due to teachers William Dean, Tina Ehsanipour, Marisol de la Torre-Escobedo, and Seth Leslie, who contributed their heart and creativity to the school's founding as well as their recollections and artifacts to the writing of this book. In addition, researchers Donielle Prince and Donna Winston participated in evaluations of East Palo Alto Academy's work and outcomes that informed this volume.

The authors would like to thank all the people whose hard work and dedication to educational excellence made East Palo Alto Academy possible.

This includes the teachers, staff, student teachers, volunteers, and parents who worked at East Palo Alto Academy from 2001–2005, and especially the following: EPAA teachers and staff Itziar Apperibay, Danielle Bahr (formerly Wright), Gabriel Bailon, Misla Barco, Raul Betancourt, Bonnie Billings, Xochitl Acosta Brent, Jane Bryson, Marisol Castillo, Sharon Cravanas, Jerry Cronin, Bella Duran, Cristina Galvan, Angelita Garcia, Jeff Gilbert, David Heinke, Beth Injasoulian, Josephine Jimenez, Staci Kavanagh, Adrian Kirk, Tim Mansfield, Maura Marino, Manny Medina, Vanessa Michel, Simone Miller, David Nyquist, Gaylen Raisler, David Ramos-Beban, Dominique Revel Uskert, Ruth Robledo, Haydee Rodriguez, Nati Rodriguez, Rachael Shea, Brandy Spong, Julie Thompson, Leah Tuckman, and Kelly Wilson; EPAA student teachers Eva Davalos, Jon Deane, Corbert Elsen, Damian Ewens, Angelita Garcia, Sonya Gee, Nayelli Gonzalez, Van Lac, Heather Marshall, Yael Natori (formerly Proskuroski), Michelle Refuge, Robert Sohovich, and Tessa Yeager; EPAA adjunct staff Antonio Altamirano, Chris Brynelsen, Coach Gunn, Charlene Huber, Dana Kawano, Remarque Loy, Jeremy Milo, Margot Parker, Robert Ryan, and Karin Schlanger; AmeriCorps Interns Katrina Logan, Katie Morton, Sarah Press, and Eric Tygenhof; EPAA parents Marcelino Lopez, Guadalupe Martinez, Jacqueline Tuliau, and Olga Valadez; California State Assembly member Ira Ruskin; and former Santa Clara County Judge LaDoris Cordell.

The authors also would like to thank the Stanford University staff and faculty who provided essential support and guidance to EPAA: Stanford University School of Education Dean Deborah Stipek; development staff Heather Trippel Coleman and Rebecca Smith; Stanford professors Arnetha Ball, Shelley Goldman, Pam Grossman, Theresa LaFramboise, Guadalupe Valdés, and Sam Wineburg in the initial years, as well as Jo Boaler, Al Camarillo, Prudence

Carter, Claude Goldenberg, Kenji Hakuta, and Andrea Lunsford, in later years; Stanford Teacher Education Program (STEP) director Rachel Lotan and director of clinical work Ruth Ann Costanzo; STEP academic coaches Nancy Lobell, Jeannie Lythcott, and Jeff Zwiers; STEP supervisors Peter Lawrence and Laurie Stapleton; STEP staff Chandelle Black, Elizabeth Chesler, and Katie Miller; the Haas Center for Public Service, especially Jon McConnell, Jackie Schmidt-Posner, and Julie Wilson; the Lucile Packard Adolescent Health Van, especially Dr. Seth Ammerman, Dr. Eunice Mata, Heather Sorenson, and Lisa Westrich; the Black Community Services Center at Stanford, especially Associate Dean Jan Barker Alexander; El Centro Chicano, especially Associate Dean Frances Morales; the Stanford Institute for Diversity in the Arts, especially Executive Director Gina Hernandez; and a host of other present and former Stanford staff and students whose hard work made an indelible mark on EPAA, including Suzanne Abel, Renita Attardi-Rosenberg, Ali Bourjian, Lisa Marie Carlson, Carl Christopher, Sandra Dean, Pamela Ellis, Jessica Gimenez, Milica Gurney, Julie Henderson, Olivia Ifill-Lynch, Fusi Mahafutau, Django Paris, Charla Rolland, Elle Rustique-Forrester, Yvette Sarnowski, Fred Stout, Nancy Wall, and Amy Yuen.

The work of EPAA would not have been possible without a number of donors whose generous commitments of time and money helped fund some of the most important school programs, especially individuals including Bonnie Tenenbaum, Tashia Morgridge, Angela Nomellini, and Bill Somerville in the early years and Mindy Rogers in the later years; and foundations including the Bill and Melinda Gates Foundation, the Hewlett Foundation, the Morgan Family Foundation, the Stuart Foundation, the Woodrow Wilson National Fellowship Foundation (especially Rob Baird and Fred Frelow), and the Peninsula Community Foundation (now called Silicon Valley Community Foundation).

We also would like to thank the community organizations and their leaders who partnered with the school to help support EPAA's educational mission: Aspire Charter Management Organization, especially Don Shalvey and Heather Kirkpatrick; Cañada College, especially President Tom Mohr, Katie Townsend-Merino, and Marilyn McBride; Ravenswood City School District and its board of directors, especially Superintendents Charlie Mae Knight and Maria de la Vega; Sequoia Union High School District and its board of directors, especially Superintendent Pat Gemma; East Palo Alto City Council; Menlo Park City Council; One East Palo Alto; and the following not-for-profit organizations: Aspen Youth Experience; Boys and Girls Clubs of East Palo Alto; Boys and Girls Clubs of the Peninsula; BUILD, especially Suzanne McKechnie Klahr; Challenge Learning Center; College Track, especially founder Laurene Powell Jobs, along with Nicole Taylor and Marshall Lott; East Palo Alto Mural Project, especially Sonya Clark-Herrera; Foundation for College Education; Girls For A Change, especially Carrie Ellett; Outward Bound; Princeton

Review Foundation, especially Jay Rosner; Sojourn to the Past, especially Jeff Steinberg; Summer Search; and Upward Bound (now called Stanford College Prep), especially Christine Solari and Cathy Avila.

A special thank you is reserved for Peg Padnos, who thoughtfully read and edited early drafts of the book, and to Maude Engstrom, who supported the editorial process and offered extraordinary assistance in securing permissions for the book.

Finally, the authors would like to thank our spouses and significant others, and our families for their moral, emotional, and physical support. We worked long hours, late nights, and weekends; you hardly complained and you were proud of the work we were doing. Thank you!

## CHAPTER 1

# The Beginning of Hope

> It's a small school, with small classes; you can get the attention and support you need. The teachers at EPAA don't stop helping. They're relentless. They get on you . . . and it works.
>
> —East Palo Alto Academy graduate, class of 2005

On a warm Friday afternoon in June, an extraordinary scene unfolds: Stanford University's stately Memorial Auditorium fills to capacity with cheering families clutching signs and balloon bouquets. Usually the site of demure chamber concerts, the auditorium has the fever pitch of a rock concert as over one thousand mothers and fathers, sisters and brothers, aunts and uncles, cousins, grandparents, great-grandparents, and neighbors from East Palo Alto's African American, Latino, and Pacific Islander communities greet East Palo Alto Academy's first class of 66 high school seniors.

They are joined by university faculty and students, along with the school's own faculty, who have worked together to build the school over the previous 4 years. Together, their cheers and applause almost drown out the sound of the traditional *Pomp and Circumstance* recording.

Leading the procession are Stanford's provost, dean of the School of Education, and faculty sponsor for the school, along with the president of Aspire Public Schools (Stanford's partner in launching the school) and the faculty and graduating students of East Palo Alto Academy (EPAA).[1] As the seniors file down the main aisle of the auditorium, families turn to watch, punctuating their cheers with blasts from bullhorns. The students wave, grinning widely as they find their way to seats in front of the stage. Eventually seniors will approach the podium one by one, some adorned with red, green, and yellow kente stoles,[2] some draped in flower or money leis,[3] each to receive a diploma from his or her advisor and hugs and handshakes from the principal and university professors. As each graduate crosses the stage, there is another outburst of exuberant and unfettered cheering, weeping, clapping, and calling out of names from the family members—some of whom have traveled from Mexico, El Salvador, Tonga, and Samoa, as well as from across the United States.

The staggering support for this small high school's first graduating class gives an indication of what East Palo Alto Academy's class of 2005 means to the community: It is the first time East Palo Alto (EPA) has graduated a public high school class entirely its own since its former high school, Ravenswood, was closed in 1976 as a result of desegregation. Since that time, only about one-third of high school students from East Palo Alto had been graduating on time from the schools to which they were bused outside the community.[4] Many had been drawn into the school-to-prison pipeline that was expanding at a frightening rate in California.

Sixty-seven percent of EPAA's seniors are the first in their family ever to graduate from high school, despite being a few miles from some of the best high schools and colleges in the country. And in this first graduating class, 95% of the seniors, admitted nonselectively and representing the full range of students in the community, are walking across the stage. What's more, 90% of the graduates have been accepted to 2- or 4-year colleges: an outcome that has not occurred in a public school in this community . . . ever.

The list of college admissions includes East Coast private schools like Smith College and Mt. Holyoke, historically Black colleges like Grambling University, selective California privates like the University of Southern California and Santa Clara University, the full range of University of California and California State University campuses from Berkeley to Sonoma State, and numerous community colleges. The largest enrollment is expected at nearby Cañada College, with which East Palo Alto Academy has an Early College relationship that allowed students to receive college credits while in high school. Five graduates plan to attend postsecondary vocational institutes, and one has elected to serve his country by joining the Marines. All are firmly planted on a path to the future of their choosing.

## A TALE OF TWO CITIES

The moment is full of anomalies: In California's brave new world of school chartering, EPAA was created by an elementary school district that lacked a high school in its community for over a quarter-century. This founding brought together two very different communities: one of the nation's most elite universities with one of the lowest-income cities in California. In the thrilling moment of EPAA's first graduation, these two communities were joined by a common purpose—to change the historical trajectory of educational failure that has robbed the futures of so many East Palo Alto young people, and to plant the seeds of new possibilities in its place.

The home of many Stanford faculty and employees, the neighboring town of Palo Alto then had a per capita income of $56,000, more than four times the EPA average of $13,000. And while 75% of Palo Alto residents had at least a college degree, a comparable share of East Palo Alto residents had less than a high school education. Nearly all of EPA's families were African American (23%), Latino (59%), or Pacific Islander (7%), while these groups constituted only 6% of Palo Alto's population, almost all of whom were White (74%) or Asian (17%).[5]

The city of East Palo Alto is located in the heart of Silicon Valley, between San Jose to the south and San Francisco to the north. A few miles from Stanford University, East Palo Alto pushes up against the brown waters of the San Francisco Bay.

There could scarcely be two more different communities than wealthy Palo Alto and East Palo Alto, which was dubbed "murder capital" of the nation in 1992, when it topped the country's homicide rate with 39 killings within its small population of 30,000 in a tiny 2.5–square–mile territory. As the *Stanford Magazine* reported a few years later:

> Gunfire was so common that some residents slept in their bathtubs as stray bullets whistled past their windows. On New Year's Eve, police officers would cower in squad cars under freeway bridges while revelers went on shooting sprees. . . . East Palo Alto had become a kind of drive-through drug store for the Bay Area, with as many as 80 percent of the buyers coming in from surrounding towns. . . . The city has the highest unemployment rate in San Mateo County. No wonder teen-agers were easily lured into the lucrative crack cocaine trade.[6]

In 2000, about the time our story begins, homicide rates had declined somewhat, but EPA was still the highest crime community in the region. Separated physically from Palo Alto by an eight-lane highway and severed economically by the results of White flight and redlining, East Palo Alto was cut off from the vast wealth of Silicon Valley in every conceivable way.

And many of its young people were cut off from hope. Given the levels of unemployment in the community and failure in the schools, the drug trade was almost the only option many young people perceived. As they became teenagers, many young men adopted a recklessness borne of the conviction they would not grow to adulthood.

East Palo Alto Academy was designed to bridge the distance between the two worlds of East Palo Alto and Stanford, and to create a college-preparatory school dedicated to the adolescents of EPA and neighboring east Menlo Park.[7] This hybrid mission—to create college opportunities for students, while not giving up on those who didn't embrace this mission from the start—earned the school a reputation for giving students a new beginning and holding on to them when others had given up.

## A SCHOOL OF OUR OWN

The idea for the school first began in the mind of Charlie Mae Knight, the long-time superintendent of the Ravenswood City School District, which serves the East Palo Alto community. Ever since 1985, when she took on the post, Knight had wanted to bring a high school back to what was then a virtually all-Black community. However, as the leader of an elementary school district, her options for doing so were limited without the cooperation of the associated high school district—in this case the Sequoia Union High School District (SUHSD).

California still preserves separate elementary and high school districts in many communities, a historical artifact of the creation of school districts serving younger children before secondary education was added. At that time, the newly created high schools typically served several elementary school districts. In this case, students came to Sequoia Union High School District from several well-heeled elementary districts in Woodside, Portola Valley, and Menlo Park, as well as the more economically and ethnically diverse Redwood City and the highly segregated, high-poverty East Palo Alto. At this point, SUHSD was not interested in re-establishing a high school in EPA.

### A Contentious History

The story of how the East Palo Alto community lost its high school and what happened as a result is a classic tale of race and class divisions in America. Ravenswood High School, which opened in 1958 in the heart of East Palo Alto, was operated by the Sequoia Union High School District. Before it celebrated its 20th birthday, this once predominantly White and working-class high school had become largely African American. Meanwhile, with the help of blockbusting in the early 1960s,[8] East Palo Alto had transformed from a working-class, mixed-race enclave to a largely African American city, sitting next to the affluent White towns of Menlo Park and Atherton (also part of the Sequoia District), as well as Palo Alto (which had its own school district).

In the early 1970s, the Sequoia District school board instituted a districtwide busing program to increase the diversity of all its high schools. This was successful for a few years, but by the mid-1970s the number of students from nearby communities wishing to attend Ravenswood High School declined. Meanwhile, racial schisms grew in a number of the district's schools, and race riots erupted at several high schools, including Ravenswood. Facing financial issues and the need to rethink its approach to desegregation, the district decided to close Ravenswood High School in 1976 and to bus all of the students to its other schools in communities across Interstate 101.

So began the legacy of schooling for East Palo Alto adolescents: With the early morning sun, Black and Brown students would arise across the city and head out to corner bus stops to await the long yellow school buses. The commute to the largely White and upper-class neighborhoods where their assigned high schools were located could take up to 60 minutes each way.

The only way to escape this fate of busing was to try to attend one of the nearby Palo Alto high schools, ranked among the top in the state and nation.[9] Even though both cities share a border and a name, the cities are in different counties, and, legally, East Palo Alto students may not attend Palo Alto schools. In 1974, Margaret Tinsley and 33 other concerned parents filed a lawsuit against Palo Alto School District, hoping to gain equal educational access for minority students.

In 1986, the California Supreme Court ruled that only a select group of students, members of what came to be called the "Tinsley" program, would be allowed to attend Palo Alto schools. In order to have their children selected, parents had to complete a complex and difficult application process. After 2nd grade, children were no longer eligible to apply. Thus, East Palo Alto teenagers could not attend Palo Alto High Schools unless they had attended Palo Alto Elementary Schools since their early years of elementary school. Since 1986, 166 East Palo Alto students—fewer than 5% of EPA's school-age children—have enrolled annually in Palo Alto schools. The vast majority of EPA children attend one of the 13 Ravenswood District schools in either East Palo Alto or east Menlo Park, which enroll 99% students of color and more than 95% low-income students.

The preservation of stark segregation has been further maintained by another set of rules in nearby, mostly White and wealthy Menlo Park. Although they are in the same county, east Menlo Park students (mostly Latino and African American) cannot enroll in Menlo Park schools west of Interstate 101 except for those operated by the Ravenswood District. However, the mostly White and upper-class students living next door to the Ravenswood District schools in west Menlo Park do not have to attend those schools. Instead, they are allowed access to the further-away Menlo Park Elementary District if they submit a petition.

If and when they reach 8th grade, East Palo Alto and east Menlo Park students receive a letter assigning them to one of four Sequoia District high schools based on their address. A follow-up letter welcoming students to their new high school district contains a school bus schedule and directions to the bus stop where they will begin their daily commute. When they arrive at their far-flung destinations, EPA students typically are tracked into lower-level classes (in what are variously called lanes, tracks, or streams), where they are segregated from most of the rest of the school population. As noted earlier, in 2000 when our story begins, only about one-third of students from East Palo

Alto and east Menlo Park would graduate 4 years later, and an even smaller number would be prepared for and admitted to college.

Despite the efforts of many good-hearted educators who sought to create a wide range of programs to address the poor outcomes resulting from this structural segregation—for example, AVID programs and Career Academies in many of the high schools, the RISE program at Menlo-Atherton, and many more—only relatively few students were enabled to succeed. Two decades after the inception of the busing program, a movement developed within the East Palo Alto community: Give us back our high school!

## A New Beginning

Several things came together to create the opportunity. One of us (Linda Darling-Hammond) had come to Stanford a couple of years earlier from New York City, where she had been on the faculty of Teachers College, Columbia University, and involved in the movement to create new, small public high schools there with innovative educators like Deborah Meier, Ann Cook, Cece Cunningham, Olivia Ifill-Lynch, Eric Nadelstern, and others. She became involved in East Palo Alto in some volunteer roles and served on the board of Center for a New Generation,[10] where she met Charlie Mae Knight, the Ravenswood City School District superintendent. Linda had begun to work with educators in the Bay Area on the creation of innovative small school models like those in New York.

One day in the late summer of 2000, Linda opened the local newspaper to find an article quoting Charlie Mae saying she wanted to start a high school in EPA and wanted to work with Stanford to do so.[11] Linda called Charlie Mae to find out what she had in mind, and learned she wanted to launch a charter school that would be a partnership between the district, the university, and Aspire Public Schools, one of California's first charter schools organizations, led by former San Carlos School District superintendent Don Shalvey. California's 1992 Charter School Act, enacted as part of an effort to create incentives for innovation while fighting off a statewide voucher school ballot initiative,[12] provided the means for elementary districts, like Ravenswood, to create their own high schools by chartering them. This would be Aspire's first high school effort.

Linda, Charlie Mae, and Don met shortly thereafter; Stanford's dean approved the partnership; a number of Stanford faculty and students volunteered to help; and by February 2001, the Ravenswood board had approved the charter. Local papers ran the story under the headline: "High School Coming Back to Ravenswood" and quoted Superintendent Knight as saying: "It's a dream come true for me."[13]

Although the charter ultimately passed the board unanimously, all was not love and roses in the months leading up to the vote. In early conversations with board members and others in the community, some voiced long-held resentments and suspicions about Stanford's commitment and motives. As in many "town and gown" contexts where contrasts of race and class are also prominent, there was what some would characterize as a "Peace Corps problem": Faculty and students who would cross the highway to "help" were sometimes less than fully skilled or culturally sensitive, and sometimes more focused on the welfare of their research studies than the lives of the people they saw themselves as "saving."

Despite some genuinely important and long-lasting efforts, like Stanford's legal clinics, health care initiatives, and tutoring supports, there were plenty of university projects that had come and gone, not all of them well managed or genuinely helpful.

It was important to demonstrate that the team involved with launching the charter school was knowledgeable about the community and its families, had a viable plan that would serve the students and the community well, was not there to "experiment" on the children, and was committed for the long haul.

The school's commitment to a small, personalized design that had proven successful in other urban districts; a culturally responsive, project-based curriculum; supportive literacy instruction for English learners and Standard English learners; and a diverse, highly professional staff devoted to parent involvement were all important to gaining the trust of the community and board. The first principal, Nicky Ramos-Beban, was a well-respected teacher leader from a nearby high school district whose welcoming manner and fluency in Spanish facilitated her relationships with parents and community members, most of whom were native Spanish speakers.

## FIRST STEPS

Despite the enthusiasm on all sides, challenges appeared from the very start. When the Ravenswood City School District board approved the charter for the new high school,[14] the old Ravenswood High School buildings had already been torn down for development of a major retail center. The school board granted the high school a temporary location: space at a run-down, 20-room elementary school that already housed two K–8 schools with declining enrollment.[15] As they phased down, the new school would grow, opening with 9th grade and adding a grade each year. Deferred maintenance led to plumbing disasters and wiring inadequacies, but these did not dampen the energy the new faculty brought to their task.

Within months of charter approval, a dozen teachers were hired, most of them graduates of the Stanford Teacher Education Program (STEP), and a handful of Stanford faculty enlisted, all working together to design the high school and its curriculum. They spent the summer working intensively with Linda, who became EPAA's faculty sponsor, and Heather Kirkpatrick, then a Stanford graduate student, who went to work for Aspire.

The founding teachers studied the best practices and design features of other small schools, specifically focusing on New York City, where the small schools movement had been thriving since the late 1980s. Teachers went on several study tours to visit schools and brought back artifacts like curriculum, bell schedules, and program descriptions. They read *The Right to Learn* by Linda Darling-Hammond[16] and Deborah Meier's *The Power of Their Ideas.*[17] They studied course, exhibition, and advisory handbooks from the schools they visited and other schools with similar visions. They also attended a school design retreat hosted by the Stanford School Redesign Network, where they connected with leaders from the school reform movement and educators who were creating other small schools. There they finalized the concrete plans that fleshed out the design of the school.

## The School's Design

The founding teachers agreed on the mission of East Palo Alto Academy: to create *a united community that educates and empowers students for high levels of success in college, the workplace and society.* An empowering education was defined in the mission statement as students' ability to

> collect information, think systematically and critically about that information, create new knowledge and effectively express and apply their thinking to real world problems. The information with which they engage may be a novel, a choreographed dance piece, a set of statistics, a newspaper report, a historical account, or a scientific article. The expression of student thinking may come in an essay, a painting, a poem, an oral presentation, a one-act play, a mathematical argument, or a scientific rebuttal. The point is that students will graduate from EPAA with the ability to access, use, and analyze information, produce new knowledge and respond critically and thoughtfully.

The school pledged to foster the habits of intellectual curiosity, independent learning, analytic ability, creative expression, moral reasoning, and empathetic action, in order to enable students to become self-motivated, competent, and lifelong learners. It adopted the following design elements to accomplish these goals:

- *Small and personalized,* with intensive, long-term adult–student relationships designed into the structure. These are fostered through a small school size (300 students), a staffing plan enabling small classes, and an advisory program in which each teacher serves as an advisor for 15–18 students for all 4 years of high school, meeting with them daily to support their academic, social, and emotional development; guiding their progress; and communicating with their parents.[18]

- **Project-based, performance-oriented, and college preparatory,** where every student has the opportunity to take a full suite of courses for college admission. Projects create opportunities to apply learning to complex problems, as well as to develop products that require written and oral expression, extended research, analysis and synthesis of information, planning, perseverance, and organization—all skills that are needed for success in college and the world beyond. Projects also link the curriculum content with students' real-world experiences, making learning relevant and valuable to their lives outside of school. Students demonstrate mastery and growth through performance assessments, which they present and defend to a graduation committee.
- **Multiple paths to learning,** including a multicultural curriculum and culturally responsive pedagogy, differentiated instruction, and many kinds of learning activities to suit different learning needs, ranging from traditional classes to local college and community college classes, online coursework, service learning, and internships outside of school.
- **Flexible supports** without labeling or tracking, which help students to negotiate the demands of challenging curriculum and assignments. These include, for example, in-school academic supports, after-school and Saturday office hours and tutoring, and advisors who are responsible for the progress of a small group of students.
- **Highly competent and supported educators,** who are well prepared, are committed to ongoing professional learning and collaboration, and agree to pursue National Board Certification (NBC) within their first 5 years at EPAA. Time for professional development and teacher collaboration is scheduled each week to support teachers in designing student-focused curriculum, pedagogy, and assessment, and learning from one another.
- **Engagement with the community** through students' community service and internships, informal community gatherings, formal meetings with parents and others to experience and evaluate student projects and portfolios, and partnerships with community organizations to benefit the education of students and adults.

In addition to these design features, the school was organized to serve as a *professional development school* for the Stanford Teacher Education Program, helping to develop student teachers under the mentoring of EPAA faculty while they complete the coursework for their teaching credential and master's degree in education. STEP and the Graduate School of Education also agreed to support professional development for veteran teachers and to partner in curricular and program development and initiatives. A wide range of faculty took up these various tasks.

Ultimately, the school also benefited from many other contributions from the university:

- A health van provided by Lucile Packard Children's Hospital to offer health services every 2 weeks
- Ongoing mental health services also provided by Lucile Packard Children's Hospital
- A mentoring program run by Stanford Law School students
- Summer school on Stanford's campus offered through the Urban Studies program
- Online courses for selected students
- Technology supports and training
- Books for the EPAA library collected by Stanford students from El Centro Chicano and the Black Community Service Center
- Ongoing fundraising to cover the costs that the state's meager public education budget would not support

## The Launch

On September 4, 2001, East Palo Alto Academy opened with its first group of 9th-graders. Tragically, 1 week into the very first semester, the September 11th attacks occurred. This national crisis cast a somber pall over the first few months of the school year. Even though East Palo Alto was far removed from Manhattan and Washington, DC, everyone felt the pain of those attacked and the weight of our nation's vulnerability. Although teachers emphasized tolerance and respect for all people, EPAA students saw many Americans responding to the tragedy with fear and intolerance toward Muslims and other minorities. They had known racism in their own lives and recognized its reach. In reflections and discussions with one another and their teachers, this first class began their high school careers engaging the fundamental American dilemma that had led to the launch of their little school.

Meanwhile, the teachers had worked hard to create a rich, discipline-based, and interdisciplinary curriculum. The veteran staff brought with them the well-honed products of their previous experiences. The newer teachers brought with them their recently acquired knowledge, creativity, and willingness to collaborate in inventing an engaging set of learning experiences for their students. The faculty was ready.

Then the students arrived. It became clear very quickly that their skill levels were not those expected of a typical group of 9th-graders, even a very

*9th graders*
*start of school year*
↑

heterogeneous one. The average reading achievement was at the 3rd-grade level; the average mathematics level was 4th grade. Some students had little or no English, while others had developed conversational skills but did not have an academic vocabulary in English. All students needed support in developing academic language.

Although staff knew in a general way that many students from Ravenswood would likely need additional supports, they were unprepared for the large skill gaps presented by what turned out to be, to a great extent, the neediest subset of a high-needs group. The effects of ongoing school budget cuts and deepening household poverty had made this one of the lowest-performing districts in a state that also was rapidly declining educationally. The effects on educational outcomes were shocking to educators who were new to the area.

Furthermore, the majority of the most academically able 8th-graders from the community were recruited by two fully subsidized private schools in the community. Of the remainder, this new school attracted many students who were viewed by their parents or middle school staff as unable to cope in the large high schools otherwise available to them. Most cumulative folders did not arrive from the district until well into the school year. So it was not until teachers met students, some of whom could barely read or write, that they fully comprehended what would be needed to support students' eventual success.

Although in most nearby high schools these students would have been relegated to a remedial curriculum dominated by worksheets and rote learning of basic skills, EPAA teachers realized their students would need to learn basic skills while simultaneously undertaking the college-preparatory curriculum the school had committed to offer. Teachers would need to figure out how to teach multiplication and division while tackling algebra, and how to teach decoding skills while bringing *Romeo and Juliet* and *In the Time of the Butterflies*[19] to life. Undaunted, staff set out to redesign their curriculum to accommodate these needs, maintaining their commitment to a school without tracking that would provide every student with the knowledge and skills that would ensure a productive future.

## THIS BOOK

At the start of that first year, with equal parts hope and trepidation, the teachers, students, and community started on a journey that continues today. In this book, we focus on the beginning years of the school, leading up to its first graduating class in 2005. We follow a small set of representative students and their teachers to illustrate how the dilemmas were tackled, how the commitments were maintained, and how the design of the school evolved to embrace opportunities and meet challenges.

In less detail, we also update the story to the present, describing both the educational and political issues the school has faced. Over all these years, through ups and downs, while admitting and holding onto some of the highest-need students in the state, the school managed to graduate its students and send them to college at rates far above the state and local averages for their peers.

*achievements*

In 2014 as this book was being written, its tenth graduating class featured, among other joys, a celebration of the first East Palo Alto Academy student to be admitted to Stanford University as an undergraduate. A few years earlier, one of the members of the first graduating class had been admitted to the Stanford graduate school's teacher education program. She is now teaching in the Bay Area. When Soledad Ramirez,[20] the first person in her immigrant family to finish high school, chose to attend Stanford after being admitted to a dozen of the most selective universities in the country, EPAA once again demonstrated what it had set out to prove: that demography is indeed not destiny.

Also in 2014, the school was finally able to return to the community as part of the Sequoia Union High School District in a new facility designed to be a real high school.

The story is at once an inspiring and a frightening tale. It is a tale of a fight to save the lives of hundreds of young people, one at a time—succeeding with most, but losing some in heartbreaking ways. It is a tale of educators partnering with a community to envision and grasp a new future—one in which its young people attain once-unimaginable success, inspire their siblings and young cousins, and return to the community as leaders.

It is also a tale of fractious education politics during one of the most contentious times in American history, peppered by fiscal crises, charter wars, high-stakes testing, and punitive accountability focused on schools just like this one: those serving students of color and English learners in communities with growing poverty, unemployment, incarceration, and violence. During these early years, East Palo Alto Academy was one of a growing number of "apartheid schools," starved of the resources needed to serve students who had become victims of what Gloria Ladson-Billings has called "aggressive neglect."[21]

The school's survival was threatened over and over again, sometimes by gangs, violence, or politics in the community, but more often by federal, state, and local government policies that have been steadily abandoning our most vulnerable children and punishing the people who are willing to serve them. In the No Child Left Behind era and the fiscal crises that followed, the strategy of testing rather than investing created incentives to narrow the curriculum, push out struggling students, and drive out all but the most committed educators from high-needs communities.

Mostly, the story of EPAA is a tale of perseverance, resilience, creativity, and grit, as teachers, students, families, and concerned people of conscience from the two communities that had pledged to work together met and surmounted one obstacle after another, day after day, week after week, month after month, and year after year.

The book is organized to illustrate the design themes described earlier. After Chapter 2, which introduces the context and the characters, each succeeding chapter takes up one of the critical elements that support students' success: personalization (Chapter 3), the creation of an academic culture (Chapter 4), the development of high standards with high supports (Chapter 5), the process of learning to teach so that students can learn (Chapter 6), and the establishment of the school as a professional place (Chapter 7). In Chapter 8, we discuss the school's outcomes, including students' experiences after high school. Finally, in Chapter 9, we describe the continuing journey, including the school's voyage through the political and fiscal shoals of a turbulent period in educational history, and its implications for addressing the issues that face so many underresourced schools in minority and low-income communities in the United States today.

We conclude that the answers are to be found not in governance changes— although chartering allowed a new approach to be tried when previous approaches clearly had failed—but in a long-term commitment to building wisely resourced, community-based schools that connect caring professionals with families and children.

This book chronicles how two communities came together to plant a new model for schooling that could transform the educational experience offered to students. These innovators followed Gandhi's advice, "Be the change you wish to see in the world." In the end, the students internalized the message that all of this effort was intended to support them and came to believe, as one of the first graduates announced: "You can accomplish anything."

## CHAPTER 2

# The Kids, the Community, and the Context

> What I like about East Palo Alto High is the attention and support we get from our teachers. . . . I like the fact that the teachers are very concerned about us students. They give us freedom to think on our own. . . . Teachers here help you with what you are doing and with what you want to do.
>
> —EPAA student

We began Chapter 1 in 2005 with the graduation of the first class of seniors from what was then called East Palo Alto High School (later to become East Palo Alto Academy). By that time, the school was serving 300 students in grades 9–12 and maintaining a waiting list for freshmen and sophomores wanting to enroll.

Because of the sharp break from the past represented by this new public high school in a community that had lacked one for a quarter-century, the unusual partnership between East Palo Alto and Stanford, and the extraordinary outcomes achieved for the students, the moment was noteworthy. Many of the seniors from the first graduating class were featured in local newspapers and highlighted on television and radio news.

One memorable television interview was with Pablo Fuentes, a graduating senior, who by his own admission had started high school as a "troublemaker" who engaged in petty theft and expected to land in jail like his older brother. Four years later, he was a leader in his class who routinely took other students under his wing and who was about to leave for college at a flagship public university in a nearby state. Intrigued by this story, a national television reporter asked to interview Pablo at the apartment where he lived with relatives. When asked to show the reporter his bedroom, Pablo pointed to a portion of the family room floor, where he slept. When he moved into his sister's small apartment, that was the only space available. Undaunted, Pablo had come to excel in high school.

Similar memories of all 66 seniors from the class of 2005 still loom large in the minds of the teachers who worked alongside them for 4 years. This book follows a small group of five students who represent different facets of EPAA's story. While the students' struggles and successes are their own, their experiences highlight the array of academic structures the school created to support them on their journey from freshman to senior year. We introduce the five students briefly below and tell their stories in more depth throughout the narrative. In addition, voices from the other 61 students of the class of 2005, as well as from graduates of other classes, many parents, and EPAA faculty speak throughout the narrative.

## THE STUDENTS

### Pablo Fuentes

By the time he graduated near the top of his class, it was hard to believe that during his middle school years Pablo was focused on getting high every morning and stealing in the afternoons. His parents recognized that he was on a fast track to jail—the same place his older brother was heading and eventually would end up. In his college entrance essay, Pablo chronicled his transformation from a youth struggling with his circumstances to a college-bound student:

> I was a boy who had a steady diet of beatings because I did . . . what my parents would tell me not to do. I witnessed my father try to kill my mother. Soon enough I was a troublesome boy taking bike rides down to the local K-Mart to steal clothes. Fortunately for me, I got caught with my brother stealing at Target. When we got back home, our parents had heard the message left by the authorities, and days later I was going back home to El Salvador. "But this home," my parents told me, "is nothing like you expect, and everything that you will hate." I did not want to go.

Pablo spent a year working in the fields of El Salvador under the blazing hot sun. The hard labor and the long walks to and from the fields made him appreciate his life in California. He vowed to himself that he would return reformed.

> I worked from 6 A.M. to 7 P.M. and had barely enough to eat. I cried and realized that what I had back in the U.S., I didn't deserve. I slowly shed my skin and became a compassionate, understanding, and, most of all, a loving person.

When Pablo returned from El Salvador, East Palo Alto Academy became his new home.

> Going to school was my only sanctuary. Before then, I did not value education because I thought it was an everyday thing and, plus, I

thought that it was cool not do my schoolwork and to disrespect my teachers. However, I would remember my stay in El Salvador and how hundreds of children hungered for an education they would never get.

Tall, lean, and strong with soft brown eyes and dark, curly hair, Pablo was not afraid to stand out and be unique. He was a charismatic mix of sweet and boisterous, sensitive and playful. He was just as likely to come to school in spray-painted jeans as he was to sport a button-down shirt with handwritten poetry in his pocket. His exuberant personality filled any room he entered. On campus he was a leader of a clique of boys who modeled their behavior on the infamous show *Jackass*. While the group often behaved outlandishly, Pablo was also sensitive, almost to an extreme.

During high school, Pablo lived with his sister, who was his main pillar of familial support, especially after Pablo's mother returned to El Salvador during his sophomore year. Pablo's sister, who had left high school just a few months shy of graduation, worked long hours at a grocery store and did her best as a single mother to provide for her two young children and for her brother. For some time, Pablo lived in a toolshed at the back of his sister's house; he preferred this solitary lifestyle so that the household noises did not distract him from his schoolwork. Later, as he told the television reporter, he slept on the floor in the family room of her new apartment. Pablo spent much of this time reflecting on his life and writing copious amounts of poetry that often moved him and his readers to tears.

After high school Pablo moved to a Rocky Mountain state to attend a 4-year university, where he studied mathematics and eventually majored in women's studies. He wanted to go away to a college where he was totally unknown, where he could reinvent himself yet again.

## Malcolm Davis

Almost the polar opposite of Pablo was Malcolm Davis, a shy and sensitive student who entered East Palo Alto Academy determined to break away from his special education status.

A checkered experience in elementary and middle school had created a student lacking self-confidence, challenged by many basic concepts in reading, math, and other staples of a core curriculum. Malcolm was an adolescent wrestling with contradictions—wanting to fit in, but so fearful of failure that he refused to participate in class.

As an elementary school student, Malcolm resented the special education services offered to him, and by the time he reached 6th grade, everything started to fall apart. He struggled to grasp multiplication, and his teacher could not understand why he was not getting it. Neither could he, for that matter. She also noticed that his reading skills, especially decoding and comprehension, were far below grade level. Malcolm would not acknowledge his learning differences so he did not cooperate with the teacher or her aide. Finally, he had to acknowledge the truth when his elementary school teacher pulled him out of class in front of the other kids to attend special education sessions. Malcolm hid under a desk when the resource teacher came into the room. "I felt like a dog being pursued by the dogcatcher," Malcolm recalled, "and when I would get pinned down to go to that other classroom with that person, I felt like a dog tag with an inscription 'special ed' had been put around my neck."

As a freshman at EPAA, Malcolm walked alone down the hallway, head bowed and avoiding eye contact, with a slow starting–stopping gait, as if he were looking for a lost object or flustered by not knowing his way to class. Malcolm wore thick horn-rimmed eyeglasses, with a wool cap pulled low on his acned forehead; he rarely smiled. His body language said it all: "Don't look at me. I want to be invisible."

But Malcolm could not be invisible at East Palo Alto Academy. He was asked to work one-on-one with his reading specialist, Simone Miller, to raise his reading ability from the 2nd-grade level, where he tested when he enrolled, to high school level, which he achieved by the time he graduated. And invisible or not, Malcolm made friends with Pablo's boisterous posse, who accepted him into their group. Eventually, Malcolm's hard work and emerging social skills yielded fruit: personal confidence and a high school diploma.

## Esperanza Ramirez

Esperanza Ramirez was a student as isolated as Malcolm but for entirely different reasons. Just prior to her freshman year, she had left her native El Salvador, traveling for 2 months, including 3 days of walking to cross the U.S. border and the Arizona desert, to reunite with her mother in the Bay Area. A petite 15-year-old freshman with fierce, dark eyes and long black hair, Esperanza spoke only a few words and phrases in English when she entered 9th grade.

When Esperanza was a baby, her mother and father had come to America seeking better opportunities, leaving their daughter in El Salvador in the care of her grandmother and older sister. A few years after arriving in California, Esperanza's father was murdered at gunpoint while walking in East Palo Alto. Esperanza's mother remarried not long after and had two children with her new husband in California.

When her mother sent for her, Esperanza traveled with other immigrants, shepherded by *coyotes*,[1] by bus, van, and on foot—including the 3 days crossing the Arizona desert—until they finally reached California. In her own words, it was the single thought of reuniting with her family on Mother's Day that kept her 4'10" body walking through the intense desert heat.

My little shadow walking with the shine of the moon reflected a weak girl who had lost her energy and could barely walk. . . . But my power came from my dreams and my goals. I wished to meet my mom and my two brothers who were born in the United States, and I intended to go to college.

Life turned out to be less than idyllic when she rejoined her family, and Esperanza was eventually diagnosed with post-traumatic stress disorder. But with the support of EPAA teachers, mental health professionals who were part of the school's wraparound supports, and the friends she gradually acquired, Esperanza regained her footing. By the time she was a senior, not only was Esperanza fluent in English and the co-captain of the EPAA girls varsity soccer team, but she also had earned acceptance to several 4-year universities. Esperanza graduated from a University of California campus, became a legal resident of the United States, and began working as an AmeriCorps Intern and then as a teacher's aide in East Palo Alto.

## Lena Fasu

As inspiring as Esperanza was, she would be the first to admit that one of her role models was another student in her class, Lena Fasu, a standout from her first day at East Palo Alto Academy. A tall Samoan girl with long black hair, brown eyes, and skin the color of coffee with cream, Lena was one of the 10% of Pacific Islanders in the freshman class. Lena was an interesting blend of "fit right in" and "stick out like a sore thumb." She was mature for her age and had a stronger idea than most of her peers about what she wanted from her life and how EPAA could help her achieve those goals.

As the eldest of five children, 22 grandchildren, and 62 cousins, Lena was not left alone to make decisions about her future. The entire family was watching her progress, taking notes, and drawing conclusions. Most important, they were all counting on her to graduate and move on to higher education. She would be the first of her generation and one of a handful in her family to attain that goal. In her personal statement for college, Lena reflected on this:

Sitting in our small Hyundai, as my two younger siblings cried in the backseat, I thought about my future intensely. I thought of my aunts, uncles, cousins, parents, and where we were as a family. We were all stuck in this box constructed by drugs, violence, and crime; East Palo Alto, California, was my home, but not where I wanted to live for the rest of my life. Every morning there was a battle to be faced, often beginning with the frustration of financial problems, or just hearing about the violence going on within my neighborhood. Still, life had to be lived, bills had to be paid, and, in my case, changes were about to be made. I took it upon myself, the oldest of 22 grandchildren, to be the first to make a difference, not only for my well-being, but for my family as well.

Although it seemed that Lena carried the weight of the world on her shoulders with these expectations, one would never know it after 5 minutes in her warm presence. Lena was immensely adept at code-switching and could just as easily fit in with a group of immature boys as she could with the fledgling staff. She consistently came to school prepared and with a positive attitude. Unlike most of her peers, she already knew she was going to college and that she would be spending the next 4 years building the best possible resume.

Lena was also a consistent example of adolescent integrity in the freshman class. Students and staff could count on Lena to do or say the right thing, whether it was setting an example by working cooperatively in class, completing all her homework, passing her exhibitions with distinction, or standing up for an unpopular idea or an ostracized peer. When teachers normed their assessments, Lena was the standard against which other students' work was measured. If EPAA had had a student body president, Lena would have been it, because her peers recognized her as a leader among their ranks.

Lena took advantage of every opportunity the school offered, excelling in both her high school classes and the college classes she was able to take as part of the school's Early College program. She completed 30 college credits while still in high school and carried them with her to a University of California campus, completing a degree in English in only 3 years. Still, she argued, "I would have been lost in the crowd at a big [high] school. EPAA provided me with the kind of attention I needed to succeed."

## Kristine Lewis

As helpful as Lena was to her teachers, Kristine Lewis was every bit as vexing. Thin and athletic, Kristine obeyed no rules of conduct except her own. She came to East Palo Alto Academy from a historically prominent and politically active African American family in the East Palo Alto community. Sadly, Kristine's mother died when she was in 8th grade, and when Kristine entered 9th grade, she was still in a state of grief and anger over her mother's death. Kristine's father was absent. When asked, she said her father was dead, but no one was quite sure whether that meant literally or figuratively dead. Kristine lived a volatile life in a violent neighborhood. She changed residences often, going back and forth between her grandmother's house and her sister's across the street. During her senior year, her older brother was murdered in her grandmother's home.

When she entered high school, Kristine had both remarkable personal presence and a great deal of anger. Kristine met Nicky, the school's principal and her first advisor, before East Palo Alto Academy officially opened, in a local television studio. The station was doing a program called *Young Pioneers*, and Nicky was invited to join three of EPAA's incoming freshmen to talk about their plans to attend the new high school. Kristine looked strong and confident wearing a University of North Carolina t-shirt over her thin frame, her hair pulled back into a tight ponytail, with no makeup or jewelry. When asked why she wanted to attend EPAA, Kristine stared straight into the camera and declared: "I think we all know that in a small school you have less violence and you learn more." Such a strong statement—"I think we all know"—was striking for a girl of 14 and indicative of Kristine's sense of self.

When asked whether she thought the violence in her community would abate, Kristine answered quickly and without mincing words: "I don't think. I know." When pressed to provide a specific example of what *she* could do to improve the situation, Kristine answered with straightforward conviction: "All you've got to do is be a good role model and do what you're supposed to do and once everybody sees you doing what you're supposed to do, they be like, 'Hmmm, she does this and they say it's OK, so maybe I should do that, too.'"

Kristine was remarkable for her sense of agency and her ability to command attention at such a young age. As the president of her 8th-grade class, she was already versed in leadership skills, and during the talk show she remarked that she led through example, "by going to class on time, making sure I have my homework in. . . . If other students see me doing that they'll want to do it too. They'll want to be just like me." This sense of a clear direction in life set her apart from many of her peers. When asked what staying focused in life meant to her, Kristine answered, "It means to set a goal for yourself and do whatever you have to do to achieve that goal. Keep your eyes on it, focus on it, make sure you're doing it."

And Kristine definitely could focus in these ways, but when and how was decidedly unpredictable; her simmering anger was always just below the surface. One never knew whether Kristine would respond to a routine question with a thoughtful answer or an epithet-laced insult. She could disrupt a class and then complain that students were not doing enough work. Her teachers and advisors spent many hours trying to figure out how to meet her needs while still developing and maintaining respectful norms in the school. Ultimately, Kristine beat the statistical odds not only as the first in her family to attend and complete college, but also as an African

American teen from East Palo Alto, who was more likely at that time to land in jail than in college.[2]

## THE COMMUNITY

East Palo Alto's reputation as a dangerous place has stuck regardless of many grassroots efforts to revitalize the city in the 1980s and 1990s and despite much outside capital investment within the past 10 years. There are more and less safe neighborhoods within the city, and there have been better and worse years, as drug traffic and economic hard times have variously intensified and eased. But the reasons for the city's negative reputation have recurred regularly and continually. In the first 22 days of 2007, there were 19 shootings and three homicides. The homicide rate in 2013 was slightly higher, and represented most of the murders within the county of San Mateo,[3] many of them gang-related incidents. Nearly all East Palo Alto Academy students know someone who either has been killed or is serving time in jail. Although the school has succeeded in eliminating gang-related activity on campus, there is still gang conflict in the community, and a number of students have family members who are actively involved in gangs.

This activity is largely isolated within the geographic boundaries that cut East Palo Alto off from the rest of the peninsula. The physical boundary of Interstate 101, which connects San Francisco at the north with San Jose at the southern end of Silicon Valley, separates most of East Palo Alto and east Menlo Park from the more affluent towns in San Mateo and Santa Clara counties.

University Avenue, which extends from Stanford's palm-lined entryway through Palo Alto and East Palo Alto to the San Francisco Bay, bisects Interstate 101 and is one of only two major streets that connect the two cities.[4] Every day, thousands of commuters drive east on University Avenue away from Stanford University, cross the 101 overpass, and head toward the Dumbarton Bridge, one of four bridges that span the San Francisco Bay. These travelers see a dramatic shift as they leave the campus, with its stately palms, broad lawns, and red-tiled Spanish architecture, and drive past Palo Alto's mansions towering behind electric gates and 10-foot hedges to reach East Palo Alto with its single-story stucco houses and two-story apartment buildings protected behind chain-link, iron, or brick fences.

If they are paying attention, these drivers see people walking past the small East Palo Alto storefronts: liquor stores, family-owned markets, and laundromats. In recent decades, these family stores have represented most of East Palo Alto's tiny commercial tax base. To this day there are no large supermarkets within East Palo Alto's borders, and before the California Bank & Trust branch opened in 2002, "East Palo was the largest unbanked city in the United States."[5] Originally an unincorporated part of San Mateo County, EPA did not officially become a city until 1983. Before the current redevelopment project began in the mid-1990s, the most exciting growth in East Palo Alto's tax base occurred at the end of the 1980s when McDonald's opened a branch on the northwest corner of University Avenue and Bay Road.

Spanning only 2.5 square miles, East Palo Alto retains some of the characteristics of a rural community, with few sidewalks, a number of unpaved roads, and streets prone to flooding and potholes. Even today, East Palo Alto still feels like a small town where many longtime residents know one another and share a sense of local history and identity.

At the beginning of the 20th century, East Palo Alto was twice its current size and wholly owned by three families, including that of Lester Cooley, who had attempted to turn a landing at the end of Bay Road (now known as Cooley Landing) into a viable port for the Bay Area. Between 1900 and the present, most of the prime land was sold by private landowners and annexed by Palo Alto or Menlo Park, the cities that share East Palo Alto's southern, western, and northern borders. Land that now hosts Facebook, the Palo Alto Golf Course, the affluent Willows neighborhood, and a bayfront industrial center all once belonged to East Palo Alto. With these losses went the most valuable portions of the tax base and the opportunity for financial resources for the community and its schools.

The only other developed commercial section of East Palo Alto was "Whiskey Gulch," a string of liquor stores, bars, and nightclubs dating back to Prohibition, which first prospered in the 1930s as a destination for Stanford students from "dry" Palo Alto. Prior to its final demolition at the end of the 20th century due to the expansion of Interstate 101, Whiskey Gulch was also a noticeable part of East Palo Alto's tax base.

Since 1995, the majority of the mom-and-pop stores have been torn down to make room for the Gateway 101 shopping center. Ironically, the jumbo Ikea, Home Depot, and two airport-sized parking lots that serve them were built over the remains of Ravenswood High School and the adjacent and crumbling Cooley Apartments. The shopping center now represents nearly 90% of East Palo Alto's sales tax revenue,[6] accounting for the city's designation as the fastest-growing California retail market between 1995 and 2000.[7] While the Gateway 101 shopping center employs some East Palo Alto residents, unemployment is still twice the county average, and the residential neighborhoods of EPA still suffer from economic hardship.

Although the students recognize that East Palo Alto has an uneven reputation, they carry a defiant pride and sense of hope about their community. During the first year of the school, the EPAA students spent a great deal of time holding discussions, making proposals, and leading a vote about what to name their new school. After much debate and reflection and an intense secret-balloting process, the large banner that was unveiled at the naming ceremony said: "East Palo Alto High School." The students explained that they had returned to this name not for lack of thought, but because they wanted to recognize and represent their community with respect and dignity.

At two later junctures, when an elementary school was added (and later closed), and when the school was rechartered under the aegis of Sequoia Union High School District, the issue of renaming was raised. Both times the students and faculty decided affirmatively to preserve the name of the community in their school, even though there were significant changes in the context and content of the school program. The school became East Palo Alto Academy High School, and then just plain East Palo Alto Academy, but it never lost this central identity.

## THE SCHOOL BUILDING

In 2000, there was not a readily available space in East Palo Alto's small territory for a new high school. The old high school site was now a shopping center, and, as we discovered when later looking for sites on which to build, the soil at many of the plausible locations had been rendered toxic and could not meet the standards for a school site.

As noted earlier, Ravenswood City School District provided space for the new high school in a dilapidated elementary school with declining enrollment. The facility had 20 classrooms, laid out in a rectangle. Like the design of most California schools, all classrooms opened directly to the outside and there were no interior corridors. The eight classrooms at the front of the school faced a small parking lot. The back classrooms opened onto a pitted blacktop, bordered on the right by a small gym with two classrooms, at the back by a chain-link fence separating EPAA from the elementary school next door, and on the left by a city-owned playing field and park. For the first year, EPAA operated out of eight classrooms at the front of the school and shared the back of the building with two elementary schools. By its third year, EPAA was the sole tenant and paid rent to Ravenswood for the space and all capital improvements.

The challenges of the site included rusty gutters with holes that poured rain onto students' heads as they walked between classes, an ancient bell system that rang at random times and added to the hum of ambient classroom noise, classroom clocks that never told the correct time and couldn't be reset, a decrepit plumbing system that overflowed during heavy winter rains into the science lab and closed down the bathrooms, an overworked and outdated computer server, an unworkable phone system with a "black hole" for voice mail, and nonprogrammable classroom thermostats that kept temperatures sweltering or frigid. Once-grand redwood and eucalyptus trees on the campus had been cut down or decapitated by district maintenance. Many classrooms had threadbare carpet, broken faucets, and ramshackle cabinets that wouldn't close. The science lab, originally designed for elementary school students, had no functioning gas jets and few working electrical outlets.

Getting the district to fix any of these things proved nearly impossible. To add to the challenges, in the summer of 2001, the district repossessed the school's classroom furniture while the teachers were away on a planning retreat. After reviewing EPAA's Memorandum of Understanding, the district business officer eventually sent rusty and dirty replacement desks and chairs. In the interim, EPAA bought hundreds of folding chairs so that school could start.

Teachers and staff became skilled at making do with what they had, learning to avoid the mini-waterfalls and puddles during the rainy season, ringing the hourly school bells by hand, hanging working clocks in classrooms, and renting porta-potties when the bathrooms were closed. Even though the students (and sometimes staff) referred to the school as "ghetto," they knew they were fortunate to have a building at all. Staff had heard the stories of some local charter schools that began the school year in public parks, empty supermarkets, or closed-down banks. The staff and students invested in making the school their own, including decorating the main hallway with a floor-to-ceiling mural painted by the students in collaboration with the East Palo Alto Music and Mural Arts Program,[8] and grew to love the site despite its flaws.

## THE FACULTY

One of the conditions of the charter was that the school would hire well-qualified staff who were committed to achieving National Board Certification within their first 5 years at the school. Schools in Ravenswood City School District, similar to other high-needs districts in California, often were staffed by a revolving door of beginning teachers, often hired without preparation or mentoring, who floundered and left quickly. Like other districts, Ravenswood had begun to staff many of its schools with young White Teach for America recruits, who would spend 2 years before going off to law school or a "real" job on Wall Street. Several members of the school board were unhappy with this "missionary model," as one of them called it, and pleased that the new high school might change this trend, although they were not sure how this would be accomplished.

The lure of teachers to EPAA was what dynamic professionals typically respond to: the opportunity to use their hard-won knowledge to create a new approach that could better serve the adolescents they cared about. As an added bonus, those recruited knew they would be working with other highly motivated individuals in a setting where they could learn from and collaborate with one another.[9] Despite a tight budget, salaries were made competitive with those in other districts by investing largely in teachers rather than non-teaching staff and by cutting every conceivable corner in other categories. But the main attractions remained the same: the mission and the colleagues.

The founding principal, Nicky Ramos-Beban, was recruited in January 2001 to hire the staff and launch the new school within only 8 months. A veteran English teacher with 10 years of experience and boundless energy, Nicky had been a Stanford undergraduate and then a graduate of the master's-level STEP program, for which she later served as one of the most successful cooperating teachers, training new teachers for the profession. A mixed-race Latina adopted by a Black family, Nicky was at home with all sorts of people, and she helped establish a set of school norms grounded in respect, tolerance, empathy, and positive intent. Nicky didn't believe in rigidly hierarchical structures, and she practiced consensus decisionmaking with strong faculty involvement. She taught 9th-grade humanities and weightlifting, and led an advisory for the first 2 years of the school in addition to being principal.[10]

The founding staff of nine was an extraordinary crew of diverse, highly committed, and highly professional teachers who were completely devoted to their students and the community. Most were graduates of the Stanford Teacher Education Program. Others came from Rutgers, UCLA, and other top teacher education programs. Just over half were teachers of color, and most were Spanish-speaking. From 30-year veteran William Dean, who began teaching in Camden, New Jersey, before reaching the Bay Area, to relatively newly minted teachers Rebecca Altamirano and Tina Ehsanipour, all spent nearly every waking hour in those first years designing—and redesigning—the school with one another and the Stanford faculty.

As faculty sponsor, Linda Darling-Hammond was most continuously involved, but the faculty also tapped, at various points along the way, STEP director Rachel Lotan, who had taught them how to design effective group-work, and other STEP professors—Pamela Grossman in English education, Arnetha Ball in literacy, Sam Wineburg in history education, Jo Boaler in mathematics education, Guadalupe Valdés and Kenji Hakuta for support in teaching English learners, and professors from other parts of the university, like Andrea Lunsford in English and Al Camarillo in history.

## THE CONTEXT

With excitement at the new beginnings, none of those involved could have known how rocky the road would be. Over the coming decade, California would continue its precipitous decline in funding that began in 1979 with the passage of massive tax cuts under Proposition 13, encountering one budget crisis after another, and slashing schools to the bone during the Schwarzenegger administration, especially in high-needs communities like East Palo Alto.

### California: From First to Worst

Plummeting from "first to worst," as John Merrow's aptly named film[11] illustrates, California would become one of the lowest-spending, most unequally funded states in the nation. When the 21st century dawned, California ranked first in the nation in the number of K–12 pupils it served, but 38th in expenditures per student, 48th in expenditures as a share of personal income, and 50th in the ratio of students per teacher, despite the influence of class size reductions during the late 1990s.[12] The state employed a greater number and proportion of underqualified teachers than any other state in the country and ranked in the bottom decile among states on access to libraries, librarians, counselors, administrators, and most other school resources.

Things got even worse throughout the decade, and the brunt of spending shortfalls was borne by low-income schools in increasingly segregated communities. With wealthy districts spending three times more than poor ones, spending on students of color in intensely segregated schools (those that are 90–100% "minority") was significantly lower than that in majority-White schools.[13] These apartheid schools were a growing share of the total, since California also was heading toward becoming one of the nation's most segregated school systems. By 2004, it was one of the five most segregated states for African American students and one of the three most segregated states for Latino students, with 87% of African American students and 90% of Latino students attending schools that served a majority of students of color.[14]

When the national average for school funding hit $10,000 per pupil shortly after this story began,[15] small schools like EPAA in high-needs communities in one of the most expensive regions in the country were receiving less than $6,000 per pupil in state funding, eliminating the possibility of "luxuries" like libraries, librarians, school nurses, music programs, physical education, sports facilities, and much more. Only the commitments of some local foundations and donors kept the small school afloat, even though it was unable to afford these "frills."

In 2000, the state's funding system was challenged by a lawsuit, *Williams v. California*, which documented the crumbling buildings, lack of textbooks and materials, unqualified teachers, and truncated curriculum available to many of California's low-income students of color.[16] The suit led to a settlement in which a small amount of money for facilities and textbooks was made available to low-income schools, but the free fall continued for another decade.[17]

### Incarceration Rather than Education

Meanwhile, the state continued its climb in incarceration rates, set in motion by policies established by Governor Ronald Reagan several decades earlier. Between 1980 and 2008, the prison population grew by more than 400%, and corrections costs climbed by 900%.[18] This meant there was less and less discretionary funding available for education and other social services, particularly in light of the recurring fiscal crises resulting from the earlier tax caps coupled with tax cuts imposed by Governor Schwarzenegger when he took office. While corrections costs climbed from 3% of the state general fund budget in 1980 to 11.5% in 2008,[19] general fund allocations for the state university systems (UC and CSU) were slashed by 25% in that same year.[20]

Although the state would not pay $10,000 a year to properly educate a young person in a community like Oakland, Compton, or East Palo Alto, it would pay more than $50,000 a year to incarcerate that same young person several years later. And with zero tolerance discipline policies in schools, harsh sentencing guidelines, and an overcrowded and abusive youth detention system that eventually came under court surveillance, there was a very large pipeline of young people making that journey from school to prison.

As the poor got poorer, the state continued to cut funding for schools, children, and families, and the prison-industrial complex grew. The proportion of children in California schools eligible for free or reduced-price lunch exceeded 50% by 2005, and in a growing number of communities, it surpassed 90%.[21]

## Testing Without Investing

Not surprisingly, schools that served high-needs children typically reported lower test scores than others. And while resources were dwindling, testing was expanding. Under the test-based accountability framework that began in the 1990s, students took 35 tests from 2nd through 11th grades before they even got to the SAT, ACT, or AP tests at the end of high school. These tests were almost entirely multiple-choice, emphasizing recall and recognition rather than applied learning.

In the name of accountability, the state's major strategy for improvement was to label schools and districts that had low test scores as failing and queue them up for sanctions. The Academic Performance Index (API)—a state metric combining several test scores into a number between 200 and 1000, which was associated with a decile ranking for each school—had a 90% correlation with socioeconomic status, so it routinely ranked the schools in line with their poverty levels. But to provide a measure of fairness, schools also were compared with 100 "similar schools" with similar demographics.

With the arrival of the federal No Child Left Behind (NCLB) Act in 2002, the ranking system became more oppressive for high-needs schools and the sanctions became more widespread and severe. These could include reconstitution (firing most or all staff), state takeovers, or interventions from state-approved vendors who typically prescribed tracking low-achieving students into long hours of drill-based remedial math and reading courses, which deprived them of learning opportunities in science, social studies, and the arts, as well as engaging, project-based learning. Closures of public schools and, for noncharters, transmutations into charter schools were also options. In some high-needs communities, schools were closed and replaced by other schools that later were deemed low-performing; these also were closed in a cycle that often occurred twice or three times, creating chaos in the lives of many families without significantly changing the outcomes.

Although state test scores rose nearly everywhere, California remained one of the lowest ranked in the country on the National Assessment of Educational Progress in the first decade of the new century. Meanwhile, the federal law created a more torturous gauntlet based on annual expectations for steeply rising test scores that supported this churn. The need to make "adequate yearly progress" (AYP) on state tests in every grade for every group of students (by race, language background, income, and disability status) in order to avoid sanctions each year had several side effects.

- Schools serving the widest range of student populations were subject to a "diversity penalty,"[22] often having to meet test participation and score targets for more than 30 different categories in order to make AYP. While penalizing the most diverse schools, this also discouraged schools from seeking to become more inclusive in terms of race, income, and inclusion of special education programs.
- Schools serving English learners were subject to the "Catch 22" for English learners; that is, although the law required a greater number of students to test at the proficient level each year, aiming for 100% proficiency by 2014, English learner students who reached a proficient level were then removed from the English learner category, so no school could ever advance to the point of 100% proficiency in that category, even if its students were all making excellent progress. Not surprisingly, all of the schools identified as the state's lowest performing under the federal law had high proportions of English learners.
- Schools had strong incentives to keep out and push out the lowest-performing students and those most challenging to teach, so as to boost average scores. This was easiest for charters that could discourage special education students or others with unique needs from applying or could require students to leave if they misbehaved, did not progress, or broke a contract signed upon admission. (Some charters also required contracts of parents, and a parent's failure to meet volunteer or other obligations could lead to a student's expulsion.) But regular public schools also had incentives to avoid serving high-needs students, and they also responded to these incentives, sometimes creating bizarre unintended consequences.

For example, in one nearby district, there were sustained battles over where a special education program would be located, since none of the schools wanted to accept a group of students who would cause average scores to dip and place the entire school at risk of being closed or reconstituted. In another district, special education students at the elementary level were moved to a different school each year so that no school would have to bear more of the brunt than any other. This was terribly disruptive to the students but rational in the face of an irrational "accountability" system.

At the middle and high school level, the incentives to push out poorly performing students were intense. This could manifest in extended suspensions or expulsions resulting from harsh disciplinary policies, which often led students to drop out, or in counseling out to another school or GED program when students became credit deficient from low grades or poor attendance. Grade retention often had the same discouraging effect. It also could occur through a transfer to "continuation schools" that were not held to the same accountability standards as other schools and often graduated few of their students. These became prevalent ways of dealing with the accountability sword hanging over low-income schools.

To be sure, there were many public schools that did heroic work and many that genuinely improved, but there were few supports and more incentives to lose struggling students than to enable them to succeed. Between 2000 and 2008, the National Center for Education Statistics (NCES) graduation rate used for NCLB reporting dropped from 87% to below 80% statewide.[23] Meanwhile, African American and Latino students were graduating at rates of just 55 to 60%.

## Local Implications

The state's priorities had several effects on young people in communities like East Palo Alto. The hard-edged testing policies had the largest effect on low-income schools where scores were lower and fear of harsh sanctions was greatest. (As noted earlier, the API had a 90% correlation with socioeconomic status.) Not counting college admissions tests or those associated with programs like Advanced Placement and International Baccalaureate, there were 21 tests at the high school level—both end-of-course exams in each core subject area in grades 9–11 and additional federally required tests in science, plus an exit exam in English language arts and math. This resulted in many schools creating a test-based curriculum, drilling for the tests in virtually all courses and settling for narrow rote-oriented instruction offering little writing, speaking, research, investigation, or project work. Students spent weeks and sometimes months prepping for multiple-choice questions, learning how to eliminate the obvious wrong answer, narrow down the choices, and, finally, guess at the answers, rather than pursuing fascinating questions, reading passionately, writing effectively, or applying mathematics to serious problems in science, social science, or engineering.

If it wasn't going to be on the test, many schools felt they couldn't take the time away from test prep to engage in it. At schools like East Palo Alto Academy, the teachers ultimately ran a dual curriculum—one focused on engaging students in authentic work and community-based projects that could demonstrate the relevance of schoolwork to real life, and the other, on the side, to prepare students for the tests. There were always outside pressures to abandon the projects and exhibitions and to do more test prep.

The testing focus also resulted in pressures to "cream and crop" students so as to raise scores, which EPAA fiercely resisted, even when wealthy donors insisted that weak students should be dropped as they saw other charters doing. All the way up to the president of the university, Stanford committed and continuously recommitted to supporting a school that served the highest-needs students in this high-needs community, even though admitting and keeping struggling students would depress test scores.

Students were admitted on a first-come, first-served basis (or by lottery when there were more applications than the number of slots) without admissions hurdles. As the school got a reputation for success with new immigrant students and with students who struggled in other ways, more of these students applied. The school took students who had failed at the large comprehensive high schools in the nearby districts and those who had been expelled from or counseled out of other charters in the vicinity. The school wrapped around those students and often succeeded in getting them to persevere to graduation and take the next steps toward a productive future.

This required more and more investments from the university and the school's donors in instructional supports (reading specialists, lab courses in writing and math, Saturday school, and others), summer school, health and mental health services, and a willingness to work with students for a 5th year of high school (not funded by the state for students after age 18), or to take students back after they returned from jail or from having had a child. These costs were impossible for many public schools in similar communities to bear without outside funding.

In addition to ongoing cuts in school budgets, the cuts that occurred in the public higher education budget meant that many of the young people who worked hard to meet the eligibility requirements for the state's 4-year colleges could not go. This was both because universities became unaffordable when financial aid was cut while tuition was increased, and because the university system eliminated slots as its budget was cut. Although community colleges were expected to pick up those students, these schools also were experiencing cuts that decimated their advisement structures and ability to offer the courses students needed to move forward in their studies.

Research and experience have shown that first-generation college students who attend 4-year colleges where they live on campus and receive advisement are much more likely to finish school than those who try to make it through community college while living at home, juggling other family responsibilities, and trying to advise themselves. We saw that firsthand with our students, who constantly were tugged away from their studies by their need to work and their perceived obligation to assist their families. There were always needs for students to assist their families with income to pay the rent, babysitting for younger siblings, translating for parents and grandparents at the doctor's office or other transactions outside the home, and many forms of crisis management.

And before the Dream Act passed in California in 2011, there was no financial aid available for undocumented students, who were a large share of EPAA graduates. It was not unusual for five or six of the top ten seniors to be undocumented and without resources to attend the selective universities that had admitted them. The teachers and donors together created a scholarship fund to support these students in attending college, but many still had to settle for starting in a community college rather than a 4-year school because the remaining costs were out of reach.

Even for students eligible for federal financial aid, the climb was difficult, because the size of Pell grants and other federal aid had dropped so much since the end of the 1970s. Whereas these grants once covered close to 80% of the costs of a public higher education, they now covered only one-third. Pressures to find funds to send students to college always competed with pressures for funding the services they needed to get ready for college.

The East Palo Alto community suffered the effects of the fiscal crises and the great recession, through cuts in social services, closed libraries and recreational services, growing unemployment, evictions, and homelessness. While Silicon Valley rebounded rapidly, East Palo Alto did not, experiencing more than twice the rate of county unemployment. Adjusted for inflation, 2010 median household income was 20% lower than in 2000.[24]

Meanwhile, the high rates of incarceration touched nearly all of the families in East Palo Alto in some way. Among adult men in California in 2010, African Americans were incarcerated at a rate of 5,525 per 100,000 (fully 5%), compared with 1,146 for Latinos, 671 for non-Latino Whites, and 43 for Asians.[25] Most students had a parent, sibling, other relative, or friend in jail, and a number had themselves been accosted or arrested by police, or been placed in juvenile detention, on probation, or even in the adult system.

With all of these challenges, it was important for schools in communities like EPA to figure out how to wrap around their students in multiple ways, to support them in their lives as well as their learning. Learning to do that was an ongoing process for the faculty. And it began with the school's many strategies for personalization, described in the next chapter.

## CHAPTER 3

# Personalizing School

My advisor always taught me—don't think just now, think ahead, think about the future.

—EPAA student

They taught us that no matter where we came from, we can get to where we want.

—EPAA senior, class of 2005

Most East Palo Alto Academy students came to school with a range of challenges in their homes and neighborhoods. Some issues were related to poverty: Students came to school hungry or with blankets over their shoulders instead of warm coats. Others witnessed violence frequently in their homes or on the streets. Many students lived in dangerous neighborhoods plagued by shootings and crime that affected their families directly. Most students were affected by gangs prevalent in the East Palo Alto community, and a few were in them. Some of these students brought their gang issues onto the school's campus, dragging other students into them.

Many students had parents who struggled with unemployment, incarceration, and substance and/or domestic abuse. Some lived with relatives other than parents, in foster care, or on their own. Others took care of younger siblings after school or even during school hours. Still others lived in overcrowded housing where they shared a room or a garage with several other family members and where there was no place to study. Seniors depicted these situations in their personal statements for college applications:

I then remembered [when I was 5], I ran to my mom and with my eyes closed, I squeezed her hand. I heard my dad's hand against her face and then a scream; she took her hand away. "Somebody help me," she yelled as she got on her knees. I stood in front of my mother and even though I was too small, I put my arms around her and tried to protect her as much as I could. I knew my dad kicked me when my knees bent to the ground, but I was protecting my mother and watching her suffer was worse than my pain. I realized it was another night with a drunken stranger who called himself my father, but only caused harm. . . . My mother would . . . say once more, "Don't hate him, he's your father."

—Magdalena, class of 2005

I see visions of my mother and father being on drugs most of their lives. The vision of three blank faces representing the two brothers and one sister that I never met. The vision of a baby in the hospital with so many wires and tubes that she looks like a pin cushion. . . . The vision of me as a baby, abandoned in a hospital, because my mother and father chose not to take care of me.

—Charisse, class of 2005

Growing up in a neighborhood filled with violence, economic depression, and drug abuse had made me detached and unsympathetic towards others. Living among violence can turn a person into a predator. I preyed upon the weakness of others. I'd yell or hit anyone who disagreed with me. People hated the way I acted and instead of keeping friends, I pushed them away. I had many verbal and physical altercations. Soon I began to hate myself, I wanted to change but I didn't know how.

—Jade, class of 2005

These three students and many like them found a home at EPAA, a community where they could redefine themselves, and a staff willing to help them develop their new identities. Nicky commented on how students' intense needs required a different school structure:

EPAA is such an intense accumulation of students with deep needs that what you have to do is create this overwhelming structure to support them from all sides. That's different from most suburban classrooms where you may have three or four students who have intense needs. But we couldn't just create another traditional, anonymous high school; it wouldn't work for our students. We had to meet them where they were.

A core belief of staff was the importance of knowing students individually: their lives, families, community, personality, learning styles, opinions, strengths, dislikes, and interests. Knowing the many facets of each life made a difference in meeting the needs of the whole student. And if students were struggling, teachers first had to understand the roadblocks standing in the way of the students' academic success and to tap into and build upon their strengths.

Even though most teachers in most schools believe in supporting their students in every way possible, there is often a tipping point phenomenon in schools of concentrated poverty, where teachers and students become overwhelmed by the level of stress and trauma that individuals experience each day. In warehouse-like, factory-model high schools of 2,000 or 3,000 students designed on the old assembly-line high school schedule, teachers see 150 to 200 students a day, and students never spend extended time with any adult. Under these conditions, it is almost impossible to address students' needs. At East Palo Alto Academy, multiple strategies were built into the structure—and others continually developed in response to these needs—that allowed staff to personalize the educational experience and meet individual students where they were. The core strategies included:

- Maintaining the school's small size and small classes
- Developing structures for long-term relationships between students and teachers through looping with the same teacher for more than 1 year and keeping the same advisor for 4 years
- Building a sense of mutual responsibility and community among students as well as between students and staff

The advisor relationship and the structure of daily advisory classes became the spine of the school, without which almost nothing else would have been able to work effectively. Key to building strong relationships and norms were the Five Community Habits developed by the staff in the first year. These habits—personal responsibility, social responsibility, critical and creative thinking, application of knowledge, and communication—were the basis of rubrics used for guidance and evaluation in every class, every year, by every teacher (see Appendix A). They helped build a sense of continuity and community. In what follows, we describe EPAA's core strategies and supportive structures, as well as some of their effects.

## THE ADVANTAGES OF SMALL SIZE

EPAA's design was developed to facilitate personalization and individualized student attention. The structure and organization of the school were based on educational research demonstrating that small schools designed for personalized relationships typically produce stronger outcomes, including better attendance and behavior, a stronger sense of belonging, greater participation in activities, and higher rates of graduation, especially for students who are traditionally low-achieving.[1] With this research as a guide, it was decided that the school would grow no larger than 320 students in grades 9–12.

The goal was to create a close-knit school community where the principal and the teachers knew every student by face and most by name. Visitors to EPAA's campus routinely commented that they could clearly see the close relationships between students and teachers. It was difficult for a teacher to walk down the hallway without being stopped multiple times by students who wanted to share a recent success, ask a question about homework, or just say hello. Two students from the first graduating class reflected on feeling supported by teachers:

> They're always there. They are always trying to help. Any teachers, all the teachers.

> I can go to any of the teachers and ask for help. I feel that they wouldn't hesitate to help or ask somebody else to help.

Because the school hired very few nonteaching personnel, it also was able to provide for smaller class sizes, a key feature that enabled teachers to respond to individual learning needs. At EPAA the class sizes were significantly lower than in a large California comprehensive high school at this time; most courses were limited to 25 students, and some had fewer than 20. Not only did the small school and class sizes support individual student learning and academic achievement, but they also facilitated the development of community. One senior in the class of 2005 reflected on his freshman-year experience:

> On the first day of school [I was] sitting in Mr. Gilbert's Humanities I class, and the first thing he said to me, and the thing he drilled for the next 9 months, was community. I can still remember him saying that our school is a community and you're going to have to learn how to interact in a community.

With teachers able to know each student well enough to build a strong relationship, and with a mission to work explicitly on building personal and social responsibility, the foundation was laid.

## STRUCTURES FOR PERSONALIZATION

Even in a small school with small classes, it is possible to replicate many of the features of a factory-model school on a smaller scale. To accomplish personalization, it is also important to extend the amount of time teachers spend with individual students beyond the fragmented structures of the traditional high school design, which usually comprise a batch of six or seven short, 50-minute periods daily across which teachers typically must divide their attention among 150 to 200 different students. Three major structures supported EPAA teachers in getting to know students well enough to support their learning and development, and students knowing teachers well enough to trust them to do so: block scheduling, looping, and a well-developed advisory system.

## Block Scheduling

An early decision, modeled after the designs of successful small schools in New York City and elsewhere, was to offer nearly all classes on a block schedule. Over the years, the length of the block ranged from 75 to 90 minutes, but the idea was always the same: to allow teachers to work more intensively with fewer students each day and each year. If teachers taught two long blocks a day plus an advisory class, rather than five or six short classes, they could spend more time with students, use more interactive strategies, engage students in project work, address individual needs more strategically, and start students on their homework with guidance.

These block classes lasted all year long. Whereas many California districts had adopted block scheduling on a semester basis (the so-called "four-by-four" block with faculty teaching a different set of four classes each semester), the research had already indicated that this was not typically a successful strategy with high-needs students. Most would not successfully learn algebra or make significant gains in their writing skills in a single semester when they started out with skill gaps and needed to gain both significant academic ground and confidence to try—which required, in turn, a high level of trust built on long-term relationships with their teachers.

In many classes, the block schedule provided three opportunities a week for teachers to meet with a group of students for 90 minutes on two occasions and 45 minutes on the third. (All the classes met on Fridays to be sure teachers could round out the week with all of their students.) However, in humanities and, from the second year on, in 9th-grade algebra, the students met in "double blocks," meaning 90 minutes every day. The decision to combine English language arts and history/social studies in a single, year-long humanities course reduced each teacher's pupil load by half so that they could support more extensive reading, writing, and project work on the part of students, building their literacy skills intensely, while also getting to know them deeply. Soon it became obvious that students needed the same intense support in 9th-grade mathematics, and a double block was created for that course as well, supporting dramatic improvements in student achievement as a direct result.

Block scheduling traded depth for breadth. It allowed for deeper relationships between teachers and students and for pedagogies that could support deeper learning. However, the trade-off was that the school could offer and students could take fewer courses. In particular, this approach reduces electives and emphasizes a more focused set of challenges for students. This was offset by the fact that in their interdisciplinary projects students often experienced much of what traditional schools relegate to electives and extracurriculars: opportunities to engage in creative work that is student-initiated, incorporates the arts, and supports students' development of a wide range of leadership abilities.

## Looping

In addition to block scheduling, the school made a concentrated effort to "loop" students with teams of teachers, especially in the early years when a new grade was being added each year. Looping means that teachers work with the same group of students for 2 or more school years. In the second year of the school, many teachers moved "up" to 10th grade with their 9th-grade students. In later years, some teachers looped with the students they taught, while others stayed in a single grade level, where they gained expertise with a particular curriculum. Most students could expect to see at least one or two of the teachers they'd known previously in each new grade, providing continuity to their school experience.

The benefits of looping became obvious to teachers as soon as they tried it. First, teachers who had looped with their students had a clear idea regarding students' knowledge and skills from the very beginning of the second school year and could set appropriately challenging goals. Second, much of the foundation for relationship building was set during the first year. Teachers remarked that a second year with a student was always easier.

Seth Leslie, the school's first math teacher, who looped with his initial math students for their full high school experience, described how powerful the experience was:

> Looping was a core component of our program, and as the first math teacher for the school, I taught all of my original 9th-grade students for the first 3 years. There was even a cohort of about 12 talented kids who stayed with me for a fourth year to study math analysis and pre-calculus. It was a first for all of us. As an educator who believes strongly in the power of relationships, I felt that I had the most leverage with the students whom I taught for the greatest length of time. Many of those students are still in contact with me today.

In addition to teaching math, Seth was the varsity boys' soccer coach and, like other coaches, he also "looped" with his team. This experience enabled the alchemy of long-term relationships for creating the personal leverage that can turn failure into success. Seth did this with the entire soccer team, eventually progressing from no-win seasons to no-lose seasons, and the team emerged as league champs in 2008.

Part of the reason the second year of teaching was often more effective for East Palo Alto Academy students was that they were often slow to open up and trust their teachers to support them and to stay for the duration. In addition to the disruptions many experienced in their home life, there had been little continuity in the elementary and middle schools they attended: Teacher attrition rates were high, and students encountered many temporary substitutes as well as inadequately trained teachers who left in midyear. Few stayed for the long haul. When students had experienced educational chaos and failure, they were unsure about whether to trust their high school teachers, and often tested them to the limit before agreeing to try to engage in learning. Over time, students began to put their faith in the staff, who demonstrated a firm commitment beginning with the simple act of showing up to teach and advise, day after day, year after year. This transformed the teaching and learning experience.

## The Advisory System

The most important example of looping was the advisory system, which paired one teacher with an unchanging group of 15 to 18 students for 4 years. The advisor's role was to monitor and support each advisee's academic progress and to support his or her social-emotional development. This work was conducted in a dedicated class period that met every day, as well as in a variety of one-on-one conversations, meetings, family conferences, and specific supports for both social–emotional–behavioral needs (discussed later in this chapter) and academic exhibitions (discussed further in the next chapter).

At a large school, it is possible for a student to be invisible and never have a deep conversation with an adult on campus, let alone develop a long-term relationship. At EPAA, every faculty member was also an advisor, and with the advisory system, student invisibility was virtually impossible. The advisory system made certain that students would have a specific time and place in which to develop a strong relationship with a faculty member that extended beyond specific content areas or classes. For most students at EPAA, the advisor/student relationship was a key component of personalization, and advisory was one of the most important structures of the school, valued by teachers, students, and their families.

Advisors sought to know students sincerely and individually, repositioning themselves as partners and advocates, not only for the students, but also for their families and the community as a whole. The advisors' commitment to know students helped them engender trusting relationships with students and families, which proved to be an essential key to the success of the school. Having worked closely with the same students over multiple years, the teachers at EPAA were much better equipped to support them. These teachers had come to know the students' experiences, the struggles they faced, and the impact these struggles had on their academic career. As one teacher put it:

> I think a big part of [developing a personalized environment] plays out in advisory. The fact that all my advisees can call or come to me at any time of the day and say, "Ms. X, I'm not coming to school today because of this. Ms. X, I need help with my humanities homework." They know that there's someone that they can always turn to for help. Whether that's at school or after school, they know that there's that resource there for them to ask for help.

Another teacher described her role in this way:

> It's like you're the mother . . . nurse, psychologist . . . immigration expert, everything. It's much better here because you spend more quality time with students. You get to know each student in a very personal way and their parents. I think that allows you to help guide them much better, because you are watching out for the person and earn their trust.

As much as possible, EPAA teachers validated the commitment to keeping students with the same advisor for 4 years, because they knew that, as difficult as some relationships might be at the beginning, there would be larger gains in the long run.

> You know students in your advisory better than other students. These are very deep relationships over a long term. You have leverage with these students that you don't with others, as [your advisees] have to learn to deal with you since they'll see you for 4 years and get their college recommendations from you. It's sort of like a family relationship in that you have to work things out with your advisor just as a family has to work things out.

The advisor's charge was to ensure that each of his or her advisees moved forward in their academic and personal development. The goal for each student was to successfully graduate and have the necessary education and tools to access opportunities for college and/or the workforce. Advisory classes initially were designed with the following goals in mind:

- To provide a daily space to check in about social and emotional issues
- To teach students how to tackle homework assignments and become independent learners

- To provide a quiet environment conducive to academic study and a dedicated time for completion of homework
- To guide students through the steps to prepare for college

Over time, it became clear that students needed more tools to support their social and emotional learning, and advisory also became a place where that kind of learning was organized. Advisory evolved in several ways over the years as staff perceived needs and organized themselves to meet them. Always, though, advisory was a place for advisors and students to discuss academic and nonacademic goals and to work together to develop plans to meet them.

All students created a graduation plan with their advisor that included regular reviews of their transcript and progress toward graduation requirements. The plan also included built-in support for navigating the college selection process, including help with registering for college entrance exams, getting fee waivers, and completing applications. Other advisor support included drafting personal learning plans with students, working with the on-site resource specialist to support individual education plans (IEPs) for special education students, implementing behavioral intervention plans, and connecting advisees to resources like doctors and counselors.

Advisors were the primary school contact for families. The advisor met at least twice a year with each student's parents or guardians. One of these meetings was dedicated to the Student Learning Conference, during which students led a conversation about their academic progress and graduation plan. Student Learning Conferences provided an important opportunity for parents and students to engage in academic discourse about the students' learning and development. Almost all EPAA families came regularly to these meetings, facilitated by their children.

Parents also leaned on advisors to provide other types of support. Sometimes parents wanted advisors to reinforce rules or encourage more communication at home. In these cases, parents and advisors worked together to deliver the same message to students about academic performance and behavior at home and at school. As students and their families grew to trust EPAA advisors, they also were called on for other supports, such as helping a student find a job after school, assisting a family applying for medical insurance, or accompanying a student to court.

Eventually the school was able to find the resources to hire a social worker who could help with some of these issues. But the advisor's role was always central in identifying needs and seeing that they received attention. The job of an advisor was daunting, and over the years new staff often struggled with—and sometimes pushed back on—the unfamiliar role, but veterans in the school had learned that the advisory program was critical to student and school success. Every time advisory was questioned, it was reaffirmed as essential by teachers, students, and parents.

## ADVISORY IN ACTION

Before the school even began, in the summer of 2001, the newly hired faculty, along with the Stanford faculty sponsor and the Aspire leadership team, met with each individual student to interview them about their personal and academic history, interests, strengths, and needs. These interviews were used to ascertain skill levels and needs and to determine advisee placements.

Rebecca Altamirano was assigned to interview Esperanza Ramirez because Esperanza spoke only Spanish, and Rebecca, like many of the staff members, spoke Spanish fluently. Rebecca had come to teaching after graduating from Wellesley College and earning her credential at STEP; she also had worked with the principal as a student teacher at a previous school. Petite, lithe, quick-thinking, and fast-talking, Rebecca was creative and entrepreneurial: In the first year she organized the service learning program, taught a mural arts course, recruited local artists to teach an art course, and took on an advisory, before becoming a humanities teacher in the following year.

So it was that one hot day in the summer of 2001, the two met in an empty classroom, with Esperanza eventually doing most of the talking.

### Esperanza's Story

Here is how Esperanza described herself: "I am a small person, happy and romantic but at the same time I have a difficult attitude. Sometimes I get angry easily." At first, Esperanza fidgeted, but she began to relax after Rebecca explained the interview was not an evaluation, but rather a way for teachers to get to know their students as future members of the new high school community. As Rebecca remembers this first encounter:

> It was like she had been holding her story in for so long, she was about to explode. She finally sensed that this would be a safe space for her to share her harrowing tale of leaving El Salvador to come to the United States. She told me that her goal was to go to college. I asked her if she had ever met anyone with a college degree. She replied, "You're the first one that I have ever met."

As we described when we introduced Esperanza in Chapter 2, her story was indeed distressing. When her parents came to the United States to make a better life, Esperanza remained in her home country with her grandmother, only re-encountering her father at his funeral, when his body was returned to El Salvador after he was killed in East Palo Alto. Later on, Esperanza would describe her father's funeral in an essay:

> My life had changed forever. I can even remember his face and my expression when I saw my dad for the last time in my life. . . . I was 6 years old with long hair, no shoes on my feet and tears going all over my face. He was sleeping. I saw him lying in his coffin, with an expression of peace and his hands were on his chest, and he could not feel me when I put my hand on his face. He was cold, hard and motionless. Because he was dead, I could not do anything for him. My heart was crying because at that moment I knew that I would never be able to hear his voice telling me that he loved me and that I was his little angel.

Many years later, Esperanza's grandmother informed her one morning before school that she would be leaving for the United States in 2 days. Esperanza's mother had borrowed money and arranged for a *coyote* to accompany her on the long trip.

It took Esperanza over 2 months to reach the American border. Shepherded by the *coyotes*, living in deplorable conditions along the way with little food or water, she traveled by bus and van, and on foot, with other immigrants. In Esperanza's words:

> I crossed the Arizona desert for 3 days walking and I didn't eat for 6 days. I fainted twice. I was very tired, hungry and thirsty. My weight was so low. I had lost 8 pounds. I was 86 pounds, not a good weight for a girl that was having her *quinceañera*[2] and becoming a young woman.

After the interview, Rebecca would come to understand that while in El Salvador, Esperanza had created a dream world of her new life with her mother in East Palo Alto. Esperanza wrote, "When I finally saw her, I was very happy but I was confused and all of my feelings were mixed together." She had imagined long heart-to-heart talks, excursions to the market, and cooking tortillas, but once the family was reunited, the soft, romantic images quickly faded. Esperanza soon realized that blood and blood alone was the common bond with her mother. She felt like a servant and a veritable stranger in her new home.

As her advisor, Rebecca learned Esperanza's story over time, using the information to monitor and support her student's academic, social, and emotional well-being. It was apparent from the beginning that Esperanza would have difficulty transitioning to high school. In her words: "I didn't know any people. I didn't speak English. I was nervous. My body was in the classroom but not my head." After the start of her freshman year, Esperanza became closed off and depressed, and Rebecca realized that Esperanza's situation warranted intensive support. Esperanza lost more weight. Her sleep became fitful. Rebecca recommended that Esperanza speak to an on-site psychologist from the Stanford mental health program, who diagnosed her with post-traumatic stress disorder.

The initial information Esperanza's advisor collected was the beginning of learning how best to serve Esperanza during her 4 years at EPAA. The first step was to address her social-emotional needs and to connect Esperanza to counseling services to help her process and move forward from her past. Her advisor created a support network for Esperanza: access to a counselor, tutors, and medical services at EPAA; personal assistance in applying to a college-prep, English-intensive summer program; and eventually, scholarships from donors for her college tuition. Even though Esperanza's situation required extraordinary measures, what EPAA did for Esperanza it attempted to do for all its students.

## The Evolution of Advisory

East Palo Alto Academy teachers who previously had taught in big high schools knew that such intimate knowledge of students' lives was not the norm. Even when they had wanted to know their students and meet their needs, the overwhelming number of students they saw in one day—often 35 in a single class and 175 in a day—made it impossible to give personalized attention to more than a few. This was one reason EPAA chose to remain small and why teachers continued to support advisory: Knowing all students well is possible only in a small learning community that is designed to create enduring and influential relationships between adults and adolescents.

Rebecca characterized the depth of the commitment teachers had to advisory in this way:

> When we first started our school, we naively thought that the students would welcome these ideals, but, boy, did they ever resist. "Why are you always up in my business?" was the statement of the year. Their resistance to our support and inquiries felt sometimes like a slap in the face, but over time, I think we came to understand it better. Our students were not used to nosy teachers who wanted them to constantly write and reflect on their behavior. And over time, they began to trust us more, though for some, it was a long battle and we all emerged with wounds and scars.
>
> Those first years, there was this overwhelming energy that we would do whatever it took to support students. We would be much more than teachers. We would be advisors, coaches, social workers, surrogate parents if need be. We would help find a job for a student's unemployed

mom, help younger siblings enroll in preschool, drive students home who were afraid that they would be "jumped" walking alone, and stay at school late filling out college applications. We would do whatever it took. Eventually they let us into their lives and they didn't let go. They called us late at night to talk, sometimes to ask a question about homework, other times to get advice, and sometimes just because they wanted to hear a calm, encouraging word before going to bed.

We felt that this was the most important work that we could be doing, that we were part of a movement that could change the trajectory of our students' lives.

Although advisory was created to provide an important support for EPAA students, the process of advising students also impacted teachers in important ways, and the student/advisor relationship was often mutually beneficial. Advisory also functioned as professional development for teachers. It was difficult for advisors to hang on to general assumptions or stereotyped notions of students when they learned a student's history, visited the student's home multiple times, and got to know their students' families.

Advisory went through a series of modifications throughout the school's existence as teachers experimented and shared ideas about the best way to use the time for students' benefit. Eventually EPAA settled on a schedule where advisors met their advisees twice a day, 4 days a week, excluding Wednesday, which was an early-release day for students and professional development afternoon for teachers. On the other days, advisory occurred once in the morning for a 15-minute "homeroom" and once in the afternoon for a 55-minute homework and life skills period.

The 15-minute morning advisory period served as a check-in for advisors to monitor which students were tardy or absent. Advisors often were seen making calls from 8:05 A.M. until 8:15 A.M. to check in on students or to speed them along if they were late. Eventually, students were expected to call their advisors if they were going to arrive late to school, and this practice had a positive influence on the daily attendance of students.

The longer afternoon advisory period allowed teachers and students to devote time to relationship building by attending to individual academic and social-emotional needs. In addition to monitoring completion of homework and "major assessments" (usually large, multipart assignments or projects), advisors checked daily reports of students' academic progress. There was constant email communication between teachers and advisors regarding upcoming events, class assessments, and students who were required to attend after-school office hours. The school also had an in-house system that alerted advisors about students who failed to complete or revise an assignment with a "yellow slip" that detailed the missing work; students were then expected to use advisory time for completion.

Creating that quiet, focused space both during and after school was a critical element of supporting success. Because students could start their work in the afternoon advisory, teachers often could figure out what the students needed and send them to after-school office hours where they could get additional help.

During EPAA's weekly staff meetings, the faculty had many conversations about how to improve advisory time to maximize its effectiveness. The teachers closely examined what was working well and what were reasonable expectations for an advisor.

In the morning, teachers liked having a 15-minute check-in to get the students settled and ready for the day. During EPAA's first years, advisors' styles varied. Some did not have a set routine for morning advisory, while others had a regular round of activities such as SAT word of the day, college of the day, read-alouds, and "connections." All staff meetings began with connections, in which staff sat in a circle and shared personal news or checked in with the group to express appreciations and concerns. Some advisors adapted this practice for use with students. After the first senior class graduated, the faculty voted to have a standard structure for morning advisory.

All afternoon advisories began with either sustained silent reading (SSR) or 20 minutes of silent homework time. Staff wanted students to become independent learners and organize their work plan, attempting to complete assignments individually before seeking out help from a peer or the teacher. They also knew this time was vital for many students, who needed a quiet, stable environment where they could do their homework and get help. Lena Fasu, EPAA's first valedictorian, whom we introduced in Chapter 2, described how hard it was for her to study in her traditional, extended-family home:

> I lived in a three-bedroom house with 14 people, leaving me to rarely have a corner to myself to do school assignments. Naturally, the many people that inhabit a Samoan house also create a tremendous amount of noise as they go about their varied lives. Sounds of adults rushing to work as children cried often surrounded me. Still I continued to press on, thinking of the future and what I had to accomplish.

## From One-on-One Support to Systems of Support

Afternoon advisories also provided time for individual conversations with students. Rebecca described how she, like her colleagues, used advisory time for one-on-one conferences:

> Every day, at the beginning of advisory, I asked my students if they had any needs. Students would ask for a calculator, graph paper, colored

pencils, etc. I then asked if anyone wanted a conference, and I wrote their names on the whiteboard. Sometimes I added names to the list if I needed to check in with a student. They quickly learned that having a conference was not necessarily a bad thing, and some of my advisees requested conferences every single day. We sat at a table in the corner of the room while the rest of the students worked quietly, and we talked. The topics ranged from the mundane to the traumatic. I worked with students on problem-solving small conflicts with a teacher or students, or they might share with me deeply personal thoughts and experiences, such as that they were thinking of killing themselves or that they had been raped. I never knew what to expect when I went into a conference, but I learned that it was important to make conferences available every day and to make sure that I reached every student.

Sometimes the issues were mundane, for example, negotiating with parents about participating in sports or having fewer home responsibilities. Other times students just wanted someone listen to them vent about a difficult day or relationship. Often during these personal conversations students would reveal shocking information, like unplanned pregnancy, drug addiction, domestic violence, or homelessness. It was not unusual for students to ask advisors to help them talk to their parents about these issues.

The advisors' first response was to marshal resources—sending the student to the on-campus health van, to see a counselor, or to seek the principal's guidance. For issues that arose frequently, the school gradually created systems of support. For example, when staff discovered that many young women were becoming pregnant, the school created a partnership with Stanford School of Medicine to provide sex education classes and pregnancy prevention groups. Young women who did become pregnant had full use of the on-campus health van during their pregnancy. If necessary, advisors would organize independent study work for mothers who had just given birth, so they would be on track when they returned to school.

As much as possible, EPAA supported young mothers to stay in school, graduate on time, and continue on to college. Girls who were not able to attend school regularly or keep up with their independent study work were enrolled in a local continuation high school that had an on-site day care and a program for young mothers. Some of the girls returned to EPAA to graduate.

The understanding that the advisory role was far more than academic was an important distinction that all community members came to understand. The entire school community saw the advisor as more than "just a teacher." One parent of a student in Nicky's advisory commented:

To me the advisory is like a social service class. [My son's advisor] is available after school; if [my son] hasn't done something, she'll flag me down. She really takes a personal interest in the students. Even for the SAT, she was there. I don't know any school that sends a staff member to the SAT site to make sure everyone's organized. [My son] has an appreciation for the advisory. He knows that he can always go to his advisor.

One of Rebecca's advisees, who had many health problems, had this to say after she graduated:

During the process of [my having] anemia, she was always there to help me become stronger, even through some hard times. I had brought her down with my anger, but she didn't give up. She continued to be there for me. She even bought me an alarm clock just so that I could get to school on time. She also made sure to call me and make sure I was up. Seeing her love and respect for me made me get up and do something. I started walking more, going out, eating the food I needed, and having other teachers help me when I was confused. I guess what I needed was someone that was there for me to help me overcome my depression. But now I know that I am an intelligent and a determined female. Yes, determined to go to college and do my best.

## Challenges for Teachers

As one might imagine, the intensity of the advisor's role posed challenges for even the most seasoned teachers. It was not unusual for first-year teachers or those who had never taught at a small school or advised before to feel overwhelmed or discouraged. As one noted:

I know that advisory is really important because students establish a long-term, 4-year relationship with an adult, a different kind of adult. I think it's a really powerful thing. I'm kind of like their parent on campus, which is an interesting thing. It's hard, though. It's hard to know what to do. It's like being a parent for the first time. [It's] hard to know how to get kids to do what they need to do, hard to chase kids around when they're not showing up. I usually make phone calls, but sometimes I'm too busy.

Perhaps an unsurprising challenge of advisory was the differing experiences students encountered. Even with common ground rules, some advisories were highly structured while others were less so. Some advisors had a wide repertoire of strategies to draw on, while others struggled to meet the range of student needs.

In response to the teachers' request for support, lead advisors were later selected to serve as mentors. Teachers began to collaborate more intentionally around the needs of students at each grade level and to plan for those needs in advisory. As the school grew, and more teachers joined the staff, grade-level standardization for advisory activities and curriculum continued. For example, freshman advisory focused on academic norms for subject-matter classes; senior advisories focused on college, the application process, and post–high school decisionmaking.

As the external structure of advisory changed, and even when teachers employed different internal structures across advisories, its essential function remained the same: facilitating strong and sustained relationships between a small group of students and an adult in order to improve students' academic success. In fact, EPAA had one golden rule that was never broken during the first 4 years: Advisors and advisees were never reassigned. If a conflict or obstacle arose between an advisor and an advisee, or between two students in an advisory, the principal and lead teachers would intervene to mediate the conflict using a nonviolent communication protocol, explained in a later section of this chapter.

## PERSONALIZING TO SUPPORT POSITIVE BEHAVIOR

Perhaps unsurprisingly, the teachers found in the first year that they had a steep slope to climb to create a safe, respectful school environment in which students interacted peaceably with one another and were responsive to the faculty. There were fights on campus; some students belonged to, or were pursued by, gangs; teachers were often shocked by profane language and angry behavior directed toward them as well as bandied among students.

Like other schools, EPAA developed a behavior code and a list of steps to follow if a rule was violated, but it differed from many high schools because it did not have a list of impersonal, standardized consequences that would be applied for each offense. The focus of the process was on understanding what had happened, why, how it could be avoided in the future, and how the student could make amends to those harmed and the community as a whole. These days, this approach is known as restorative justice, and more schools are developing systems to support students in learning responsibility rather than merely being the subject of external rules and punishments.

Today East Palo Alto Academy has a formal curriculum for conflict resolution and a process for restorative justice, although when EPAA began, that concept was alien to most California high schools. A zero tolerance approach had been incorporated into the state education code, and most schools listed offenses subject to punishments that were almost entirely punitive and exclusionary, focusing heavily on in-school and out-of-school suspensions leading to expulsion.

Through trial and error, the school developed its own approach focused on student redemption, by seeking to develop a sense of student responsibility to the community along with the development of skills and tools that could help reshape behavior. The advisor eventually became the point person for disciplinary issues, because knowing how to proceed required knowing the student well.

As mentioned earlier, being an advisor was the best professional development a teacher could receive for culturally responsive teaching. Working closely and partnering with students and their families over the course of 4 years, advisors learned many details of students' experiences and gained a nuanced understanding of their emotional, social, and academic characteristics and needs. This process of seeking to understand a student and then having to advocate for him or her helped to undo many stereotypes or preconceptions that teachers may have had about students based on race or socioeconomic class.

Likewise, students and parents, who had developed a habit of mistrust due to past negative experiences with schools and teachers, learned to trust advisors and their intentions. The process of advising forced teachers to drop unproductive assumptions about groups of students and find real ways to meet individual students' needs. One teacher shared his experience before working at EPAA:

> One thing I didn't like about [my last school] was that there was always a line of Latino and Black kids, Polynesian kids, outside the principal's office. They were always getting in trouble. It seemed to me like they just were trying to be pushed out of the school.

That perspective had to change at EPAA. Because 100% of the students were students of color, and most lived in households near the poverty line, the effects of race and class on student interactions were mitigated. In large comprehensive schools where students of color are the minority, they often feel marginalized or are targeted more for disciplinary action. At EPAA, students of color did not have to struggle with the issues of race and privilege in the same ways that students in the neighboring high schools had to. One student in the class of 2006 reflected on this phenomenon:

> In [my last high school] people of color don't get as much attention
> . . . because of stereotypes basically, saying that "Oh yeah, they're lazy

or whatever." They only give attention to the children who ask for it. And here . . . the teachers make you realize that [school] should be something that you should be caring about.

## The Challenges of Creating an Effective, Personalized Approach

Most teachers at EPAA agreed that the school's philosophy was to meet students' needs and build on their strengths so that students would graduate high school and prepare for future endeavors. However, some teachers voiced concerns over the fact that keeping difficult students who consistently disrupted the learning environment, rather than expelling them, posed a risk to the culture of the school and interfered with other students' learning. A number of students posed sufficient challenge that the concern was legitimate, yet the school was committed to doing all that it could to serve each of its students. Figuring out how to do this while building a positive culture was an intense journey.

The commitment to personalization coupled with a lack of precedents in a new school meant that in the first year behavioral concerns were treated on a case-by-case basis. This was possible to do with only one grade level and a school that was amply staffed. However, teachers came to believe that a more explicit and standardized structure for behavior management would help students understand what was expected of them and the steps necessary to fulfill those expectations. One teacher recalled:

> At the beginning it was all of us running around trying to figure everything out in a small amount of time. And so, even with the organization and structures in place before our first year, it was very difficult to understand our behavior policy. We didn't really have one. It was just kind of come as you go, and you might get different answers from different people.

Faculty found themselves balancing the desire for more standardized approaches with the need for some individualization that allowed students to change unsuccessful behavior and redeem their academic reputations. Finding the balance depended in part on developing common norms and in part on understanding students more fully. As Nicky remarked in the third year of the school:

> We have such a better sense of our students now. I remember the first year I made a lot of mistakes. I didn't know how to back off and where to push and where not to push. Now I make fewer mistakes. It's kind of a delicate balance when you work with students—when to accept what

they are giving you even if it's not exactly what you want, and when to push for the things you do want.

In year one, we learned that the students try to play us against each other. We learned in year two and three how to stop them from playing us against each other. And we learned how to all say the same thing so students would get the same answer when they talk to different teachers. And we're learning the concept of steps and boundaries and not letting the kids stretch the boundaries within the classroom.

## The Discipline Process

The faculty created a behavior code that listed all school rules and infractions, as well as an accompanying intervention system for the school, which tracked incidents but allowed students to revise their behavior and redeem themselves. Except for offenses that required mandated suspensions (physical fights or weapons on campus), the steps that followed an incident focused on recognizing and rectifying the problem, to the greatest extent possible, beginning with the "FICA," a student-written narrative about his or her behavior and an opportunity to make amends. In the FICA essay, used since the school's inception, a student describes the *Facts* of what occurred, the *Impact* his or her actions had on the teacher and other students, the larger *Context* of the incident, and the further *Action* the student will take to try to rectify the situation. (See Appendix B for the FICA template.)

If that did not work, the process might move to daily progress reports and a behavior contract. If needed, parents would be called in for consultation to reinforce the plan. If this was unsuccessful, the process would lead to a disciplinary hearing with the family, which could be followed by suspension or expulsion.

However strict the behavior code was, the emphasis was on revision and redemption of behavior; as much as possible, interventions were structured so that the student had the necessary support to succeed. Advisors worked with the principal and vice principal to decide on appropriate consequences and interventions. One advisor commented on the effectiveness of personalizing discipline through advisory:

> The advisors are much better at [discipline] because [you] know the kids better and because you're not overwhelmed with 12 situations in a day. You may have one kid in a day. You can deal with it. You can make the phone calls home. . . . The advisors are also much better at understanding where a kid is. Personalization, knowing the kid, and knowing the situation [are key]. And I think that the advisors take a lot of pride in that these are my kids, I'm going to handle it. I want them to

succeed, and so I'm going to try to figure out ways to motivate them to do better rather than just punish them and move on.

Another teacher commented on the benefits of advisor support for students' behavior in their classes:

> I think the advisory system is very, very strong. I see students regularly, and I have intimate relationships with them. I can really get to them in terms of the needs they have, behavior issues they have, academic issues they have. But also, if I have a concern about a student in my class, I can be very well assured that I can talk to that person's advisor and their advisor will be assisting me with that student. So there's this back and forth . . . that is very beneficial to the students . . . and also in helping us reach the students. . . . I've seen students make improvements with that kind of "double teaming," I call it.

Generally, classroom teachers tried first to talk to students to teach them about the inappropriate behavior in the situation, and then worked with the students to help them rectify it. Classroom-level interventions included instructing students to apologize in person and in writing, return something taken, clean up a mess, modify behavior with another student or teacher, or even write out or rehearse a strategy for behaving differently in the future. Students also were referred to after-school community service where, under Nicky's watchful eye, they gave back to the school by picking up trash, cleaning walls and windows, or scraping gum from the underside of desks.

## The Importance of Student Reflection and Responsibility

If the classroom teacher's interventions did not yield the desired response from the student, or if there was an incident in class that needed immediate attention, the course instructor sent the student directly to his or her advisor (or in certain circumstances directly to the principal or vice principal), and the student formally entered the behavior intervention system. Most advisors had a table set up in their classroom where advisees could wait if they arrived when their advisor was teaching a class. Advisors were expected to immediately assign a FICA, as well as speak individually to the student when time permitted and contact parents as needed.

Students were instructed to write the FICA using "I" statements, taking responsibility for their own actions in whatever situation occurred. Often students had to write multiple drafts of their FICA until they accurately portrayed what happened and accepted responsibility for their part in it. The FICA also was translated into Spanish, and students could write in whatever language they felt comfortable.

The FICA became a common tool that served several functions at East Palo Alto Academy. First, it gave the student a chance to calm down if an incident was emotionally heightened. The act of sitting quietly and writing often de-escalated agitated emotions or situations. Second, the FICA gave students the opportunity to tell their side of the story in their own words and guarantee that their voice would be heard. Finally, responding to these questions gave the students the time and space needed to reflect on the incident, to think about how their behaviors affected the school community, and to imagine what could have been done differently. Behavior policies in large comprehensive schools often leave out the space for student voice, which is why some students use their actions to speak and make statements. Also, behavior policies often omit a formal step for student reflection, which is one reason why many students repeat the same disruptive actions over and over again.

For students who had chronic behavior issues, other interventions were used in addition to the FICA and conferences with advisors and parents. After three incidents, students were assigned 2 weeks on a "green card," a daily progress report that was signed by the student's teachers, his or her advisor, and the parents or guardian. This process required daily reflection on the part of the student, in concert with these adults. Students who successfully completed 2 weeks on a green card with fewer than three negative reports no longer had to carry a daily progress report.

Students who were unsuccessful on green cards moved to yellow cards for 2 weeks, then to a behavior contract for a period of weeks or months. All behavior contracts required meetings with the student, his or her advisor, the parents or guardians, and either the principal or vice principal, and everyone in attendance signed the behavior contract. Students who successfully completed the terms of their behavior contracts would work their way back down the hierarchy of consequences in the behavior intervention system, through yellow and green daily progress reports to writing FICAs. However, students who broke their behavior contract repeatedly were assigned to a formal disciplinary hearing, where a final disciplinary contract was generated.

A small percentage of students reached the level of the disciplinary hearing, and a tiny number were put up for formal expulsions for offenses that, under state law, required an expulsion hearing—carrying a weapon, setting a fire, drug possession. However, all students who were put up for expulsion in the first 4 years of the school received suspended expulsions and were allowed to reintegrate into the EPAA community under a strict postexpulsion contract.

Students also could be suspended from school because of major or persistent infractions like fighting. Wherever possible, Nicky preferred having a student attend school during an in-house suspension and work on class assignments with his or her advisor or the principal, rather than staying home and watching TV. Often this was coupled with a community service activity.

The goal was to have the student continue to work on academics while trying to improve his or her positive participation in the community.

Nearly all of these students made it through high school, gaining in maturity and interpersonal skill along the way. "Can you believe how I used to act and how much I have changed?" was a common question seniors asked teachers and advisors, and a conversation that adults freely engaged in to take the opportunity to praise students for their growth. One graduate from the first class commented:

> The biggest thing they did was help me with my attitude because basically I was [stubborn]. I think before I act now. I've learned how to understand people a little bit better, not to take things that people might say the wrong way.

The emerging maturity of the first class of juniors and seniors made a significant impact on the school culture. Because these maturing students recognized the nonproductiveness of their earlier behavior, they often called out the freshmen and sophomores for engaging in similar antics. Due to the close relationships developed at EPAA, upperclassmen began to act openly to protect the school community and, especially, their advisory classmates. Students would tell their advisors to check in with certain peers who were involved in a conflict or were thinking of fighting, were worried about a family situation, or were confused or depressed about a teenage issue like pregnancy or drug abuse.

Sometimes juniors and seniors would counsel younger students about their behavior, or they would approach Nicky and Jeff, the vice principal, about a student who had done something wrong and lied about it. This is truly remarkable because the act of snitching is taboo in most teenage cultures and is especially dangerous in communities like East Palo Alto, where retaliation for snitching is serious. Many of the staff became skilled at leveraging their relationships with students to get them to confess what they had done and make amends. The effect of this type of intervention was that students themselves would be able to work to repair the damage to the community created by their actions.

One parent commented about the effectiveness of this commitment, as seen in the school's fourth year:

> When I come after school, I notice the staff try to really talk to kids and find out what the problem is and work with them. Kids have other issues that cause them to do things. They try to work with them as opposed to a larger school where there is zero tolerance. There are not a lot of problems here.

Still, some teachers questioned the role of advisor in this process. Novice teachers and those new to the school often were used to the model of a central administration that dealt with discipline and they felt out of their element. One new teacher noted:

> Discipline is mostly carried out by the advisor. There are pluses and minuses to this. As a new teacher, I was inexperienced in disciplining students and not confident about discipline decisions. In retrospect, I made good decisions, but it was hard to see this at the time. I was not able to support consequences with good reasons because I was not sure I was doing it right.

The tension that this teacher described was one that arose periodically among the staff, leading to discussions as to whether advisors should have any responsibility for student discipline. Even though the staff revisited this topic yearly, the fact remained that teachers saw the benefit of the advisor, the person who had the closest relationship with the student, informing the decision about appropriate consequences and supporting the student's learning process.

## The Value of the Long View: Kristine's Story

Kristine Lewis's story illustrates how personal involvement in students' lives over a substantial period of time influenced not only the students but the teachers who became their advisors. As we described in Chapter 2, Kristine had lost her mother to illness during middle school and would lose her brother to violence in her senior year. She lived in a crime-ridden section of the city and had seen far too much for a person of her age. Her anger lived just under the surface at most times and would erupt without apparent cause or warning.

As her advisor and the principal, Nicky was always in the position of enforcing school rules, which was made more complicated by the fact that Kristine often would push back publicly, challenging the school culture and encouraging other students to do the same. During daily advisory, Kristine often would respond to Nicky's questions with silence or verbal rage: "Don't talk to me!" or "F--k this."

Because Kristine was a leader on campus, her influence was often in direct conflict with EPAA's academic culture. She seemed to be trying to test the teachers because she felt everyone had failed her before and she wanted to see whether EPAA would fail her, too. As a freshman, Kristine could barely interact with adults when she was angry without being offensive; she continued this tone in her many FICAs, which she usually had to rewrite. After many eruptions in multiple classes, Nicky put Kristine on a strict behavior contract with the following two provisions, focused on respect and responsiveness:

1. I will follow all directions given to me by an adult, including answering questions.
2. I will talk respectfully to adults and will not use profanity at or around them. This includes using respectful words and using a respectful tone.

The benefits of advisory looping over multiple years and building enduring relationships with students were most obvious after a student had been at EPAA for at least 2 years. Nicky persisted in holding Kristine to a high standard and requiring her to reflect and take responsibility. Like other students who used to explode in anger and a tirade of epithets, Kristine eventually learned that this method of responding to problems was unproductive. During her senior year, Kristine had to write only one FICA—and this one she professionally typed.

Even then Kristine was not easy to understand. Rebecca inherited Kristine as an advisee in her senior year, when Nicky needed to pass on her advisory to tend full-time to the needs of the growing school. At first, Rebecca admitted feeling intimidated by Kristine's in-your-face manner, but knowing Kristine was interested in the military (she had decided to enroll in ROTC), Rebecca decided to assume a caring but no-nonsense approach: "I wouldn't negotiate with her. I would state my decision and stick to it. . . . I spoke to her in a more formal manner than I did with the other students, and it seemed to work."

When Kristine's brother was shot and killed during the spring of her senior year, Rebecca attended his funeral and organized EPAA teachers to send flowers and donate money to the memorial fund. In a packed church, a sobbing Kristine, wearing a white t-shirt with a picture of her dead brother on it, allowed Rebecca to hug her for the first time. "I remember thinking what a big deal that was," Rebecca recalled.

Getting Kristine through the last 3 months of school was another major hurdle. Rebecca wondered:

How could I maintain the structure that she needed while giving her the space she needed to grieve? She would come late every day and some days not at all, but I still tried to maintain the standards and push her, but not too much because I thought she would totally shut down. When she talked about dropping out, we refocused her on staying in school, on envisioning herself on graduation day.

Indeed, Kristine did graduate on time and went on to earn a bachelor's degree from a West Coast college. As was often the case between advisors and advisees, Rebecca kept in contact with Kristine, coaching her through some academic and personal challenges in her first year at college. Rebecca wrote in a letter of recommendation, "Kristine had to make conscious choices to stay focused on her goal: college graduation. Students who do not have Kristine's inner strength would have stumbled and fallen many more times, but Kristine is an example of powerful resilience." That resilience was cultivated by the adults who worked with Kristine to channel her anger, leadership, and energy more productively—adults who were, themselves, resilient in their relationships with her.

## NONVIOLENT CONFLICT RESOLUTION

Kristine was not alone in her flashing temper. Many students could get angry easily in a public place, venting in a classroom or in the lunchroom, rather than to a friend or parent at home. The short bursts of anger sometimes escalated into full-blown fights, mostly among freshmen new to the school's culture, but sometimes among older students. Most fights were really public squabbles, and most students responded to teachers quickly separating them and instructing them to write their FICAs. Individual students usually were suspended for fighting, but once in a while fights were large, involving many individuals, and split along racial lines.

A memorable fight occurred one October between Tani, a Tongan girl, and an African American boy, Dante. Tani and Dante exchanged words, and Dante pushed Tani. During lunch that day, Tani told her brother, Sese, what had happened, and her brother immediately exploded in anger, cornering Dante in the gym cafeteria. A crowd of students gathered; the school's most senior teacher, William Dean, intervened and stood in front of Dante to protect him.

Sese picked up a 32-gallon plastic garbage bin and threw it at Dante; it missed him, spilling leftover lunches everywhere. After the commotion subsided, William directed Sese to pick up the garbage, and the students were suspended. By this time Sese's anger had turned the fight into a racial incident, with the Tongan siblings and cousins on one side and Dante and his African American friends on the other.

Clearly, a larger and more comprehensive intervention was needed to build and restore community. Nicky turned to a set of nonviolent communication techniques she had adapted from *Nonviolent Communication: A Language of Life* by Marshall Rosenberg.[3] These strategies had been used on campus for some time, mainly in small sessions with two or more students who had a conflict. On this occasion, Nicky invited all involved students and their advisors and families to a meeting on campus at night. The meeting was required before students could return from their suspensions. Everyone sat in a circle of chairs in a classroom, each group of students on opposite sides of the circle flanked by their parents and advisors.

The entire meeting was scripted, like a ritualized response to heal the spontaneous rupture caused by the fight. Nicky set the ground rules: First the students would talk, then the parents. Nicky began: "We're here because of what happened, but we are not going to belabor the details. We all think we know what happened, but what is more important to heal the community is to look at how we *feel* about what happened and to think about where we are going from here."

Nicky instructed everyone to share what they were feeling when the incident happened. Tani shared that she was hurt when Dante teased her. Dante shared that he was scared when Sese threw the trash can, and Dante's friends shared their anger at Sese for publicly threatening their friend. Nicky then asked each side to repeat something a person on the other side had said. If one couldn't remember what the other had said, the other repeated it. This continued until everyone's feelings had been remembered and restated correctly.

Nicky then asked each person to say what he or she needed for this conflict to end. Tani said she needed the boys to stop bothering her. Likewise, Dante and his friends said they needed Tani to keep her comments to herself when she walked down the hallway. They repeated and remembered one another's statements.

Finally, Nicky asked what each person could give to end the conflict. Tani said she could set a better example for her cousins and peers by not getting angry so quickly. Dante's friends said they could check their facts before rushing to Dante's side.

Then the parents spoke, and they had nothing but praise for their children's words of peace. Having the parents' respect did much to heal the wounds between the children. It also made their peace public.

Even though students only shared words and promises of improved behavior at these peacemaking meetings, the conflict resolution worked. Twice during her 5 years as principal, Nicky called these large roundtable meetings. Both times they worked to resolve a complex conflict and gave the campus a chance to breathe and heal.

## THE IMPACT OF DETERMINED PERSONALIZATION

This approach took a lot of effort that did not come easily in the press of all the demands of starting a new school and meeting students' other needs. It required perseverance and determination, and did not work for every single student. It also provoked a lot of conversation among teachers about whether they should keep trying to work with students whose behavior suggested they did not want to be there, and whether that undermined the school's reputation with more "promising" students already focused on academic investment and college. Nicky often reminded the faculty, "We don't look at our school as a push-out school. We see it as a place to help and nurture students." The teachers came to understand that long-lasting personal change takes time. This meant giving students multiple chances to reflect on and change their behavior instead of emphasizing punishment that led inexorably to pushing them out.

There were risks involved. East Palo Alto Academy did not want to be known as a "last chance" school or a continuation school for students who left or were expelled from the public school system. However, it also was committed to taking all students who walked through the door and were dedicated to their education, regardless of their special needs, English language proficiency, or academic abilities. EPAA's advisory and the behavior intervention system were designed to give students multiple opportunities to learn how to succeed, including recognizing destructive habits and learning to change them. It was a delicate balance between giving students chances and letting them take advantage of the school's culture of revision and redemption. Nicky commented in the spring of 2005, before the school's first graduation:

> We believe in our mission . . . that this environment is actually good for the large majority of students. This is the kind of school that we've set up. . . . We are about retention versus kicking kids out. Our mission is we work with you as hard as we can. [We] make the guarantee to parents and students that if you come to school every day, do all the work we ask you to do, and accept the help we offer, you will absolutely graduate and have the opportunity to go to college. I can make that guarantee because we've set up our school to deliver on that promise.

And it was certainly true that many students who would not have graduated and would not have gone on to college did so in this context. Time and again, the graduates said that personalization made the biggest difference in their experience at EPAA. When interviewed after graduation, nearly all mentioned their teachers' and advisors' persistent support and high expectations. Even beyond graduation, EPAA teachers stayed in touch with alumni, providing academic and personal assistance. The words of several alumni illustrated their ongoing communication and relationships with their advisors:

> We catch up. We talk about everything from classes to how my parents are doing, how his family is doing.

> It was my first time in college, and there was a lot that I didn't know. [My advisor] told me what to take in college, how to get a math tutor. I went ahead and did it and I passed math with a C.

We talk all the time. Most of the time, she's asking me how I am doing in school. If I need help, I call her for suggestions.

[My advisor] came to my mom's funeral.

My advisor told me she's my advisor for life. If I'm having a rough time, if I need help with my resume, she's there.

One graduate who had to leave college temporarily due to financial issues talked extensively with her advisor and other teachers about adjusting her college and career plans so that she could stay afloat in the short term and return to college when she had raised enough money. These teachers also helped her with job applications and preparation for interviews.

Many years after their seniors graduate, advisors are still in contact with their advisees. To this day, teachers joke, "Once you're an advisor, you're an advisor for life."

Quite often the most appreciative students are those who initially had the hardest time with school. In the words of one:

Thank you for your love and support and especially to my advisor . . . because I [am always] acting up and he always, always, always still believes in me and helps me and never judges me and supports me.

And another gave staff this advice:

Don't give up on them. You probably [are] their only hope for them to actually do good because they know you won't give up.

## CHAPTER 4

# Creating an Academic Culture

> One thing about the school is that they have actually thought about the academic program, and it's not something that is just thrown in front of you. The assignments we do in class have something to do with tackling a problem in the world, something that you're going to have to deal with far in the future. Those are two main things that set up East Palo Alto Academy from the rest.
>
> —Graduate, class of 2005

EPAA was committed to ensuring that every student would have the opportunity upon graduation to pursue higher education if they chose. But students had to want that opportunity, and be willing to pursue the path to getting there, and that was not a given. Creating a strong academic culture was one of the toughest hurdles that the teachers of East Palo Alto Academy faced. In this chapter, we describe the initial obstacles to establishing academic norms that students could buy into and the many approaches used to overcome those obstacles.

## CONFRONTING THE CHALLENGES

The first part of the challenge was to create high expectations—instilling the idea that academic engagement was expected and achievable and that college was a desirable and attainable goal. The second part was to help students develop the work habits necessary for academic and life success.

The obstacles were numerous, as many of the students who attended EPAA did not have the benefit of a stable K–8 academic experience. Students often told stories of school dysfunction in their middle and elementary schools, and this dysfunction was witnessed often by faculty when they accompanied EPAA students to middle schools to recruit incoming 9th-graders. Once, for example, when Nicky and her student ambassadors[1] went to make a recruitment presentation at an East Palo Alto middle school, they encountered a scene that Nicky described as follows

> We walked into a classroom that had a substitute teacher and found the room in total disarray. The teacher was sitting at his desk in the corner,

ignoring the students, who were spread out around the room doing what they wanted. All the desks had been pushed out of rows and there were textbooks on the floor with covers ripped off. Pushed up in the front corner were four students sitting in two rows of two desks working diligently on schoolwork; the rest of the students were clearly goofing off. Before we could make our presentation, we had the students pick up the trash on the floor and rearrange themselves into rows. I started the presentation with a short speech about students respecting themselves as learners.

Generally, EPAA freshmen did not have a history of sustained and positive academic experience, and were, in Nicky's words, "educationally malnourished." Many had lost faith in teachers and schools. This, compounded by underdeveloped academic skills and identities, often led to disruptive classroom behavior.

Tina Ehsanipour was one of the teachers who especially took up the challenge of creating an academic culture, building on her experience attending an academically rigorous, private high school in the Bay Area and her commitment to make that quality of education available to those who typically had little access. Tina also drew on her undergraduate years at Berkeley and her training in STEP. As she explained:

> We dealt with angry adolescents who had no problems defying authority, swearing at teachers like it was what they had done all their lives. We struggled as a team to create engaging curriculum that would not only prepare our group of mostly low-skilled students, but that would also spark their energy and passion.

In Farsi, Tina's native language, the name *Tina* means flower, and Tina was tiny and delicate-looking, with long, curly black hair. But appearances can be deceptive. Tina held a black belt in jujitsu, which she could activate at any time, and was a spoken-word poet and a creative writer. She was also a teacher-revolutionary, passionate about changing the world one mind at a time. Tina never relented in asking students and staff to think deeply.

And critical thinking in the classroom context was one of the challenges for a group of students whose previous academic experiences had been spotty at best and mostly dominated by fill-in-the-blank worksheets. As one teacher commented:

> And as far as I can ascertain there was not much training at all in their early education [on critical thinking]. They don't look to me like students who were expected to formulate thoughts. They behave like students who frantically try to get the right answer, what they think I

want them to say, or they shut down because they seem to have a sense
of despair over not being able to get the answer that they think I want.

Students were, on average, multiple grade levels behind in reading, writing, and arithmetic skills, and most lacked confidence that they could rise
above their inadequate prior education, even with strong academic and personal support. In most years, the entering freshman class had average reading
and math skills at the 3rd- or 4th-grade level; very occasionally, a cohort of
students reached the 5th-grade level, on average, in their entering skills.[2] Although many students performed low academically, they often displayed high
levels of critical thinking and problem solving in their everyday lives. Many
had adult responsibilities in their work and home lives, but had not learned to
bring these skills into the school environment and transfer them to academic
work.

As a result of their earlier experiences, many young people who entered
EPAA did not know how to be *students*. Many had not ever before done work
in class, much less homework outside of class. They did not know how to read
for understanding, write beyond a few sentences (often without punctuation
or capitalization), take notes, ask questions, manipulate numbers, conduct
research, or engage in academic discourse. Most had not been asked to reason
their way through a problem, develop an evidence-based point of view, discuss a piece of literature, or debate a social question. When asked to do these
things, they did not know where to start, and many resisted. This did not seem
like school to them; it challenged their sense of themselves and raised insecurities and fears about whether they could succeed.

Of course, there was a range in student capacities and needs, which is well
illustrated through our focal students. Earlier we described Malcolm Davis,
who had struggled throughout school within the special education program in
Ravenswood, as one of most underprepared students. Malcolm entered high
school with a 1st-grade reading level and almost no academic confidence.
The challenge for students like Malcolm was helping him build skills in a very
purposeful way and convincing him that he ultimately could succeed, so that
he would try things well beyond his comfort zone.

Like Malcolm, Esperanza Ramirez had to travel a significant distance to
acquire the skills and self-confidence she needed for college, having entered
the United States and the school with no English after a set of traumatic experiences that left her scarred and shaken. Kristine Lewis was intelligent,
well-spoken, and a born leader, but she was often angry and oppositional,
and inclined to push away from the goals that adults wanted her to embrace.

Pablo Fuentes entered with academic promise but without an academic
skill set. He had spent middle school getting high and getting into trouble, and
he needed to learn how to attend school, use his abilities, make up for lost
time, and get serious about schoolwork. While Pablo was ready to settle down

after he returned from El Salvador (where his parents had sent him to work
in the fields), he lacked the educational experiences that normally prepare
students for high school work, and he sometimes could distract himself and
his peers from classroom tasks.

We introduced Lena Fasu as one of the most focused students in the first
class, who took advantage of every opportunity, graduated first in her class,
attended a prestigious University of California campus, and graduated from
college in 3 years. However, even Lena felt sorely underprepared when she
entered high school. She described her feelings this way:

> EPAA provided me with the kind of attention I needed to succeed. Never
> before had I received such support within the classroom. Before high
> school, teaching went as far as being given a packet [of handouts] for the
> week; this was definitely not the case in my high school. Not only did
> my teachers support me, but they also pushed me past my limits.

There were times when Lena felt not only constrained by the shortcomings of her prior educational experiences and pushed beyond her limits, but
also frustrated by the poor behavior of many of her peers, who were often
off-task and disruptive in class. As Lena herself later said:

> It was already difficult enough to try to succeed in high school, but to
> deal with students like these made the task that much harder. . . . [If my]
> classmates were frustrated and didn't understand the work, they would
> have outbursts. That was what was distracting. But I understood that all
> students have individual needs, and some needed more help than others.

Thus, the other parts of building an academic climate were:

- Engaging all students in the work that only some initially wanted to
  learn to do
- Teaching them the skills that they should have been, but previously
  were not, taught
- Managing the psychology that led many to act out in order to distract
  attention from their lack of skills
- Keeping them committed when they were "pushed beyond their
  limits"

Teachers often discussed the challenges of getting all of their students to become as invested in the school's academic culture as Lena was.

One final consideration was the fact that few students had relatives who
had graduated from high school or gone to college, so the idea of doing either

was fairly abstract and mysterious. Relatively few families held postsecondary aspirations for their children, beyond getting a job that could help pay the rent. Motivating students to put forth the effort needed to make huge progress in high school required that they develop a vision of where they wanted to go and what it would take. In the words of one teacher:

> They struggle to be self-sufficient learners; they want to be, but reading hinders them. Regular student stuff is hard, too. Getting assignments done, getting engaged, there are so many things that challenge them. One of the biggest [challenges] is that there aren't that many community, neighborhood, or family members who have graduated high school and even fewer who have graduated from college. They have few role models. The default state is to drop out.

Another teacher reflected:

> Most students still wonder if they want to be in school, if school is important. Trying to get students to jump from the idea of dropping out of school to that of going to college is a huge leap.

## DEVELOPING STRATEGIES FOR BUILDING CULTURE

Many key components were necessary to create an academic culture that would prepare students for college and the workplace. As we have described, the school hired a cadre of dedicated and qualified teachers, change agents who would not back down from the on-the-job challenges. East Palo Alto Academy strove be the antithesis of the traditional factory-model high school where students switch classrooms every 50 minutes and face a whole new set of expectations and regulations in each room. Instead, the faculty deliberately created consistent academic and behavioral expectations across all classrooms. The school operated under the principle that all students can learn when given an opportunity to experience success rooted in tolerance, acceptance, and belonging. Faculty designed and taught a rigorous and engaging curriculum, and developed systems to support all students, including longer class periods and looping so that students stayed with the same teacher for more than 1 year.

The staff named each classroom in the school after colleges the faculty had attended: Stanford, UC Berkeley, Wellesley, Duke, San Jose State, and more. This gave staff a hook for talking about their own experiences and what different colleges are like. Advisors took their students to visit colleges, and teachers sought to set expectations at every opportunity, beginning sentences with phrases like, "When you're in college . . ."

But more was needed, and there was no silver bullet. The staff constantly worked and reworked their strategies for building an academic culture that could focus students on intellectual work while helping them believe in and care enough about their own educational success to invest their energy in school. There were three major strategies that proved critical in the first years:

- Establishing habits of mind
- Creating a rigorous and relevant curriculum
- Bringing college to the campus

Each of these strategies is explored in the following sections.


## ESTABLISHING HABITS OF MIND

As introduced in Chapter 3, the centerpiece for building an academic culture was the Five Community Habits, East Palo Alto Academy's statement of the essential skills and habits that staff desired students to internalize by the time of graduation. The staff wanted a clear statement of expectations with a built-in barometer that measured their own and students' success against these standards.

The process was launched by beginning with the end in mind. What did teachers want students to know, do, and be like when they graduated? Teachers knew that good students demonstrated particular personal and social skills necessary for success, but these skills were rarely taught explicitly. EPAA faculty wanted to instill lifelong, positive habits that would foster critical thinking skills, expertise in collaborating with others, and high levels of emotional intelligence,[3] all of which are essential for success in the 21st-century world.[4]

Jeff Gilbert, the Humanities Department chair and school's vice principal, explained the process of developing EPAA's schoolwide standards:

> You hear so often from teachers, I can't teach these student skills because I'm teaching content, but it became obvious to me that whenever you are teaching content you *are* teaching skills like communication and creative thinking.
>
> We wanted to describe more than the mental processes at work and include a richer description of what kind of person we wanted students to be when they left school. We were planning backwards. I remember during our first school planning meetings that we broke into groups and we all tried to describe the ideal graduate. Then we came back and compared notes. We had to go back and forth, but there was consensus pretty quickly.

EPAA's Five Community Habits were (and still are):

- *Personal responsibility*—Being prepared and punctual, participating in classroom activities, and working hard to produce academic work
- *Social responsibility*—Interacting with others respectfully, resolving conflicts peacefully, collaborating well on group tasks, taking responsibility for oneself and one's actions, and contributing positively to the school and broader community
- *Critical and creative thinking*—The ability to ask questions and pose problems; predict, hypothesize, and infer; investigate, gather, and organize evidence; answer questions by analyzing, synthesizing, justifying, imagining, and creating; and reflect, make connections, and revise by seeking other perspectives and taking them into account
- *Application of knowledge*—Demonstration of content knowledge, conceptual understanding, and content-related skills in relation to the curriculum standards, and ability to apply knowledge and skills to new tasks or contexts, and to integrate them with other knowledge and skills
- *Communication*—The ability to communicate ideas clearly, organize thoughts, and present effectively in oral, written, and visual forms

These habits guided the development of curriculum, the rubrics used to evaluate student work on every assignment in every class, the feedback students received, and the design and evaluation of yearly public exhibitions of student work (described further in Chapter 5). In short, the Five Habits were used to teach students in a consistent and persistent manner what it meant to be a student, a worker, and a member of a community at EPAA (see Appendix A). This consistency was hugely important in developing an academic culture in the school. As one student noted, "The [Five Habits] rubric has been the best thing for me over the last 4 years." This student reflected on how useful the rubric was in helping her to grow academically because it gave her a clear understanding of what standards she was meeting and what she had to improve upon.

Having schoolwide habits also influenced the way teachers designed curriculum and instruction. Jeff explained:

If you were going to assess students on critical and creative thinking, communication, or how to work in a group, you had to teach these skills. I have never met a social studies teacher who said it was most important to master facts. They always said students need to think critically, consult sources, and problem-solve, but they don't usually teach these skills. At EPAA, we developed a clear set of skills that drove our curriculum.

## MAKING SCHOOL RIGOROUS AND RELEVANT

If the soul of EPAA was relationship and personalization, then a rigorous and relevant curriculum, with a litany of adaptive supports, was the heart. In every subject area, teachers sought to create a relevant curriculum that reached students where they were, but then rigorously accelerated them forward in their learning toward the critical thinking skills and deep understandings of concepts embedded in the Habits. Teachers collaboratively developed curriculum by first looking at state content standards and then looking at student achievement data for the particular subject area and thinking about both of these in light of their deeper learning goals.

### A Commitment to Revision and Redemption

In addition, the faculty continually modified curriculum based on weekly formative and summative assessments, and took time every year to reflect on curriculum units and how students responded to them. Formative assessments—reflections, discussions, quizzes, homework, or classwork—were used to gauge student progress toward mastery of a skill or concept throughout a unit of study. Summative assessments used to evaluate achievement at the end of a unit or semester were usually projects or presentations, and sometimes tests. As described in the next chapter, these were never the end of the story for students or for teachers. Through the school's commitment to "revision and redemption," students were encouraged continually to revise and improve their work and their rubric scores. And teachers also continually revised their curriculum, assignments, assessments, and instruction as they saw how students responded.

The first task faculty faced in developing an academic culture was to create work that students would want to do for intrinsic reasons. The traditional extrinsic incentives used in high school—"do this to get to college," or "if you don't do that, you'll lose points or fail"—were ineffective because students did not believe they would go to college (and did not know why they would want to, since they did not know anyone who had gone). Furthermore, when threatened with failure, many simply would succumb, since failure was a familiar way to cope with the experience of school.

As we describe below, the curriculum was carefully crafted to offer intellectually challenging and engaging experiences for students, as teachers knew that while their students often needed to acquire basic skills, this need not and should not be equated with rote learning. They had active, inquiring minds that needed to be put to use acquiring those skills in the context of meaningful curriculum and engaging pedagogy.

## The Power of Authentic Engagement

Especially in the first year, there were quite a number of students who had not developed the habit of doing work during school and even more who had never done work outside of class time. With so much ground to cover, the teachers knew that had to change. One of the most powerful and school-transforming experiences was developed in the first year by the 9th-grade humanities team. William Dean and Jeff Gilbert created an inquiry project in which students were to learn about the history, geography, context, and culture of East Palo Alto in order to present—through written essays and videography—a set of mini-documentaries about their community to Stanford faculty and master's students in STEP. (For the STEP students, this offered an opportunity to see and engage with authentic assessment, as they evaluated the students' exhibitions.)

The work began, and when a date was set for the exhibition, the level of motivation skyrocketed. All of a sudden, with a real audience wanting to learn about something the students deeply cared about, they had a reason to want to work hard—to do their research and find effective ways to present it, to meet a high standard. To be proud of their presentations was to express their commitment to and pride in their community.

For the first time, every single student was engaged and working, not just in class but beyond class time as each completed the research, wrote and revised, filmed and edited, rehearsed and polished. When the day came, it was an emotional experience for both high school and university students. The collective video was aired in an auditorium at Stanford; both on that stage and in classrooms where individual projects were showcased, EPAA students presented their stories and analyses—from the deeply personal to the seriously sociological. Stanford students asked authentic questions of the authors and learned about the community as well as the depth of understanding of the students; they scored the presentations using a rubric and offered feedback. The EPAA students felt like bona fide scholars when they left the university campus.

This experience and others like it informed the evolution of curriculum for each of the major subject areas offered at EPAA, as described below.

*Humanities.* The decision to combine English language arts and history/social studies in a single, yearlong humanities course was based on a desire to make curriculum more relevant and engaging. Integrating these two subject areas reduced each teacher's pupil load by half so that the teacher could support more extensive writing and project work on the part of students. Because students earned credit for two classes (social studies and English), humanities met twice as long as other core classes, and because students stayed with the same teacher for two periods, humanities teachers typically taught 40 to 50 students, rather than the 150 or so an English or history teacher would see in a traditional high school structure.

The humanities curriculum initially was conceptualized and designed by Jeff Gilbert and William Dean, two of the school's wisest and most senior faculty members, along with the principal, who also taught humanities. Like Nicky, vice principal Jeff Gilbert had been a Stanford undergrad and STEP graduate many years before. Before coming to EPAA, he had been one of the most beloved social studies teachers at nearby Hillsdale High School, to which he later returned to create small learning communities founded on the principles he helped develop at EPAA. (Also supported in its reform agenda by faculty at Stanford, Hillsdale's later redesign was so successful in raising achievement and reducing the achievement gap that it was later profiled by *Newsweek* and the *Washington Post*.[5])

Jeff thought deeply about matters of learning and about how to organize a school and curriculum to support every student and teacher in becoming a more thoughtful, competent, and caring person. In faculty meetings, Jeff had a reputation for quietly asking the right question at the right time to move a stalled conversation forward. Despite his low-key demeanor, he loved sports and was highly competitive. In addition to his vice principal duties, Jeff also taught a section of humanities and coached the boys and girls basketball teams.

William Dean was a Rutgers University graduate who had been teaching English for almost 30 years first in his home state of New Jersey, then in Las Vegas, and finally in the Bay Area. Mr. Dean, as he was known by everyone, was by all accounts the students' most beloved teacher, a father figure to the young staff, and the best-dressed man on campus. A dignified Caribbean American gentleman, William came to EPAA to finish out his career and retire: Before he left, he served as a humanities teacher, a coach for beginning teachers, and even the school's vice principal (dubbed "Dean Dean" by the staff and students) for a year. He was also one of the school's first National Board–certified teachers and helped coach others through the process.

Jeff Gilbert and Mr. Dean co-designed and individually taught the humanities course that blended English and history/social studies in a project-based curriculum. Nicky contributed key ideas and curriculum units to the early design as well. They organized humanities curriculum content across the four grade levels as follows:

> *9th grade:* Introduction to Social Studies and English Language Arts
> *10th grade:* World History and World Literature
> *11th grade:* U.S. History and American Literature
> *12th grade:* U.S. Government, Economics, and Modern Fiction and
>     Nonfiction

Authentic learning experiences occurred at each grade level. In 9th grade, students studied their own community and wrote an autobiography. In conjunction with studying the Holocaust and World War II, sophomores visited the Museum of Tolerance in Los Angeles. Upon their return, they created their own museum of tolerance, relating their learning of Holocaust facts, such as the persecution of homosexuals under the Nazi regime, to current issues like homophobic hate crimes.

Sophomores also studied imperialism and re-created the South African Truth and Reconciliation hearings of those who murdered Amy Biehl and Steve Biko, transforming themselves into lawyers, defendants, and witnesses. They held live court sessions in the Redwood City Courthouse that were presided over by local community leaders, including lawyers and professors. Family, friends, and community members were invited to witness student presentations.

Juniors studied the Civil Rights era in depth, and some had the opportunity to participate in Sojourn to the Past,[6] a 10-day journey to the South where students visited important historical sites and met people who were part of the movement themselves.

Seniors learned about the Supreme Court and the Constitution, and did an in-depth study of selected Supreme Court cases that they presented to law students in the practice courtrooms of Santa Clara University (SCU). These trials were a series of civil liberties cases that had been argued in front of state supreme courts or the U.S. Supreme Court. Some of the cases students reenacted included: *People v. Woody, Johnson v. Santa Clara County Transportation Agency, National Socialist Party v. Skokie, Ill., Stanford v. Kentucky,* and *U.S. v. Chadwick.* An SCU professor worked with students to design the project, and then he, along with two SCU law students, hosted the mock trials at the law school where they acted as judges for the cases.

In the area of economics, seniors wrote a personal financial plan for a fictitious future, learning how to budget responsibly in the process.

Projects like these created opportunities for students to explore history and the world through a social justice framework, which helped to empower them when they thought about their individual and collective ability to influence change in their lives, community, and the world. Thus, school curriculum was not only about learning facts and analyzing them, but about building students' capacities to be change agents.

These authentic experiences often had a lasting impact on students. One student who went on the Sojourn trip wrote in her senior personal statement:

> Non-violence was my goal and my trip with Sojourn to the Past was
> my ticket. . . . I never pictured myself sitting in front of Martin Luther
> King's grave, much less touching it. But that day when I sat under
> the rain face-to-face with the man that fought against racism and

discrimination through non-violence, my views changed. For me, it became a reality check. I realized that violence has never been the answer and that instead of granting me power, it would only destroy me. To see the grave and Dr. King's Baptist Church as the center of the city and as a reminder of his struggle for freedom confronted me with a truth: violence has a duality. It makes you feel powerful yet inside its hatred slowly poisons you.

*Mathematics.* Curriculum development in mathematics followed a progression similar to that in humanities. Mathematics teachers, led by Seth Leslie, had a great deal of flexibility in designing a curriculum that best suited their students' needs. Math courses went through a series of modifications, evolving from an integrated mathematics approach in the first year of the school to a more traditional sequence of Algebra, Geometry, Algebra II, and Math Analysis (trigonometry and precalculus) in the following years. This shift was in response to California's state testing and accountability system, which made it more difficult for schools to offer integrated mathematics.

Even though EPAA adopted the traditional sequential approach to math content, it did not give up the highly scaffolded and spiraled systems embedded in an integrated mathematics curriculum, where concepts are taught with an emphasis on understanding versus procedural fluency. Teachers taught students how mathematical concepts were relevant to their lives and how to represent mathematical processes in multiple ways. Projects included:

*Algebra:* A "$y = mx + b$" book where students showed their understanding of linear relationships through connections between graphs, tables, equations, tile patterns, and student-created word problems

*Geometry:* An investigation of similarity, congruence, ratios, proportion, and scaling through the measurement of Barbie dolls and their human-sized counterparts

*Algebra II:* An instruction book for marking a soccer field, which students completed by using trigonometry and the Pythagorean Theorem; a banking project where students explored exponential functions to better understand the social justice issues that governed the savings and investing patterns of affluent versus poor people

*Math Analysis:* An election analysis in which students computed the minimum number of popular votes needed to win the presidential election of 2004

Although the majority of students entered high school with significant gaps in basic multiplication, division, fractions, and negative numbers, the school refused to track freshmen, instead firmly adhering to the principle of heterogeneous grouping as well as to the commitment to offer a college-prep education to all students. Consequently, the school adopted a daily block of algebra for *all* 9th-graders in 2004–2005, which supported the expectation and realization of stronger mathematics achievement. Seth commented on this approach:

> Teaching algebra to kids without basic math skills was challenging. When it comes to math, people seem to love it or hate it. There's no middle ground, and the choosing of sides appears to happen at a young age. In general, I think it is fair to say that about 25% of my students love math and feel comfortable working with numbers, while the rest struggle with their confidence and their competence. I found that success came more easily when we were able to provide activities and exercises that developed mathematical thinking skills. These helped to grow confidence and gave kids new entry points into improving their number sense and computation skills.

Students in algebra were given double the amount of instructional minutes required by the state, and this proved to be very effective in accelerating their acquisition of math skills. To illustrate, EPAA students first took the California High School Exit Exam (CAHSEE) in the spring of 2003, with a first-time pass rate of 23% on the mathematics portion of the exam. By 2008, when double-block algebra was in effect and the faculty had fine-tuned the curriculum to accommodate both basic skills and algebra content in a project-based context, the first-time pass rate had jumped to 74%. Another benefit of the double block for freshmen was the increase in numbers of students completing higher-level math courses beyond Algebra II, leading the school later to open an Advanced Placement statistics class.

***Science.*** Two talented teachers who did their undergraduate studies in science at Duke and Berkeley, respectively, and learned their teaching craft at STEP, built EPAA's science program. Danielle Wright and Cristina Galvan were hired in the second year of the school, shortly after they graduated from STEP, and quickly became a fearsome twosome, tasked with creating EPAA's science curriculum while also navigating their first year in the classroom. Their mentor, Jeannie Lythcott, who taught science curriculum and instruction at STEP, met with Danielle and Cristina frequently throughout their first 2 years to plan lessons and assessments, as well as to observe classes and give feedback.

The science curriculum, aligned with California's science standards and driven by EPAA's Five Habits, had a focus on authentic learning by connecting scientific concepts to real-world problems. Cristina and Danielle were also each other's best supports, collaborating on all their lessons, venting about the day's trials and triumphs, and attending professional development opportunities together. Both were skilled at advocating for their needs and bringing outside resources into their curriculum and classroom, even acquiring secondhand lab tables and cabinets from a local private school that was upgrading its facilities. Cristina set up a snake habitat and a goldfish tank. However, the snake escaped once into the laptop cart with the help of a student and later mysteriously disappeared for good.

For the first 3 years of East Palo Alto Academy, students took biology, physics, and chemistry. However, Cristina and Danielle noted that it was difficult to teach sophisticated science concepts, as entering students typically had little or no science in elementary school—a condition not uncommon in underresourced, low-income communities strapped for cash and teachers, and focused primarily on the high-stakes reading and math tests. Because students demonstrated so little familiarity with basic science knowledge, the teachers, with Jeannie, their mentor, decided to create a Foundations of Science class for freshmen. Beginning in September 2004, Cristina and Danielle taught the fundamentals that students would need for their future science courses. Danielle commented:

> The reason we decided on this Foundations of Science course, is that [we] both had to spend the first 2 1/2 months teaching things that students should have learned in the 7th and 8th grade. In biology, they had no concept of what a cell was or where you would find a cell. They had no concept of energy, of matter, of motion. [It was necessary to] go back and fill in some holes for knowledge . . . and skills that they didn't have. We relied heavily on concept mapping to help them understand concepts and how they're related. And we relied heavily on investigations, experiments, and writing up lab reports.

Cristina added:

> This course was really about teaching adolescents how to become students in a science classroom. This is how you do lab reports. This is how you do inquiry. This is how you use lab equipment. We got to address basic skills like measuring. We can be confident in any science class now that students have a basic understanding.

In Foundations of Science, Danielle and Cristina taught an integrated biology, chemistry, and ecology curriculum, covering the components of cells, DNA fingerprinting, laboratory skills, waves and energy, and culminating in a unit on earthquakes and plate tectonics. For the last, students researched and taught a lesson about earthquake safety to a local elementary school. For the DNA unit, the teachers facilitated a biotech forensics lab on fingerprinting, with the help of Gene Connection,[7] a high school outreach organization. Students learned basic biotechnology and how to use biotech equipment, then applied that knowledge to a class project combining studies of science with social justice issues. Students analyzed the case of the Central Park Five, where a group of Black and Latino teenagers were wrongfully convicted of the rape of a young woman. Students engaged in a laboratory simulation where they analyzed DNA samples of the men convicted and found that the samples did not match the DNA from the crime scene. They then matched it to the DNA of the man who eventually confessed 15 years later. Gene Connection adopted parts of Cristina and Danielle's curriculum in their work with other schools, including the scaffolds to support English language learners.

Cristina and Danielle found that the focus on teaching basic concepts raised test scores in biology by a large margin and that students were better equipped to understand both content and the scientific process in their future science courses. As Cristina observed:

> Part of this was building the science skills and the content background so they could be prepared for the science exhibition in their sophomore year where they had to design a controlled experiment with independent variables and repeated trials.

***Spanish.*** In order to balance the budget of the small school and to avoid scheduling challenges that would impede cohorts of students from looping with teachers over 2 years, EPAA had to streamline course offerings in all subjects, including world languages. Where traditional high schools offer a variety of foreign language options, EPAA taught only Spanish, with a strong emphasis on Latin cultures and language mechanics. The school's focus on Spanish reflected the 70% Latino population of EPAA and the fact that the Spanish language is widely spoken in California. EPAA offered Spanish I and II, Spanish for Native Speakers I and II, and AP Spanish.

Despite the plentitude of Spanish speakers in the area, it was frustratingly difficult to find a native speaker who could teach the language well. For the first few years, EPAA teachers jokingly spoke of the *Spanish curse* after enduring a string of Spanish teachers, none of whom worked for more than a full school year and a few of whom even left in the middle of the year or were asked not to return. The curse was dealt its death blow with the arrival of Misla Barco.

When the school where she was teaching lost its charter and closed, Misla accepted the invitation to join EPAA's staff, bringing a group of her students with her. The school community—parents, students, and teachers—immediately fell in love with Misla, whose hearty laugh and positive, can-do attitude energized them. Misla had the added responsibility of outreach to the parents and local community, which she approached with gusto. She soon organized a loyal and dedicated group of parents who attended school events and community meetings, packing classrooms for parent meetings and celebrations such as *Día de los Muertos* and Ninth Grade Poetry Night. As the unofficial school photographer and honorary mom for the soccer team, Misla, sporting EPAA bulldog gear, frequently was heard cheering on the sidelines, her wild, curly black hair spray-painted silver and waving in the breeze, representing the team's colors.

When she joined the EPAA faculty, Misla was the only Spanish teacher; eventually she taught every Spanish course offered at EPAA. As of this writing, Misla is still teaching at EPAA, along with her younger colleague and STEP graduate Ventura Garcia, who also is beloved by the students.

Students in Spanish I, II, and the Native Speakers classes focused on the four goals of foreign language instruction: listening, speaking, reading, and writing, with constant emphasis on grammar and syntax. In addition, there was a strong emphasis on understanding the difference between colloquial and academic Spanish. Specifically, in AP Spanish, students learned to read and write analytically and studied the format of the persuasive essay. They built their literacy and writing skills through the study of their own Latin cultures, heritage, and history.

In later years of the program, with the encouragement of Stanford professor Guadalupe Valdés, who created a Young Interpreters' Program, all students had opportunities to produce translations of school documents and written advertisements for actual school events, as well as serving as translators in other contexts. Misla developed a wide range of authentic projects, including a cross-cultural exchange with students in Guatemala and Argentina. She explained her approach this way:

> I try to use the community for my Spanish classes and take advantage of all community resources. For example, in my Spanish for Native Speakers class, we had a big unit on immigration because that's something that touches them. So they had to interview two different people who emigrated from different countries and find the pros and cons of coming to a new country, and they had to present that to the class and write a paper about it. We had textbooks, but I have created 80% of my curriculum and followed the national standards and the benchmarks for California standards.

For many years, Misla's students have had a near-perfect record in passing the AP tests in Spanish and, in more recent years, in achieving the California Seal of Bi-Literacy.

***Electives and Art.*** One challenge that faces most small schools is how to provide a strong core curriculum in humanities, math, and science while also providing electives that acknowledge student expression and interests. However, the "shopping mall high school"[8] approach that offers a wide variety of electives ultimately precludes the more focused staffing model that allows for small classes, block scheduling, advisory, and grade-level teams.

Among the few slots students had for electives, EPAA included support classes that enabled students to fill in gaps in their fundamental skills and knowledge while they were still taking college-preparatory classes. Thus, instead of tracking students in math, science, or humanities by their prior achievement levels, those classes were heterogeneous, and some students also took a "Math Lab" or a "Reading for College" course to backfill skills they were missing.

Students also took electives through the Early College program, described below, which enabled students to take college-level courses and earn college credits while still in high school. Depending on the interests and expertise of the core staff, other elective courses also became available: Art I, II, and III, journalism, creative writing, weightlifting, yoga, internships, service learning, and leadership.

Initially, though, there was neither an art room nor enough money for an art teacher. Having been raised in a home filled with artwork, Rebecca decided the students needed an art program, so she found two local artists to teach a daily class to freshmen and sophomores, while she herself taught a mural arts class. By the second year Rebecca had turned an initial investment of $300 into $3,000 through the sale of the students' work, which also hung in the main offices of the school. A huge student-designed mural depicting the twin cities of East Palo Alto and Palo Alto hung in the gym.

By the third year, the school had a credentialed art teacher, Staci Kavanagh, who built a more complete art program and remained at the school for many years to see it flourish. Known for her larger-than-life personality, biting sarcasm, and well-organized curriculum, Staci also served as athletic director and volleyball coach. She held her students to high standards, mentoring those who wanted to pursue their creative talents and encouraging them to work toward art degrees after high school. She modeled a lifelong commitment to art, earning National Board Certification and exhibiting her own work at several galleries while teaching at EPAA.

In Staci's Art I, II, and III classes, she taught color theory and art history, as well as basic technique and design. Student projects usually involved research, writing, collaboration, and a final exhibition of their art. The walls of her classroom, a converted dance studio, were covered with student art, including a huge painted map of the United States with each state bird meticulously rendered. Shelves were lined with student projects from her sculpture classes, such as papier-mâché statuettes inspired by Native American Pueblo Kachinas and Congolese power figures representing a student's best and unrealized self.

## CREATING LIFE GOALS AND A COLLEGE-GOING VISION

Finally, the staff developed an academic culture by bringing college and other enrichment experiences directly into the life experiences of their students. Very few EPAA students knew anyone, except for their teachers, who had gone to college. Few had ever been on a campus, met a professor, or even seen a college catalogue. The notion of preparing for college was for them, therefore, utterly mysterious.

There were a number of strategies for bringing college to the students: developing summer opportunities, creating an Early College program, and creating other partnerships for learning on the Stanford University campus. We describe these below.

### Accessing the World Beyond

Beginning in its inaugural year, the East Palo Alto Academy staff spent much energy connecting students to enriching summer opportunities. From many conversations with students and parents, teachers found that most students did not have the opportunity to engage in learning activities during the summer, such as camp programs, library reading programs, student leadership trips, and local business internships. EPAA staff knew instinctively what research shows: that by high school, as much as two-thirds of the difference in achievement between affluent and low-income students is the cumulative result of summer learning loss for those who lack such opportunities in contrast to the gains that advantaged students experience.[9]

During the first year of the school, advisors worked individually to get their advisees into programs. By 2002, EPAA created a Director of Summer Programs position, shared by Maura Marino and Rebecca Altamirano. The goal was for every student to access enrichment experiences in the summer, with a focus on academic or leadership development. In addition to a summer school that EPAA teachers created and ran for their students, plus opportunities to attend classes at Stanford as part of the Early College program, the co-directors researched and contacted different programs that would fully fund EPAA students whose families were hard-pressed to make a financial contribution.

The school built partnerships with organizations such as Upward Bound, College Track, Summer Search, Outward Bound, Experiment in International Living, and Phillips Exeter Academy to create an extensive menu of summer programs. Maura and Rebecca ran application workshops, wrote numerous letters of recommendation, and reviewed every application before it was sent out. Advisors also supported the process for their advisees.

EPAA teachers noticed that students who were involved in summer programs returned to school changed, refreshed, and with a work ethic that was contagious. Like Pablo, who returned from Stanford's Upward Bound program[10] in the fall of 10th grade, other students returned more studious and focused on not just completing assignments, but completing them to the *best* of their abilities. They inspired other students in their classes to make school a top priority and to buy into the academic culture.

As a result of their summer experiences, students came to understand that education is not something done *to* you but something you can choose and reach out for yourself. As Maria put it:

> [Teachers] show you how to go after your education and not sit and wait for everything to just come to you. I know from experience. I took a college course at the University of Michigan this summer, and if you don't go out there and try to get an education and try to involve yourself, then it's not just gonna come and land in your lap. The teachers here teach us to grab at things we want. They try to be there every step of the way to help us, not to hold our hands but [to act] as guides.

Students expanded their worlds as they met and became friends with people who were completely different from them. One student, for example, spent his summer at a program in Italy; once home, he maintained contact with his host family and Italian friends. Another traveled to Guatemala through GLEAN (Global Education and Action Network) to research education; as a result, she aspired to become a teacher, which she ultimately achieved after finishing college and attending Stanford's Teacher Education Program.

Some students who had limited English proficiency or learning disabilities went on monthlong Outward Bound courses and had life-changing experiences. Kinesthetic learners were outstanding students in the outdoor courses, and others became group leaders. Returning with glowing reports from their Outward Bound instructors as well as newfound confidence, they demonstrated marked improvement in their academic work.

Esperanza was one such student: Having entered the school in 9th grade with no English at all, she attended a 4-week wilderness course sponsored by Environmental Traveling Companions the summer after her sophomore year. While on the course, she was surrounded by native English speakers and was pushed to practice and develop her language skills. At the same time, she had the opportunity to develop her leadership abilities:

> I did so many things like backpacking, rafting, and kayaking. The first day of backpacking I was worried that my backpack would kill me because it was too big. I was also excited because there were many feelings inside of me. I was about to have a big adventure. I was nostalgic for my family, yet I was happy to meet new people.

Upon her return, Esperanza was more confident, and her English was greatly improved:

> This summer experience gave me the opportunity to know myself and learn about myself like I never did before. I learned how to know what is inside of me, what I want to do in my life, and why I am doing it. I am stronger now. During the trip I took time to think about my life, dreams, and my family. I want to keep going with my dreams and my goals because I can do it if I want to do it. Also now I can be more open with others because on the trip I learned to tell the big and bad moments of my life.

## Bringing College to Campus: The Early College Program

In order to give students a taste of the college experience and a chance to earn college credit while still in high school, East Palo Alto Academy joined the Early College movement in 2003. Initially funded by the Woodrow Wilson National Fellowship Foundation and the Bill and Melinda Gates Foundation, Early College programs were created "to serve students underrepresented in higher education—low-income students, students of color, English language learners, and students whose parents did not graduate from college—regardless of prior academic performance."[11]

The Early College mission and vision expanded EPAA's academic offerings, giving high school students direct experience with college-level learning and expectations. Students who enrolled in the EPAA Early College program took courses through Cañada College, a local community college committed to serving students from East Palo Alto and east Menlo Park. Some students also attended a specially designed Early College Summer Institute at Stanford University, with liberal studies and robotics courses taught by university professors.

All students were eligible to take part in the Early College program after the first semester of their freshman year, and EPAA regularly had eager second-semester freshmen taking college-level classes, earning college credits that they ultimately would transfer to their undergraduate institutions, saving them money and time, and reinforcing the bridge between high school and college. As Rebecca, who became Early College Director, remarked, "It was pretty incredible to have a 14-year-old student who would be the first in his family to graduate from high school complete a college class in his freshman year."

EPAA students could choose from a variety of courses, among them Academic Reading Strategies, Writing Development, American Politics, Career Options, College Success, Cultural Geography, International Relations, and

Music of the Americas. Students also could choose classes from two high-interest strands—early childhood education and health careers—with courses like Health Basics, Health Career Options, Introduction to Biology, Communicable Diseases, and Introduction to Early Childhood Education. A course in peer counseling also was offered to support EPAA's Peer Leaders program.

In general, EPAA offered Early College courses that had particularly strong instructors, were popular among students, or served as prerequisites for transferring into the California State University System. The Early College team, which included Linda, Nicky, and, later, Rebecca, met regularly with Cañada College's Humanities Department dean and college instructors. The Early College program was designed so students could continue their studies in the two strands of early childhood education or health careers once they matriculated into Cañada College or could use the credits in the pursuit of an associate's or bachelor's degree at another institution. Having completed some of the required coursework while still in high school, it was easier for Early College students to earn a career certificate, an associate's degree (AA), or a bachelor's degree (BA).

When the Early College program began in 2003, most of the class of 2005 and a handful from the class of 2006 took at least one college course during the year. Three years later, almost 50% of the entire student body, or more than 130 students, were enrolled in Early College courses, and almost all students took at least one college course before they graduated.

Early College programs have been shown to improve the likelihood that students will matriculate into and graduate from college.[12] Indeed, at EPAA the program positively impacted students' confidence and willingness to apply to college, as well as their comfort level and success once there. In the words of Sofia Bracamontes, an alumna from the first graduating class and now a graduate of a selective New England college:

> Being part of the Early College program helped me to get a feel for what college could potentially be like. The Cañada College classes helped me work on my personal responsibility and self-discipline. Having had the opportunity and experience helped me know what to anticipate in college.

Esperanza also commented about the influence of the Early College program on her future studies:

> It helped me have some understanding of what a college class was like and how I could be more prepared to succeed in college. It also helped me to think about a major. While in high school, I took a Latin American studies course and in college I decided to major in it because

I wanted to learn more about Latin America and the different struggles that Latinos face in the U.S.

Due to difficulties with transporting students to classes on Cañada's far-away campus and communicating with college instructors there, the program eventually brought all community college courses to the high school campus. Rebecca explained the main advantage of bringing classes closer to home: "Here at EPAA, we can put in supports and are getting constant updates on students, whereas when the courses were at the college campus, we never met most of the instructors."

In addition, Rebecca formalized the support system for Early College students. This included two AmeriCorps[13] members who attended each class with EPAA students. They tracked students' attendance and assignment completion, took class notes, collected homework, led study sessions, communicated with advisors about missed assignments and upcoming projects, and provided support on assignments where needed. Other supports included a Cañada counselor assigned to the high school campus 2 hours a week and a student liaison, a current Cañada student, who informed EPAA students about programs and events on the college campus. Each semester, Rebecca worked with the Cañada instructors and the AmeriCorps members to create individual plans for students who needed extra support or challenge. Early on, if it seemed that a student would not be able to pass the college class, the student was withdrawn from the college roster, but remained in the course to complete it for high school credit, under the supervision of Rebecca and the AmeriCorps members.

The results for the school were positive. By the end of the 2007 academic year, 88% of EPAA's Early College students completed Cañada College courses with a passing grade, earning a total of 503 college credits (an average of 2 per course). Such results were celebrated at the end of each semester, with *cum laude* honors given for the highest Early College GPA. Cañada College followed through with donations of food and prizes, including college gear, and with course instructors participating in the ceremony.

Understandably, the EPAA Early College program encountered challenges as part of its growth and improvement. EPAA had to maintain course enrollment of at least 25 students per course in order for Cañada to receive state funding and to prevent having to pass on the financial responsibility to the high school. Sometimes, Cañada's course offerings did not match the interests of enough students and the school had to recruit students for particular classes. Students encountered college-level practices in Cañada courses that were different from practices at EPAA—larger class sizes, an absence of scaffolding for major assignments, and fewer opportunities to revise assignments or redeem low grades. Also, Cañada College instructors were not specifically hired to teach EPAA students, and the fit between instructors and students sometimes varied.

In later years, the school and college were able to learn from each other, finding and developing instructors with a broader repertoire of teaching strategies who were able to teach high school students effectively, without reducing the rigor of the course expectations. EPAA also added supports for students to learn how to study and keep up in the college context by using AmeriCorps volunteers and the Early College director as coaches and mentors for the participants.

Another significant challenge arose when the grant supporting the Early College program ended in 2009 and the Gates Foundation discontinued its support for the nationwide initiative it had created. Although EPAA was one of a few schools in the state to get an additional year of funding and fundraising efforts were under way, the long-term financial support of the program remained uncertain. Rob Baird, the vice president for school–university partnerships at the Woodrow Wilson Foundation, which served as an intermediary for Gates, described the challenges this way:

> Over the last six years, the Woodrow Wilson Foundation has seen how truly transformative early college can be for students and how it can dramatically change the culture of schools. The challenges that remain—paying for all of the costs of early college, ensuring ongoing commitment from every partner and policy-maker, and figuring out if early college is scalable, in short, capable of improving the lives of many thousands of more students—are challenges that can only be solved through the collaborative work of our network of schools and partner colleges.[14]

Over the years since then, and continuing through this writing, EPAA, Cañada, and Stanford have figured out how to keep the program going, with funding from generous donors and a range of in-kind contributions from both Cañada and Stanford. California's dual enrollment policies also have helped keep the cost of enrollment within reach, if not easily affordable. All involved have dug deep to keep Early College going, because the value of bringing college to a community where it has been absent is indeed priceless.

## REALIZING AN ACADEMIC CULTURE

Gradually, the school moved toward a tipping point in the number of students actively engaged in and dedicated to their education. Students reacted well to the small class sizes, relevant curriculum, consistent contact with their advisor, similar schoolwide expectations spelled out in the Five Community Habits, and resilient teachers who made themselves available.

## Year Two: Reaching a Tipping Point

The continuity of staff and expectations, all voicing confidence that students could do the work and get to college, made a palpable difference between the first and second years. One founding teacher commented:

> I've seen [students'] progress, because I also had them last year. And that's one of the really encouraging things because I look around in my classroom when it's work time and there are two kids maybe not doing what they're supposed to be doing, and everyone else is annoyed with those two kids. The other kids are thinking, "Can you *stop* talking so I can do my work?!"

By the end of the second year, the progress was even stronger. Teachers observed:

> That shift, it took 2 years, but that shift, it's huge! It's that they're starting as a *group* to value their education as opposed to a few, which is what I felt like when we started. . . . I see more kids trying to "exceed the standard," more kids doing more than what they were asked to do. Approaching the standard isn't good enough anymore, they want to meet and exceed [it]. And more kids are looking at the rubrics to see, "What did I do well? What could I have done better?"

> They are [making this shift] for a lot of reasons. Some of it is maturity, and some of it is being here for 2 years with the same teachers saying the same things . . . over and over and it's finally getting through.

> I think some of them are finally realizing that we're not out to get them, that we've stayed committed to them for 2 years and that we plan on doing it for 2 more to see them graduate. They can't just be mean to us, and then we write them off. We're really not going to give up on them. And I think they're finally getting that.

Students remarked about their teachers:

> They set [expectations] high for you. . . . You know they set them high *for* you. . . . They say, "I know you can do it. I know you can go to college."

They are definitely pushing me. . . . They know who I am and they know what I want and right now they are throwing options to me for how to get there. I know where I want to be; I know where I want to end up, but as far as how I get there I am still deciding.

The principal also noticed that over time students became more proactive in regulating their behavior and monitoring their peers' conduct: "And that's the thing that changed. Our kids don't actually enjoy being bad anymore. They come to me and say, 'You've got to talk to this teacher because he lets us get away with stuff.'"

## Year Four: Creating a College-Going Culture

An even stronger shift in the academic culture of the school occurred during the fourth year, when the senior class began applying and getting accepted to college. As younger students watched the seniors moving through the college application process, receiving acceptance letters, and making plans, it had a powerful influence on the climate of the campus. Even if students chose not to attend college, the act of applying left an enduring mark. One senior from the first graduating class commented:

My principal wrote me a letter, which made my cheeks go up so high I couldn't stop smiling. She made me feel better than what I used to feel. I really hope that the violence, hurting drama comes to an end because we kids are too young to be dying. . . . When I graduate, everyone who told me I could not [succeed is] going to be shocked because I am a new person.

Both teachers and students commented on how strongly the first senior class positively impacted the academic culture at EPAA:

And I'm just like wow, if they can make it there, I know I could go [to college]. It encourages you, definitely.

—EPAA junior, class of 2006

Now the freshmen have seen all the seniors doing all their applications, getting into college. They see that everything they are doing is about going to college. So that really strengthens the academic culture.

—EPAA teacher

Ironically, the same students who initially resisted EPAA's academic culture were now among its strongest proponents, urging the younger students to focus on their education through the Five Community Habits. One teacher reported:

> The seniors actually get why our school exists and they tell it to the younger kids. And they're just great role models. I heard one senior telling a sophomore who was mad and didn't want to take the exit exam,[15] "Just suck it up and go take it. You have to take it." I hear them talking about colleges they are going to apply to or that they got into.

This set the stage for the next cohort of students. Many who had never thought about college before high school found it hard to resist EPAA's emphasis on college and their teachers' faith that they could succeed, and ultimately surprised themselves:

> When I first arrived to this school, I did not have any inspiration to go to college. Now I am very happy that I am going to UC Berkeley.
> —Valedictorian, class of 2007

Teachers perceived that the academic culture on campus had improved every year. At the same time, most agreed that constant surveillance of the college-going culture was needed. With a yearly influx of new teachers and students, the school had to be vigilant to sustain its original standards, expectations, and mission. Each summer, Nicky organized a staff retreat to revisit the mission, guiding principles, Five Community Habits, and schoolwide behavior norms, and to focus on any needed areas of professional development. This helped integrate the new staff, and for veteran teachers, it reinforced the principles behind the school's structures, policies, and pedagogical choices.

And each year there were refinements and revisions so that the culture, climate, and practices could continually improve. Just as EPAA set high standards for the students, it set high standards for the faculty and for itself as an organization. As the next chapter describes, these high standards also required high supports.

## CHAPTER 5

# High Standards with High Supports

> They are very focused on helping us to succeed in life and going to college.
> . . . These teachers have plans that everyone will go to college or at least be
> presented with the opportunity to go to college.
>
> —Senior, class of 2005

The staff began to see that an academic culture required clear expectations for behavior and engagement in learning that were *taught* and reinforced in all classes, as well as a rigorous and relevant curriculum that was *made accessible* to students. Quite often, high schools set behavioral and academic expectations around which they manage, judge, and grade students without explicitly teaching students the skills to meet those expectations. EPAA faculty aimed to provide both the standards and the supports to enable students to meet them.

Faculty learned that authentic engagement in academic work occurs when students complete meaningful and complex tasks in a supportive environment, and are evaluated on both the *process* and the final *product*. This means that all skills needed to complete the academic tasks had to be taught in a highly scaffolded way, sometimes over the course of multiple years.

For EPAA, the Five Community Habits rubric helped to serve these multiple purposes, as it addressed the development of both social-emotional skills and academic skills, offering a framework for designing assignments that supported deeper learning while guiding feedback, support, and revision. An explicit means of offering rich and detailed feedback is critically important for leveraging substantial learning gains, as students who previously have not had specific academic experiences can acquire them more rapidly if they attempt a task, learn what they need to do next to improve it, and immediately undertake to do so. Indeed, research has demonstrated that extended practice, guided by informative, nongraded assessment and opportunities for revision, is one of the most powerful strategies for learning.[1]

The alternative, especially for students who are academically inexperienced, is the traditional method of giving out information, giving a test or assignment, giving a grade, then—without opportunities for more practice or revision—moving on. The low grades that often result from this practice discourage students and eliminate opportunities for them to act on feedback so that they can gain skills, along with confidence that with effort they can improve their learning and achievement.

In this chapter, we describe how the school set high standards by using the Five Community Habits rubric and a system of performance assessments tied to academic exhibitions. We also describe how the school developed a system of strong supports to enable students to reach the standards.

## SETTING THE STANDARD: THE FIVE COMMUNITY HABITS

Described in Chapter 4 as a schoolwide rubric that was used by all teachers in all classrooms, the Five Habits were used to communicate feedback on assignments, assessments, and exhibitions throughout a course (see Appendix A). The rubric became an essential tool, as the founding teachers realized that the traditional approach of assigning points or letter grades to signify student achievement was not useful when it did not give sufficient feedback about what the student was doing well and what needed improvement.

In addition, students who were accustomed to not succeeding in school did not respond well to points and grades as motivators for improvement.

Students received five rubric scores—one for each community habit—in all their classes. EPAA report cards were a mixture of rubric scores and detailed comments from teachers. Seth, the math teacher, eventually created an algorithm that translated rubric scores to letter grades for transcripts sent to colleges as well as to other institutions or programs requiring a letter grade or grade point average. Students were trained to read their teachers' feedback closely on the rubrics and to consult their transcripts and grades only to monitor college readiness.

Student performance could fall into one of five categories on the Five Community Habits rubric: exceeding the standard (XS), meeting the standard (MS), approaching the standard (AS), emerging competency (EC), and no evidence (NE). Although feedback on assessments was not reported by letter grades (A–F), in general the staff agreed that work evaluated as meeting the standard was equivalent to a low A, about 90%.

One teacher described the value of rubric feedback versus grades in this way:

> In a traditional school, when a student receives a B– on an essay, what does that grade really mean? Did the student turn the essay in late? Were there multiple spelling errors? Did she have good ideas but didn't provide textual evidence? With the Five Habits rubric, teachers are able to clearly communicate what a student is doing well and what she needs to improve upon. Maybe she wasn't personally responsible enough to

turn the essay in on time, but the essay met the other standards for clear communication, solid critical thinking, and application of knowledge.

Another teacher commented on the value of explicit feedback on the schoolwide habits:

> The goal of the rubric system was to not only make our expectations for students clear, but also to give them authentic feedback that would highlight their areas of strength and weakness. We wanted students to look beyond a grade and actually use the feedback to revise and therefore improve. The Five Habits we finally decided upon represented for us what made students successful both in school and life beyond.

For most students, the Five Habits were useful guidelines in school that were also culturally relevant and reinforced in their lives outside of school. Lena said, "In the Samoan culture, personal and social responsibilities go hand in hand."

Because of the consistency in using this rubric, students grew to have a thorough understanding of the standards, commonly referenced them, and knew what was needed to meet them. Ericka, a student from the first graduating class, demonstrated her deep understanding of the habit of social responsibility as she reflected at her senior exhibition:

> It was hard for me, because freshman year I was just really a cocky individual. I thought I knew it all; I didn't want to work for anybody else, because I was big-headed. And part of this habit is how well you interact in a group. How well do you work with people who are not like you? If I put you in a group with [two other students], can you work with them? Can you get the job done? How do you move your group forward? . . . Are you interrupting me every time I'm trying to speak? . . . I would apply this [to the challenge of] being able to work with people who are not like you, who have different backgrounds from you, who have different viewpoints from you. Being able to tackle that in high school I think [will make it] easier for me to tackle when I go to college.

Initially, students and parents alike reported that they had trouble understanding the Five Community Habits rubric and the way the school graded students. The practice of being awarded letter grades was hard for parents and students to give up. However, this uncertainty with the new system, often heard from freshman and sophomore students and parents, changed tenor in the junior and senior years. As they became more familiar with the system, they came to see its benefits. Two parents from the class of 2006 explained how they learned to appreciate the system:

> I like the rubric. . . . Grades, you just get an A. But with the rubric, that tells you more. . . . Social responsibility is not discussed at other schools. Here it's about community, responsibility.

> One good thing about grading here is on report cards and progress reports, they make comments. [Another] thing that they do here is that [students] can revise work. If they get EC or AS, they can do revisions, so they can see what mistakes there were and that they can improve. This has really helped my son.

Teachers new to EPAA also had to learn how to teach the Five Community Habits and how to assess students' performance. Jeff explained his approach to coaching new teachers in the Humanities Department:

> Learning to use the Five Habits rubric may have been more difficult for experienced teachers who were new to EPAA and had not helped to create the Five Habits. I think that some staff didn't initially buy into it because they didn't have a chance to develop it with the founding teachers. How do you give people the freedom to develop new ways of doing things but respect the work that has gone before? It's hard to get rid of the neatness of summing up all learning into one grade. We hoped new teachers would see the logic in having rubrics and categories of skills, versus blunt numbers and letter grades. The Five Habits rubric is really an elegant thing.

Teachers used the Five Community Habits rubric to evaluate most student work, including assignments, major tests and projects, and yearly public exhibitions. Habit 4, the "application of knowledge" component of the rubric, often would be elaborated for individual assignments to reflect the content-specific knowledge and skills reflected in the assignments. In other cases, teachers might use appropriate sections of the rubric to measure student performance of specific skills and knowledge. For example, daily homework might be assessed only on Habit 1, personal responsibility: Did the student complete the assignment fully and turn it in on time? An in-class group activity might be evaluated using parts of the rubrics for personal responsibility, social responsibly (Habit 2), and critical and creative thinking (Habit 3). Rubrics for major projects, like an end-of-unit essay, usually included all of the components, with some fleshed out further to reflect the specific learning goals of the project (see Appendix C for a sample essay rubric).

Each year the staff revisited the schoolwide rubric and made modifications regarding standards for key skills and levels of content knowledge in the different academic disciplines. As Tina commented, "The system wasn't perfect; it was constantly growing and changing. The important thing was that we were dedicated to using a rubric. All of us were dedicated to assessing our students in an authentic manner." Nicky summed up EPAA's vision of assessment: "We were dedicated to being transparent with students: Here are the skills and content knowledge we expect you to learn, and here is what it looks like to demonstrate these skills and this knowledge at different levels of mastery."

## ENACTING A PHILOSOPHY OF REVISION AND REDEMPTION

Teachers at East Palo Alto Academy believed that assessment occurred throughout instruction, from informal and formative evaluation of students' responses, questions, and interactions in class to more formal and summative evaluations through exams, essays, projects, and yearly exhibitions that measured students' progress against the Five Community Habits.

To this end, the school developed a strong policy of revision and redemption. Teachers believed that students should have the opportunity to receive feedback and reflect on their own learning and performance, and have multiple opportunities to use that knowledge to revise their work and redeem poor performance. Seth often said, "In traditional high schools, time is the constant and quality is the variable; but at EPAA, quality is the constant and time is the variable."

This meant that instead of moving on before students had demonstrated mastery of a skill, students would take the necessary time to revise their work until it met the standard of quality. Sometimes revision was planned into the curriculum for major assessments, especially papers and products where several drafts were anticipated. Other times students worked on revisions of their work after a unit had been concluded, or even in the summer. Students were expected to revise if they failed a major assessment, and they were encouraged to revise at other times as well, in order to improve their work, their understanding, and their grades.

Although students often were initially mystified by the expectation that they would do something more than once, and they needed to learn how to accept and use feedback, virtually all spoke highly of this practice once they had come to understand it. An often-heard comment from students was one like this: "What I like most about EPAA is the chance that students [have] to revise their work and make their grades better."

Although teachers were firmly committed to the process of revision to improve work and meet standards, there existed some debate between teachers as to whether there should be rigid due dates for revisions of major assessments. One challenge with revision and redemption is that at some point the work that students are revising may no longer be as relevant as it was when they first began. Since the goal was to deepen knowledge and understanding of concepts and skills, revision simply for improved grades could run counter to the spirit of revising for mastery. The staff compromised and decided that teachers would emphasize revision and redemption for major assessments but not necessarily for all of the smaller assignments.

## DEMONSTRATING THE STANDARD: PERFORMANCE EXHIBITIONS

Like the schools teachers studied to inform the design of EPAA, the new school adopted a stance that student work is the centerpiece of the school and should be supported, exhibited, discussed, and recognized. Throughout the year, students did work that they exhibited publicly. As in many schools, they exhibited artwork (and created large murals to cover school walls); they wrote poetry and performed poetry slams; they undertook mock court trials and debates; they created their own Museum of Tolerance exhibits; they wrote and produced products that were on display in classrooms; they designed brochures on health topics like diabetes and distributed them in the community.

These were part of the ongoing activities that teachers organized within the curriculum. They were designed to represent what David Perkins calls "performances of understanding."[2] As we noted earlier, when students are called upon to produce meaningful work and share it with an audience beyond the teacher, motivation and pride increase, as does students' drive to work toward a standard of excellence.

In addition to these kinds of activities, the school defined a set of major summative assessments given annually, which constituted a graduation portfolio, much like those of the New York schools they had visited, most of which are now members of the New York Performance Standards Consortium.[3] Students had to pass these exhibitions in order to graduate. In the first years, three major projects representing key content areas and skills were defined, and each was allocated to a grade level (9th, 10th, or 11th), where it was taught and exhibited. The senior exhibition was based on a portfolio that collected work conducted over the 4 years that demonstrated accomplishment of the Five Habits. Whereas some schools save much of the graduation portfolio work for 11th and 12th grades, the staff felt it was important to establish the culture of exhibitions early and to begin to acculturate students to developing their work for an audience beyond the teacher. They also felt that one major exhibition per grade level would make the process more manageable for the staff.

Initially, as we describe below, the Humanities Department carried the weight of the exhibitions, with an autobiography project in 9th grade and a history research paper in 11th grade. In 10th grade, students completed a mathematics project. Soon, however, the science department was ready to sponsor an exhibition, and while the autobiography was still taught in 9th grade, the major exhibitions were allocated to a mathematical modeling project (9th grade), a science investigation (10th grade), a social science research paper (11th grade), and the senior portfolio in 12th grade. These have continued to evolve over the years, but the requirement that students complete major projects in their classes and an exhibition each year as part of a graduation portfolio has not changed.

## A Schoolwide Focus on Learning

Exhibition weeks were defining moments in the school's academic culture. For 3 to 4 weeks every school year, classes ended early and community members and parents flocked to the school for exhibitions. Young adults in suits and dresses replaced adolescents carrying backpacks and wearing jeans. For many students, in particular, presenting their exhibitions was the first time that they became true scholars. The purpose of the exhibitions was fivefold:

- To foster authentic learning experiences for students
- To prepare students for college-level assignments
- To help students attain skills required in the 21st-century workplace and world
- To challenge students to demonstrate important academic skills
- To challenge students more intensively to master the Five Community Habits

To prepare, students worked for months, laboring over complex projects, conducting research, and preparing their presentations. Teachers met before exhibition week to judge a live practice exhibition and calibrate their scores on the exhibition rubrics. Students could receive the following scores: pass with distinction, pass, pass with contingencies, or revise. Students who passed with contingencies had to rework some part of their exhibition, and students who had to revise were expected to completely redo their exhibition and present it a second time.

One of the major benefits of the exhibitions was that all teachers were engaged in scoring students' work and developing a common sense of what quality work looks like. Teachers learned to design successful project-based units and how to support student learning from the artifacts and conversations that surrounded the exhibitions. The Five Community Habits came alive in this process for teachers, students, parents, and partners, and the school strengthened its commitment to its mission while it enacted these common standards.

During exhibition weeks, school ended early, and all teachers reported to their assigned classrooms to judge student presentations for the rest of the afternoon. Students, dressed in their Sunday best, paced nervously up and down the hallways, clutching their sweaty note cards, waiting to begin. (In later years, exhibitions became more technology-based, and students clutched their laptops or memory sticks.) Advisors were nervous, too, as they had to participate in judging exhibitions for all their advisees and were responsible for coaching them to pass.

Students presented their exhibitions alone in front of a panel of four or more judges, including their advisor, another teacher, a student, and one or more outside community members. These community members could include Stanford faculty and students, employees of local businesses and nonprofit organizations, school board members, and donors, as well as parents and other family members. The panel was generally four members, but there were frequently other community members, especially friends and extended family members, in the audience. Students had to defend their ideas and answer any question posed by the judges. In general, most students in American schools would not experience such an intensive individual critique of their thinking and scholarship until college or graduate school (e.g., at their thesis defense), but at East Palo Alto Academy this happened for every student every year.

Students responded differently to exhibitions. First-year students were the most anxious and resistant to exhibitions, and complained that they were too hard to complete, or that friends at other schools did not have this requirement. These complaints reflected the fact that most students had never been challenged in this way academically, being expected to complete a project that involved multiple steps over an extended period of time and present it for evaluation in a public forum.

Virtually all EPAA students ultimately felt they learned a great deal and grew in their confidence and competence because of exhibitions. One student commented, "Big projects always get me motivated into doing my work and it highly supports my learning, since it makes me think more deeply [about] what I'm actually doing." As each year progressed, and students completed exhibitions successfully, they became more positive about the exhibitions and took pride in their results. They also became more competent and confident. Teachers saw this trend. As one put it:

> The freshmen are really scared about the autobiography exhibition. They don't know what to expect and for some of them this is the first public presentation they have ever made. For some of them this is the best

work they have ever done in school. After they complete it, there is an incredible sense of accomplishment. Each year they get more confident in their presentation skills.

The founding teachers originally thought they would require nine separate exhibitions for graduation, but quickly learned that the work required to support each and every student was substantial, and the coordination needed to solicit judges and manage the presentations was time-consuming. The faculty realized that many of the projects they thought useful could be done within the classroom and that *one* major exhibition a year at each grade level could serve as a public extension of the ongoing work done in classes.

In what follows, we describe the initial exhibitions, how they were designed, and how they affected students and faculty.

## Freshman Exhibition: The Autobiography

Ninth-graders were expected to write about a series of linked autobiographical turning points focused on life-changing experiences within their family, friendships, neighborhood, and school. In freshman humanities, students read *The House on Mango Street*[4] and other autobiographies; they studied Howard Gardner's theory of multiple intelligences[5] and Abraham Maslow's theory of the hierarchy of needs,[6] and they connected these to the texts and their lives. During the exhibitions, students introduced themselves, shared their major turning points, read a selected piece of their autobiographical writing aloud, tied the incident to Gardner or Maslow, presented their long-term goals, and reflected on their learning. Humanities teachers regarded this in-house assessment as a major benchmark for 9th-graders' academic growth and designed their course curriculum around this major project.

***The Design and Rationale for the Autobiography.*** The freshman exhibition was significant for many reasons. First, the choice of an autobiography was strategic for 9th-graders who entered the school unaccustomed to writing more than a few sentences, and who needed to engage intensely in literacy activities to substantially strengthen their reading and writing skills. By allowing them to read about others who had encountered obstacles and to write about what they knew best—themselves and their families—the autobiography project was highly motivating and helpful in supporting their reflection about their emerging identities and goals. Because of the subject matter and the fact that they would be presenting to others, students were willing to revise their vignettes multiple times to tell the story well and to reach a higher standard of writing proficiency.

In the process, students learned a great deal about the writing process and strengthened their abilities in organization, grammar, syntax, spelling, and language use—a foundational necessity for work at the high school and college levels. Students who were recent immigrants and did not speak much English when they enrolled could write their autobiographies in their native language—typically Spanish—but they would translate the portion they intended to present into English and read it in English to their panel of judges. This, too, provided a major jump-start for developing their literacy skills and their confidence in using the language.

For the vast majority of students, the presentation of their work to a panel of judges was an intimidating experience, and the public exhibition added weight and authenticity to their work. In addition to supporting the development of academic identities for students, the autobiographies also gave teachers and staff access to pivotal experiences in the lives of their students. Many told deeply personal stories for the first time. Esperanza, for example, shared her story about crossing the U.S. border. Another student wrote about how his father had been killed outside his house when he was in middle school. As William Dean put it, "This project was an emotional and visceral experience for students, staff, and community because our students publicly revealed their . . . feelings and thoughts about themselves."

***Malcolm's Freshman Exhibition Story.*** Malcolm Davis posed a challenge for his humanities teacher because Malcolm was dead set against performing in public. Embarrassed about his special education status and with reading skills below the 3rd-grade level, Malcolm needed significant support with the project from his humanities teacher, Mr. Dean, and his reading recovery teacher, Simone Miller. (Simone's work with Malcolm is described later in this chapter.) However, the public presentation was the real terror for Malcolm. Although he had participated in group projects in Mr. Dean's classroom, Malcolm always hid behind his classmates when his group presented at the front of the class. When Malcolm realized the exhibition was one in which he would stand alone, he panicked.

The day William Dean introduced the assignment to the class, Malcolm waited until lunchtime and returned to his teacher's classroom: "Mr. Dean, I don't want to do this assignment. Why do I have to present to people I don't even know?"

William responded, "Malcolm, most of the people you already know, like me, your advisor Mr. Gilbert, a classmate, and the other teachers. You will be fine because all you have to do is talk from your heart, showing the panel how much you know about yourself and the impact your learning has made."

"How about if I just write everything and you can read it to them?" Malcolm asked.

"No, you know that's not the way it works. As we go through our preparation, I'm sure your confidence will build, so let's just take it one step at a time."

From claiming to not get along with certain classmates to pretending to not know what to write about, Malcolm was persistent in trying to get William to relent. William found his insistence amusing to some degree, because by now Malcolm knew his teacher well enough to know he was not going to budge.

William asked, "Why don't you write about your new friendship with those boys you socialize with during lunchtime? You can start thinking about the impact these fellows have had on you since you began to hang out with them."

The thoughtful and effervescent Pablo had reached out to Malcolm to bring him into his group. They were an eclectic bunch that claimed their turf on the campus and spent lunch doing crazy but harmless stunts: daring one another to eat sand, consuming a concoction of chili peppers and orange juice. The group had an undeniably unique persona; they were an exclusive fraternity. Yet they reached out to Malcolm to be a part of their posse. This was an interesting olive branch since Malcolm had resigned himself to being alone at lunch, reading his books on the bench. As William encouraged Malcolm to trust his experience with Pablo and his new friends, and write about what he knew, Malcolm's fear of the autobiography exhibition began to subside.

Eventually Malcolm conceded, "I guess I can write about that but I don't want them to know."

"Okay," William replied. "I will not require you to share that turning point with any of them until you feel confident. You need to keep in mind, though, that one of them may get to participate on your panel."

After Malcolm finished his rough draft about his friendship turning point, he brought his writing into William's classroom during lunch. Malcolm had attempted to describe and explain his newfound friendship. Although somewhat shaky and disorganized in its first draft, the essay nonetheless included a coherent recognition of Malcolm's turning point. Here is an excerpt from the revised version:

> The event which caused me to have a turning point can be placed in the category of belonging and love on Maslow's hierarchy of needs. This event goes under these needs because I got to make friends with a bunch of boys. I had not admitted it to anyone that I was in need of friends, especially since I was starting high school and wanted to fit in.
> This change was really important to me because becoming friends with those guys who did not make fun of me or ridicule me was a big deal. They accepted me as I was and they never questioned anything about my personality.
>
> I used to sit on the school bench and read my book. I thought I liked doing this alone so I was always saying something negative about almost everyone. I assumed a lot of people made fun of me mainly because I felt insecure about myself. That's why I hung out by myself.

What I learned about myself was good for me because I was able to find out that I really do care about being liked and it's O.K. to be myself. If I want to fool around with the group I can, and when I don't want to I don't. This was a big freedom for me.

When the day of the exhibition arrived, Malcolm dressed up for the presentation, and although he was anxious, he showed a new maturity unseen before by his teachers. Malcolm presented to his panel, receiving constructive feedback. He ended his first year of high school with a significant academic breakthrough. In fact, most of Malcolm's freshman peers rose to the occasion, and 90% of the class passed the first autobiography exhibition on their initial attempt. The others revised as needed and passed the exhibition the following year.

## Sophomore Exhibition: The Math Project

As the head of the exhibitions study group (see Chapter 7) and as the resident technology guru, Seth Leslie organized all the staff meeting calibrations and created the online schedule and sign-up process for teachers, advisors, and community judges, whom he recruited. Seth also led the process for vetting and finalizing the exhibition rubrics and brought them all to the staff meeting for review and consensus. As the sole member of the Math Department for EPAA's first year and the linchpin of the team for the next 4 years, Seth also developed the math exhibition and supported the first cohort of sophomores through it. Seth commented:

Lifting the math exhibition the first year was a monumental task. I really had no idea where I was going and how it would work, but I thought it would be best to start with passion. So we did, and kids chose to study and make scale replicas of some interesting objects: pyramids, basketball courts, tessellations, even a guillotine! At the end of the day, the management of so many unique projects and ideas was too much to manage and we all struggled with the exhibition. However, much was learned about how to manage a task of this magnitude, and later iterations of the project were much more successful.

***The Design and Rationale for the Math Exhibition.*** Like all exhibitions, the math exhibition went through a series of changes each year at EPAA. The goal of the exhibition was to help students explore an aspect of mathematics deeply, modeling a problem, and using multiple representations to solve it and demonstrate their understanding. The exhibition pushed students beyond the use of algorithms and rote procedures to a more comprehensive understanding of a problem, forcing them to reason and communicate about mathematical principles and ideas.

In general, sophomores chose a complex math problem from a list given to them and presented multiple solutions in depth. They also could propose their own problem. Students were encouraged to choose "big problems" they had encountered previously in algebra and geometry, since most sophomores had taken these two courses. Examples of exhibition topics included ways of proving the Pythagorean Theorem using geometric concepts and using exponents to predict the yearly dollar appreciation of fast cars like Porsches and Mustangs.

***Kristine's Sophomore Exhibition Story.*** For her sophomore math exhibition, Kristine Lewis chose to study the Golden Gate Bridge, figuring out proportions and ratios in order to create a scale model. She spent hours working on math equations with her teacher, Beth Injasoulian, who was also her basketball coach, and with Nicky, her advisor. Kristine progressed from trying to build a scale model with Popsicle sticks to attempting to fit a large-scale drawing of the bridge on a long roll of butcher paper. Her work was a good representation of the goals of the project.

However, what caused Kristine to fail her first math exhibition was neither her math knowledge nor major errors in her equations, but her social responsibility skills. Nicky, a judge on the three-person panel, described what happened:

> Kristine started out fine, with her usual self-composure and strong presence, standing straight and introducing herself to each judge with a firm handshake. She was slightly sarcastic while going over her slides, adding flip remarks occasionally, but I attributed this to normal nervousness. Unfortunately, during the question-and-answer period Kristine had a hard time with some of the questions and started to make snide comments to the judges.

After Kristine's presentation, she, like all students, was asked to leave the room so the judges could deliberate. Nicky recalled:

> I remember sitting there thinking that I didn't see any evidence of Kristine's social responsibility. She didn't even qualify for the emerging competency score because she had refused to modify her behavior when we told her during her presentation that she was being rude. The three of us talked about it and we agreed. We ended up giving Kristine *no evidence* for social responsibility and because of that she did not pass her math exhibition.

Figure 5.1 shows the social responsibility portion of the math exhibition rubric.

**Figure 5.1. Habit 2: Social Responsibility, Math Exhibition**

|  | Exceeding the Standard | Meeting the Standard | Approaching the Standard | Emerging Competency | No Evidence |
|---|---|---|---|---|---|
| **Interact Respectfully** Classroom Behavior | Student acts and speaks respectfully even when faced with conflict. | Student acts and speaks respectfully. Personal and school property is treated appropriately, with safety in mind. | Student acts and speaks respectfully or self-corrects when behavior, language, or use of property is inappropriate. | Student attempts to act and speak respectfully and corrects his/her inappropriate behavior, language, and/or use of property when reminded. | |
| **Build Bridges** Community Interactions | Student helps generate a positive view of school and creates healthy relationships with the community. | Student represents school in a positive way with appropriate behavior and use of language and property. | Student acts in a way that neither harms nor helps the relationship between the school and the community. | Student takes action to modify behavior when inappropriate in order to better represent the school. | |

When Kristine came back into the classroom to get her feedback, she took the comments stoically, only asking, "Why?" when she was told she did not pass and would need to re-present. This was a difficult lesson for Kristine. After the explanation, she left the classroom abruptly and threw her drawing of the Golden Gate Bridge into a trash bin. Nicky rescued the drawing and kept it along with Kristine's other exhibition materials. Eventually Kristine came to the understanding that she had to redo her exhibition in order to graduate. In her senior year, Kristine completed a second math exhibition on a new topic and passed easily, having no problem with social responsibility the second time around.

It was rare for a student to fail to meet the standard on social responsibility during an exhibition. But staff valued more than just demonstration of content mastery; they were committed to preparing students to enter and succeed in the professional world.

## Junior Exhibition: American History Research Paper

In their junior year, students selected a key figure or event in American history and wrote an 8- to 15-page paper. Students were expected to have a solid understanding of their historical figure or event as well as the related historical context. Sections of the paper included an analysis of the historical figure or event's background, contributions, defining moment, and legacy. Students ended the paper with a personal connection. In their presentations, students also were expected to engage in metacognitive reflection about their strengths and weaknesses as researcher, writer, and presenter.

***Design and Rationale for the History Exhibition.*** The history research paper was designed to reinforce critical skills of inquiry, the use of evidence, and informational writing, as well as critical thinking skills needed to analyze, synthesize, and evaluate information, and to draw well-grounded conclusions. For students attending college, the ability to find and use primary and secondary sources in researching a question is a central skill—one that too few students have encountered in high school in an era of multiple-choice testing that discourages this kind of work in many schools. Students experienced small versions of this kind of work in 9th and 10th grades at EPAA, but the 11th-grade exhibition was still a challenging task for most of them.

Tina Ehsanipour, who was trained as an English teacher, designed the exhibition with her 11th-grade humanities colleague Marysol de la Torre, who had trained as a social studies teacher. Tina described the process they undertook with their students:

> We began with our students' passions. We did a variety of activities during class to help students explore their interests. Some of these activities consisted of asking students questions like what they were willing to die for, or having them skim the history textbook and write down topics that caught their eye. The goal of these activities was to get our students thinking about possible topics they would want to explore further. Once students had chosen their topics, we worked with them individually to formulate research questions to guide their work. For many, this was their first experience with independent research so we helped jump-start their research by pointing them to valid sources.
>
> We modeled every step of the project using a sample research topic of our own. For example, before students were asked to complete their first of at least 10 research organizers, we modeled one on the overhead as a class. Modeling how to gather evidence and analyze it was extremely important to make our expectations to students clear and allow them to feel more comfortable with the research process.

***Lena's Junior Exhibition Story.*** Students were urged to choose a person or topic that was not highlighted in traditional American history textbooks. Lena decided to conduct a family history project and research the Samoan Diaspora and her family's immigration to the Bay Area.

She began the project feeling completely overwhelmed. She said, "When receiving the assignment for the research project, I initially dreaded it. Fifteen pages and a ton of research did not sound at all appealing." It wasn't long, however, before the feelings of anxiety and fear were transformed into enthusiasm and empowerment. Lena became increasingly engaged as she could feel the work's direct connection to her life and her experiences. She said:

> I felt that I was the minority in the minority. Black History Month, Hispanic culture—it was never me. We were only 11% in East Palo Alto, not much, but enough that we should learn about it. This had to be my favorite assignment to do; I researched online, checked out books from the library, I even had chances to conduct interviews with my grandparents and family friends [to understand why] they decided to come to America. I thought it was just going to be that they just wanted to come, but I learned about the first and second waves of immigration. I interviewed church members who had just come from Samoa [in the second wave] and I learned about the first wave [in the 1950s to 1960s] from my grandparents. I also learned that my family was one of the first Samoan families to live in East Palo Alto.

Lena wholeheartedly met the teachers' challenge for students to make connections between the junior exhibition and themselves. Lena even wrote this striking poem about her Samoan identity:

> Don't worry though, because I can't communicate with my
> People, long since dwelling in
> your land.
> Perhaps, they have lost their
> Way, just as they have forgotten our language,
> Settling for just English
> Intertwined with bursts of
> Samoan,
> Raped by angry tongues.
> Complaining of Faa Samoa,
> Money, church, fa'alavelave
> And needy relatives,
> Of culture and traditions,
> Ones that still embrace me,
> Because it identifies me.

Not only did Lena learn how to do library research, conduct interviews, organize a research paper, and present her ideas to a panel of judges, but she also came to understand her role and responsibilities underpinning her identity and pride in being a Pacific Islander in the United States. Lena passed her junior exhibition with distinction.

## Senior Exhibition: Senior Portfolio and Exit Interview

For their final exhibition, seniors provided evidence of their understanding and growth in EPAA's Five Community Habits by creating a portfolio of work primarily from their junior and senior years. Students had to describe each of the Five Habits in their own words, include evidence of growth for each one, and reflect on their progress as scholars and human beings. Students in the first graduating class were required to include key pieces of evidence such as their financial plan, 2004 election project, and Bill of Rights Supreme Court argument from their government and economics classes. They also could choose other pieces of work to show evidence of their growth during high school.

William, who taught humanities to both freshmen and seniors from the first graduating class, commented:

> The senior exhibition had a twofold purpose: to showcase and reflect on a collection of work during the students' 4 years and to demonstrate the students' understanding and growth in the Five Community Habits. Because the habits are our school's expected learning outcomes and our grading system, it makes sense for the students to be held accountable for their growth in them.

> Students provided varying kinds of evidence. Esperanza brought in her attendance record to prove her personal responsibility. She explained how she woke up every day before 5 A.M. to get a ride to EPAA from across the bay, where she had moved after freshman year. Other students, like Pablo, brought in their personal statements for college applications and their acceptance letters to prove their communication skills.

*Pablo's Senior Exhibition.* Most of Pablo's senior portfolio comprised work he did during his last 2 years of high school, when he experienced the most academic growth. His portfolio also was filled with pictures of friends and family, inspiring quotes such as, "Let passion be the passport of your life and make dreams your future," as well as poetry, his personal passion. Pablo's portfolio was substantial and included all of the required work as well as numerous additional items to prove his evidence of growth in each habit. He was most proud of his personal statements for college applications and corresponding acceptance letters, and used this as evidence to prove his communication skills. He reflected, "My personal statement took me a long time to write. I had so much to say but I did not know how to start and in what order to put in everything I wanted to include. . . . It is one of the best essays I have ever written."

Students also were required to write answers to the following exit interview questions:

- In what habit are you the strongest? In what areas do you need to continue to grow?
- How have you grown over the last 4 years?
- Why do you deserve to graduate?

Pablo used the prompts as an opportunity to write a thoughtful and poetic 4-page reflection essay titled "Change." His essay, a metaphor about metamorphosis, elicited a powerful emotional response from the panel of judges. It read, in part:

> Life is ever changing and since I began high school 4 years ago, I have shed my skin multiple times. Coming into high school, my mentality was in no way optimistic. I thought I was a good-for-nothing and would never amount to anything; I was the epitome of the minority stereotype but most of all I was looking for someone to show me they cared. Someone to give me love and care, the love and care my parents neglected to give me. I never thought that all I needed I would find at East Palo Alto High School. . . . Going to school was my sanctuary. Before then, I did not value education because I thought it was an everyday thing, and plus, I thought that it was cool that I did not do my work and disrespected my teachers. However, I would remember my stay in El Salvador and how hundreds of children hungered for an education that they would never get and one that I would not cherish. I shed my first layer of skin, my ignorance.

Pablo reflected on each year of high school and explained the obstacles that he overcame both at home and at school. He recalled that during his sophomore year on the day of his math exhibition, his mother told him that he had to choose between living with her or his sister. When he responded that he couldn't choose, Pablo's mother left, the last time he would see her for 2 years. When the hour arrived to present his math exhibition, Pablo was in the midst of an emotional breakdown and "failed miserably." He writes, "I felt completely alone in the only place I called home. I shed another layer of skin, the child inside of me."

Pablo explained that he later joined Stanford Upward Bound and the experience helped to pull him back on track. Rejuvenated from his uplifting summer at Stanford, he went on to have a great junior year. The highlight of his academic growth was presenting his junior exhibition, a 20-page essay on the music of World War II, as well as singing a song that he wrote. "I yet again shed another layer of skin: I became a mature young man." Pablo closed his exhibition with this final thought:

> I know that nothing will ever be handed to me and being that I'm a minority, the odds are stacked against me, but I live in the land of opportunity and while some windows are already closed because of my past ignorance, many more will open with the education I have gained here at East Palo Alto High School.

## Exhibitions and Academic Culture

Exhibitions became a central part of the academic culture of the school. Students' sense of what they needed to learn and be able to do was made real through exhibitions. Students helped one another rehearse and attended one another's presentations. They learned to use the rubrics to evaluate their own work and their peers' efforts. Teachers explained their curriculum plans in terms of how learning would accumulate to produce this kind of high-quality work. For example, 9th-grade teachers told students that as freshmen they were beginning to prepare for the junior research paper when they learned how to write structured body paragraphs, draft thesis statements, and support an argument with evidence.

Over the course of the exhibition week, names of students who passed their exhibitions appeared on their advisory classroom's Wall of Fame or were written on the classroom windows for all to see. At the end of the week, advisories celebrated exhibition success with parties and trips out to lunch. Staff celebrated student growth on the exhibitions and were thankful that students had risen to meet their high expectations. Graduates were thankful as well, as these statements illustrate:

> Exhibitions helped me with public speaking. The last couple of weeks of school, I was involved in a presentation to the president of my college and to foreign visitors, and I felt really ready.

> Exhibitions helped me participate in college, in class discussions.

> They gave us a lot of exhibitions. Even though I hated it, it worked. It prepares you for your future, for going to college. Now when I have to give a speech in front of the class, I remember that I did this before. I like that I did it before.

One graduate from the class of 2006 described using his exhibitions skills during an interview for a bank teller position. He said, "I was really nervous at first, but then I remembered what I learned when I did my exhibitions. I dressed professionally, I stood up straight, I shook their hands, I looked them in the eyes, and I answered their questions honestly. I got the job. This is a big deal for my family."

Teachers learned that in order to foster the fledgling academic culture, they needed to respond to students' complaints about the difficulty of the projects by providing more support instead of lowering standards. In what follows we describe some of the many supports that EPAA put in place to enable students to meet the standards.

## LINKING HIGH EXPECTATIONS WITH STRONG STUDENT SUPPORTS

To help students meet these high expectations, EPAA put in place a number of structural supports. These included supports for literacy development (including, for some students, reading recovery instruction), English language development, special education, and a variety of supports for individualized help with homework: tutorials, office hours, Saturday school, and time in advisory. This web of supports was made more responsive and effective by having an advisor at the hub, helping to inform other staff about the student's progress and needs, and helping to support the student to take optimal advantage of the opportunities available.

One way to see how the support system operated in action is to see how it worked for Malcolm. Determined not to be labeled a special education student and nervous about other students knowing his academic status, Malcolm tried to hide his learning differences and his efforts at first created a number of challenges. Mr. Dean, Malcolm's 9th-grade humanities teacher, reflected on his initial interactions with Malcolm:

> When I first met Malcolm in our humanities class, I immediately regarded him as a sensitive kid who did not make eye contact when talking to others. His peculiarity caught my attention because he made it known to me right off the bat that he was not going to engage in learning the way I had planned. He seemed dead set on isolating himself on day one. He was against being part of the community I intended to build. The first time we met he told me, "I need to work alone, and I need to sit alone. I do better when I can be by myself, so is that possible in here?" I also was surprised at his attitude about how he wanted to learn since Malcolm understood the school's mission was to build a new community and instill effective work habits in all students. . . . Malcolm began his freshman year as a challenge to us; we had to convince him that this school would work well for him, especially considering that his elementary and middle school years were not rewarding.

Malcolm's experience at East Palo Alto Academy was qualitatively different from his previous traumatic years of school. EPAA mainstreamed all special education students, practicing a "push-in" versus "pull-out" model for delivering services. The school wanted all students to receive personalized attention, so in this way Malcolm was no different from his peers. William explained: "We are a staff that regards all students as special people who need to see and know that we are sticking by them through thick and thin. These students deserve our support." Malcolm received one-on-one support from his resource teacher during his elective block. He began to relax and feel more comfortable because the entire school didn't have to know about the special help he was receiving.

Malcolm also had one-on-one time scheduled regularly with his reading teacher, Simone Miller. Simone was trained in reading recovery methods, a strategy generally used with primary-grade students who have not yet learned to read comfortably. Because EPAA had a number of students in that category, Simone used the same methods, while adjusting the texts to content appropriate to older students.

Simone established a routine with Malcolm during their class time. She focused on his decoding skills and vocabulary development, followed by oral reading of short passages and comprehension questions. Often their question-and-answer sessions turned into conversations in which Malcolm elaborated on his knowledge or opinion about his reading. Simone recalled:

> I wanted to get to know him so I could rely on his experiences as a resource for him to identify with what he was reading. When he started to open up during the discussions about his reading, I was able to focus on his metacognitive skills, without playing the role of a clinician. I enjoyed working with Malcolm, especially after I established a trusting rapport with him by getting him to feel comfortable and safe working with me. I had to start off slow and gentle for him to understand and know that I was not going to put him in an embarrassing situation or get him to feel stupid. He made it very clear to me that he did not want to relive his elementary and middle school days.

Before long, a pattern emerged, with Simone encouraging Malcolm to select books to read during their sessions, and Malcolm beginning to ask Simone questions about her reading, which turned into questions about her likes and dislikes. Eventually, after she had helped Malcolm solidify his decoding skills and comprehension strategies, Simone assigned outside reading for him. And this is when he started reading on his own, especially during lunch and after school. Now, whenever anyone saw Malcolm on campus, he had a book in his hand: *Holes*, *The Boy Who Lost His Face*, *Fahrenheit 451*, *Rite of Passage*, among others. Over the course of this 1 year, he gained several grade levels in reading, and the books he tackled reflected his rapid gains. And, of course, the more he read, the better he read, and the more he enjoyed it.

Despite Malcolm's progress in reading, and although he had acquired more than a dozen friends and acquaintances, his feelings of difference and isolation lingered, and he thought about dropping out. The long shadow of "special education" hovered over Malcolm and created great insecurities. Having Jeff Gilbert as his advisor was one of the main reasons Malcolm did not give up on school. Jeff described his relationship with Malcolm:

> I saw that Malcolm was shy, somewhat withdrawn, and nonresponsive. I made sure not to antagonize him; instead I communicated gingerly with him. Malcolm was a hard nut to crack. One day I would make progress and then the next day it seemed like we'd taken two steps back. It seemed that Malcolm was always fighting us when we were pushing and encouraging him to do his best. For some reason, Malcolm acted like he did not want to do well, but when I think about it more, I think he was fighting the fear in him grounded in the possibility that he would fail. He lacked the self-confidence to achieve.

Malcolm's reluctance to learn resurfaced when attention turned to his math skills after he failed his sophomore exhibition. Malcolm resisted attending math tutorial, just as he had done during his middle school days. This time, however, he just flat out refused to attend. Instead, during tutorial time, Malcolm would sit on the bench in front of a classroom reading a book. It wasn't until Jeff arranged for a tutor who knew about TV wrestling—something that Malcolm loved—that he agreed to be tutored. Jeff and William secretly prepped the tutor with wrestling information to break Malcolm's standoff. It worked: Malcolm gave in. He agreed to be tutored and presented his math exhibition. Although it took a few tries for him to succeed, he eventually passed.

Episodes of Malcolm's resistance to school occurred less frequently during his remaining high school years. By the time he was an upperclassman, he was academically responsible and accepted with equanimity the decision that he had to repeat a humanities course in his senior year:

> I felt somewhat comfortable so I worked hard my last year to make sure I was going to graduate. I knew that I had to finish school like my brother had who had gone on to college, which is where I wanted to end up. Teachers and staff made sure [I] stayed on top of [my] work, if [I] liked it or not, because they wanted to make sure [I made] something of [myself]. They made sure I at least got into one college and got all my papers done and in on time.

Malcolm's story is one example of how East Palo Alto Academy was committed to serving all students with a college-preparatory curriculum, and how faculty created a comprehensive system of supports tailored to the needs of individual students. Staff found that students needed to build foundational skills in reading, writing, math, and science, as well as get assistance outside of their classes when they struggled with work. The supports that enabled Malcolm to meet the standards and reach his goals emerged in structured form as staff came to understand students' needs and evolved in each year of the school. This network of supports continues to play a critical role in student success. Here we describe some of the major approaches.

### Literacy Development

As the school's first reading specialist, Simone Miller designed professional development for the staff as well as working directly with students. The rest of the faculty adopted a number of the key reading strategies that Simone used with Malcolm and her other students. Students learned to pre-read titles, captions, and graphs; identify key words and phrases; clarify words in context; ask surface-level and deep questions; summarize passages; and make predictions. The schoolwide approach to reading enabled all students to receive consistent literacy instruction in order to decode grade-level texts. After Simone's departure from EPAA, Rachael Shea, the next reading teacher, continued the schoolwide literacy program.

The reading program also involved special classes for some students during their elective period, and the reading specialist was available to observe classes and work one-on-one to support classroom teachers facing specific challenges such as decoding and comprehension. In time, EPAA replaced its reading classes with a more comprehensive academic literacy program that was required for all 9th-graders. That program, too, evolved over the years to support both reading and writing, alongside humanities. Expectations that all teachers will support literacy in their instruction have been constant and have included common strategies supported by coaching as well as periodic professional development sessions.

### English Language Development

A growing number of recent immigrants entered EPAA each year speaking little or no English. As the school's English language learner (ELL) population grew, so did the English Language Development (ELD) program. Large comprehensive high schools in the nearby area typically would assign newcomers to a segregated set of classes in which they were to learn English, but that were not part of the college-preparatory sequence for the California university system. This "ESL ghetto," as it often was called, while frequently caring and comfortable for students, did not provide them with English language models or with strong academic content.

EPAA maintained its commitment to offering supports for all students to take college-preparatory courses in heterogeneous settings. In the first year, the small number of students with limited English proficiency enabled the staff to work closely with them one-on-one, allowing them to take the regular sequence of courses with their peers. Because of her Spanish fluency, English credential, and training in sheltered English instruction from STEP,[7] Rebecca Altamirano was assigned to teach the recent newcomers, with coaching from local experts in the field. Rebecca reflected:

> I loved working with the ELL students. My coach, Jeff Zwiers, a local ELD expert, guided me to focus on academic discourse and to teach grammar and vocabulary in context. For example, in the second year of the program we planned a weekend camping trip, and in preparation, we learned all the vocabulary and phrases associated with camping. When we returned, students wrote essays reflecting on their experience.

ELD students also received tutoring from their bilingual peers. One student reflected on this experience in her senior personal statement:

> When I was in school a lot of students came from Mexico who didn't know how to speak English. That reminded me of my situation when I first came to the U.S. When I was a freshman, one of my teachers asked me if I wanted to be a tutor in the ELD class . . . I was delighted to hear that I was going to be part of the ELD class. I was going to be able to work with people who were learning English. I knew how it felt to not understand another language and how hard it was to do all the work in English.

In year two of the school's existence, a large influx of monolingual Spanish-speaking students entered the freshman class. This was due in part to the reputation the school was gaining for being particularly attentive to the needs of students new to the country with limited English ability. Nicky recalls: "I was pretty excited we earned a reputation for serving our ELL students well. People walked in the door and said, 'Oh, I heard about your school. I just moved from Mexico. Can you take my kid?' We got that a lot."

The following year, Rebecca again taught ELD to the incoming freshmen, as well as a section of sheltered humanities with the same ELD students. Rebecca looped with her sheltered humanities class, staying with them into their sophomore year. Two years later, Rebecca taught the ELD cohort again as students in her senior humanities classes. Thus, the second cohort of EPAA's

English language learners had the same teacher for both ELD and humanities for 3 years of their high school career.

> Having the same group of students for so long made a huge difference in being able to accelerate their English learning. I developed strong personal relationships with my ELD students, and two received full scholarships to study at a local University of California school after graduating at the top of their class. I think their success had a lot to do with the quality of individual attention I was able to give them over the years. I worked closely with these two throughout their college career, helping them choose their classes and edit their papers. They continued their education and earned master's degrees in public health from a California State University.

With the regular influx of newcomers beginning in 2002, Rebecca and Nicky, with the help of Jeff Zwiers and Guadalupe Valdés, a Stanford professor, designed the school's future ELD program. For the third cohort of students, Marisol Castillo took over the ELD program and continued to work with Jeff Zwiers to develop the program's focus on academic language. Students were tested in English fluency at the beginning of each school year. Students who were assessed as "monolingual Spanish" were assigned to one period of an ELD class that provided direct instruction in English grammar and diction. These students also took humanities, science, and math classes, covering the same content as their peers, but with sheltered instruction from bilingual teachers. After 1 or 2 years of intensive ELD support in these classes, students were fully mainstreamed for their remaining years of high school. If additional assistance was needed, students received it either through elective support classes in reading or math, or individual tutorials.

It is noteworthy that the ELD students were among the most successful at EPAA and produced the valedictorians for the classes of 2006 and 2007. Marisol Castillo offered this explanation:

> The supports that the school provided to our students recently arrived to the United States and learning English were unheard of to them. As a result, there was a feeling among the students to take advantage of these resources. There were a lot of teachers telling them that not knowing English shouldn't be an excuse for giving up on the idea for academic success. Our message to students was relentless, and many of us had embodied it with our own life stories: regardless of where you start with us, the end point can be the same for all of us—college. By seeing all the first kids succeed, it was a great message for later students. These kids started off not knowing English, succeeded in high school, and entered great colleges.

## Special Education

For its first 2 years of operation, East Palo Alto Academy was part of the local Ravenswood elementary school district for purposes of special education, as the default option for charters in California is to receive services from the chartering district. However, the school found that this system did not adequately complement the mission and needs of EPAA and its students. In addition to the fact that Ravenswood was not set up to work with high school students, it was struggling with its special education program and was under court monitoring.

We found that numerous students arrived as freshmen with significant undiagnosed learning differences. EPAA worked quickly to identify those students and get them the accommodations they needed. By the school's third year, EPAA had established itself as a Local Education Agency (LEA), hiring its own special education teachers and contracting with local psychologists and service providers.

EPAA's current special education program functions much more effectively than previous strategies to meet students' needs. Using the "push-in" model described in Malcolm's story, the special education teacher enters classrooms to work with students—and to consult with their teachers—instead of pulling them out. The special education teacher is also available during specified periods to provide additional assistance with the work done in regular courses.

This structure is beneficial to students for two reasons. First, it ensures that students do not miss crucial material presented in class. Second, since the teacher enters the classroom and works with all students, special education students are not singled out as they would be in a pull-out program. This structure helps reduce the stigma of receiving extra services and, potentially, the psychological damage associated with the special education label.

Another aspect of the program was, and continues to be, collaboration between special education and mainstream teachers about how to best support special education students. This takes the form of meeting with mainstream teachers around planning for students' instruction and accommodations, and observing them in the classroom so that special education teachers know how to best complement the instruction provided in their students' courses. Mainstream teachers also received ongoing professional development in modifying instruction for students with learning differences, such as a series of workshops offered by the Charles Armstrong School,[8] a local private school for students with special needs.

## Tutorial

After-school tutoring provided students with opportunities to complete their homework with the assistance of tutors. The majority of volunteer tutors were

Stanford University undergraduates or community members. Depending on the due dates of major assessments or special projects, there might be a few students or a deluge—40 or 50—in a single day, deadline pressures for exhibitions and critical assignments being the driving force. Otherwise, student attendance was either voluntary, conditionally based on a behavior contract, strongly advised by advisors, or absolutely required due to an academic deficiency.

In addition to after-school tutoring, students' advisories were used 3 to 4 periods a week to help students finish homework and incomplete classwork. Teachers reported that this monitoring system greatly improved students' assignment completion. In essence, advisors were the students' main tutors, routinely staying late, often coming in on weekends to work with students on all different kinds of assignments—from essays to exhibitions to SAT prep.

Over the years, the format for academic support evolved, including office hours that teachers offered after school so that students could get additional guidance directly from them on specific assignments, credit-recovery classes during and after school, and Saturday sessions for extra help, especially around exhibition time.

Nicky says that the motto of EPAA should be: "Show up, do the work, accept help." Inevitably, EPAA's simple philosophy proved to be a powerful watchword, virtually guaranteeing that students who took these "commandments" to heart would graduate ready for postsecondary opportunities. Indeed, there was no successful student who didn't do all three, and no student who did all three had ever failed to graduate. William aptly summed it up:

> The truth is that the first year of East Palo Alto Academy taught the staff to be realistic. They learned how to deal with many different kinds of students, realizing with each one that their role was to coach them, and that sometimes it would take even more than those 4 years to give them the support they needed to make it out there on their own. However, teachers never stopped hoping that their interventions would succeed in changing the social and economic life trajectories of their students, and they celebrated each student who seized the advantages given to them by the school to actually begin to change the material circumstances of their lives.

Ayisha, a graduate of the first class, echoed William's sentiments:

> They taught us to see ourselves as students. They prepared us to look toward college and to exceed the standard and go above and beyond what we were asked. They helped us by having us thinking logically and critically of our next steps . . . having us apply what we learned in our classrooms to the real world.

## CHAPTER 6

# Learning to Teach So Students Can Learn

> If we taught babies to talk as most skills are taught in school, they would memorize lists of sounds in a predetermined order and practice them alone in a closet.
>
> —Linda Darling-Hammond

As emphasized throughout this book, East Palo Alto Academy sees its primary mission as providing students from East Palo Alto with the opportunity to choose higher education after high school. In order to achieve this goal, the staff has focused on developing curriculum and instruction that foster high performance standards with flexible supports and has evaluated students through authentic assessments. The mission was embedded in multiple structures that supported the learning of students. The following guiding principles, written by the faculty and school advisors, formed the foundation of teaching and learning at EPAA:

- Learning occurs within the context of activities that produce something authentic and valuable.
- The various cultures of the community are respected and examined. This process of understanding other cultures helps shape the social and academic culture of the school.
- Schoolwide standards, the Five Community Habits, emphasize the knowledge and academic and social skills necessary to succeed in college and the 21st-century workplace. Habits are used across disciplines and focus on depth rather than breadth.
- Teachers focus on personalized learning in mixed-ability classes that tap students' passions, develop their interests, support their learning, and build on their potential.
- Teachers develop integrated, project-based curricula focusing on application of knowledge in real-world contexts, along with public exhibitions and assessments of student work.
- Education is a long-term commitment that must include the community in a reciprocal relationship where parents, employers, and community members participate in student learning. Core curriculum

is enhanced through structured experiences in the community such as internships, service learning, and mentoring. (See also the Student Guide, Appendix D.)

These guiding principles informed every part of the teaching and learning structures at EPAA, including the curriculum (*what* content and skills were taught) and pedagogy (*how* content and skills were taught). In this chapter we focus on the pedagogical strategies teachers used within the structures that had been established to accomplish these challenging goals: what they did instructionally to engage students, build their knowledge and skills, and develop positive dispositions toward learning, school, and a caring and socially responsible community.

## THE CONTEXT FOR TEACHING

Teaching always occurs in a context that shapes what is needed and what is appropriate. In this case, as described earlier, all core classes were college preparatory and fulfilled basic requirements for entrance into the University of California and California State University systems. All students participated in college-preparatory classes from their freshman year, and by earning a C or higher in each required class, they automatically met the requirements for UC and State university admission. The curriculum balanced a focus on culturally responsive material with content that taught and inculcated students into the culture of power. Thus, for example, students read and analyzed *I Know Why the Caged Bird Sings* by Maya Angelou as well as Shakespeare's *Romeo and Juliet*, and learned the political theories of Martin Luther King and Malcolm X as well as John Locke and Thomas Hobbes.

Because EPAA eschewed tracking, all classes were heterogeneous and included mainstreamed special education students as well as English language learners at all levels of proficiency. In the upper grades, some students ultimately chose to go further than others in a strand of courses (taking mathematics beyond Algebra II, a fourth year of science, or Art III, for example), but no students were tracked out of any course, and sections were designed to be heterogeneous. The courses were on a block schedule, allowing for more than 90 minutes in order to explore content in depth (see Appendix E for EPAA's daily schedule). Students were assessed in all classes on the Five Community Habits schoolwide rubric that evaluated student progress as well as proficiency. In addition, the school's culture of revision and redemption stressed ongoing improvement of work to reach a higher standard of quality.

These strategies made the school unique. In traditional comprehensive high schools, students from underserved minority groups usually are tracked into remedial and non–college–prep courses. Tracking initially was developed and has been justified over many decades for two reasons: (1) the more efficient sorting of students into the experiences that guide them toward what has been viewed as their appropriate futures, and (2) the easier and more efficient instruction of students who are, presumably, ready to learn the same things in the same ways, based on their prior achievement levels.

While there has been extensive research that illustrates the shortcomings of tracking as an instructional tool, especially for lower-achieving students,[1] the process of de-tracking is difficult: It requires that teachers learn to provide meaningful work to students who have widely varying experiences and skills, and it requires that students and parents accept a heterogeneous learning context. Teachers must challenge those who are already knowledgeable to keep moving forward in their learning, while ensuring that those who are less experienced or skilled make accelerated progress so they are neither falling behind nor holding others back.

Teachers also must manage the psychological aspects of learning in such settings: motivating students to engage and put forth effort, providing intellectual challenges without discouraging or embarrassing them, managing groups so that all students feel safe and accepted in the classroom. This is a tall order, and it requires a substantial repertoire of teaching skills, as well as the disposition to continue to inquire and learn about how to solve teaching puzzles.

## STRATEGIES FOR TEACHING DIVERSE LEARNERS TO HIGH STANDARDS

We describe here some of the most important instructional strategies teachers used in this setting to teach the very diverse group of learners they encountered, without sacrificing the deeper learning goals to which they were committed:

- *Responsive teaching* based on an understanding of what students know and think
- *Explicit instruction and scaffolding* to demystify academic work
- *Differentiation* to provide students opportunities for academic success
- *Complex instruction* to create a collaborative classroom that accelerates learning
- *Teaching of academic habits* to provide effective learning tools

### Responsive Teaching

In planning sessions before the school opened, the faculty researched best practices of teaching and learning, planned an engaging curriculum, and set up structures that could help personalize the educational experience. The school had promised the East Palo Alto community that its teachers would provide a rigorous and relevant education in an environment where the students were cared for, respected, and kept safe.

***Supporting Diverse Learners.*** EPAA teachers worked hard to challenge all their students in heterogeneous classrooms, despite students' profound differences in skills. The complexities of teaching in this way were many. About half of the students entered EPAA with reading levels below 4th grade, while others, like Lena, were reading above the 9th-grade level. Many began with inadequate study habits, had only a tenuous grasp of key concepts and skills within core academic disciplines, and, perhaps most concerning, seemed to possess low motivation. A Stanford student teacher working at EPAA remarked:

> The different levels in the classroom were so challenging! I would be working with one student who could barely write a complete sentence and then move to the next student who was writing at almost a college level. It was hard meeting all the students' needs.

To deal with the different levels in the classroom, and in order to balance high standards for performance with gaps in students' knowledge, the teachers needed to develop pedagogies to narrow the distance between what the students could do and what the teachers wanted them to do. Getting to know the whole child at the school was not just a matter of caring. It was also a matter of understanding what individual students knew and could do, what their learning styles and strengths were, and what could best support their social and academic growth.

***Creating a Two-Way Pedagogy.*** Teachers used many approaches to come to understand their students' concerns and learning styles. They asked students to complete journal entries or surveys at the beginning of the year in which students described their educational histories, as well as their goals and fears about school, and how they felt they learned best. They listened in class as students responded to questions, worked in groups, talked offline to their neighbors, and sometimes complained, with brutal honesty, about what they thought of the assignments or why they felt they could not do the work. They used all of the information at their disposal to bring the curriculum to the students, as well as the students to the curriculum.

William Dean and Jeff Gilbert, the first two humanities teachers, led the way for the staff. William and Jeff began to teach their curriculum using highly engaging pedagogies grounded in education research: complex instruction, whole-class Socratic or student-led discussions, project-based learning, and rubric evaluation. They planned humanities classes together using the backwards planning approach of Wiggins and McTighe,[2] starting with what they wanted their students to know and be able to do by the end of each unit and

how they would assess student performance on their objectives. They adapted the schoolwide rubrics for their subject, using many of Robert Marzano's
ideas,[3] which called for giving students clear feedback on the development of
specific skills and measuring improvement.

Initially, they were faced with resistance, confusion, and doubt from the
students. As William put it, "Surprisingly, we learned early on that many of
our students were not ready to assume a disciplined independence in their
learning." During their staff collaboration and lesson-planning sessions, faculty struggled with how to teach students to approach this type of education
in a way that would diffuse their confusion and resistance. William, already a
veteran teacher of over 3 decades, described his experience teaching EPAA's
first freshman class with Jeff, a 10-year veteran teacher:

> Both of us felt like beginning teachers again, trying to secure guidance
> and information to help us reach these kids. Whether we appealed to
> Stanford's experts or read research to enhance our knowledge, we were
> determined to get it right. And the only way to accomplish this was
> to pay attention to how we saw our students trying to participate in
> activities in the classroom. For instance, when we conducted groupwork
> in the form of complex instruction, the students were overwhelmed by
> this approach. Freshmen could not handle having to play an assigned
> role with specific duties and responsibilities, as well as adhering to group
> norms while staying completely on task. Because they spent too much
> time arguing about the roles and the extent of duties placed on them,
> they did not focus on the task at hand long enough to complete it.

Jeff and William had to go back to the drawing board, realizing that their
students' former education had consisted of completion of isolated worksheets, without teaching for analytical thinking and logical reasoning.

> Jeff and I did not think that this challenge was impossible although there
> were many days when we felt like it was. We just knew that we had to
> come up with different strategies that would work for our students. The
> good news was that through our collaboration time we would find ways
> to get students to produce because the bottom line was that these kids
> could learn. So how would we accomplish this?

To deal with these realities, the staff reaffirmed their commitment to a
common curriculum based on thematic units, performance-oriented activities, project-based assessments, and heterogeneous groupings. Jeff and William realized that more scaffolding was needed: Students would need to take
many small steps in order to learn how to engage in complex activities and
projects. They developed well-scaffolded lessons to teach explicitly the skills

necessary for their students to achieve the learning goals. They differentiated content, instruction, and assessments to allow multiple ways for different types of learners at different ability levels to connect with curriculum and demonstrate proficiency. They allowed students time for reflection and revision, and they listened to what students said when they reflected.

Abandoning preconceptions about how students would learn, EPAA faculty learned directly from the students what students felt, and they learned from what students demonstrated they needed in order to succeed. Rather than just imparting content, they came to see their job as bringing the curriculum to the students as well as leading the students to the curriculum. They came to see the teachers' challenge as providing stimulating and engaging learning that would keep students moving toward ambitious goals, undaunted by the fact that students would not initially be able to perform certain tasks at grade-level competency.

Teachers did not eliminate those tasks or give up on higher-order thinking and performance goals for students. They learned to teach the skills that high school teachers normally assume are present, rather than failing students for not having already brought these skills with them. Part of what their responsive teaching taught them is that sometimes you have to go slow initially in order to go fast later on. It is important to meet students where they are and bring them along with you, rather than to leave them floundering in the deep end of the pool where they might drown.

## Explicit Instruction

A first lesson was the importance of explicit instruction. In this regard, the faculty drew inspiration from Lisa Delpit's book *Other People's Children*[4] when designing their approach to teaching habits and skills: All of them were taught explicitly. This does not mean that rote learning replaced inquiry, or that lower-level skills replaced higher-level ones. The kind of pedagogy that builds skills while fostering higher-order thinking has been a matter of some puzzlement for many researchers and practitioners. A false dichotomy between skills and process, drill and inquiry, teacher- and student-centeredness has characterized a debate that often has placed students of color in highly scripted settings focused on lower-level rote learning and White students in inquiry-oriented classrooms focused on critical thinking and creativity.

Part of the confusion is that explicitness in the teaching of skills that students may not have encountered at home or in their previous education often has been mistaken for a rote curriculum. In her influential essay "Skills and Other Dilemmas of a Progressive Black Educator,"[5] Delpit argued that students of historically disadvantaged social backgrounds need direct access to skills instruction to ensure that they gain access to the culture of power. She pointed out that process-oriented approaches, which allow students to direct much of their own learning, may assume that they bring considerable knowledge with them, and thus fail to provide enough direct instruction to ensure that children acquire the knowledge they need to succeed in the larger society.

While arguing for a more structured approach that provides the building blocks needed for success, Delpit often was misunderstood as embracing a "basic skills only" approach to teaching children of color, when in fact she sought, and described in her accounts of successful teachers, a pathway to critical thinking and empowerment through a blend of methods, combining explicit teaching of decoding and the rules of grammar alongside and embedded in opportunities to read and write critically and creatively. Delpit notes:

> I do not advocate a simplistic "basic skills" approach for children outside of the culture of power. It would be (and has been) tragic to operate as if these children were incapable of critical and higher-order thinking and reasoning. Rather, I suggest that schools must provide these children the content that other families from a different cultural orientation provide at home. . . . Although the problem is not necessarily inherent in the method, in some instances adherents of process approaches to writing create situations in which students ultimately find themselves accountable for knowing a set of rules about which no one has ever directly informed them. . . . In this country, students will be judged on their product regardless of the process they utilized to achieve it. And that product, based as it is on the specific codes of a particular culture, is more readily produced when the directives of how to produce it are made explicit.[6]

Accordingly, staff taught students how to write sentences, then paragraphs, then essays; how to decode text; how to take notes; how to engage in a discussion or debate; how to study for tests; and more. Whenever possible, they reinforced similar strategies across classrooms, so that these approaches would become second nature. For example, faculty determined that it was challenging for many students to comprehend a grade-level text. In response, they adopted a schoolwide set of literacy practices that were directly taught to all students beginning in freshman year. One of these techniques was called "talking to the text," an active reading strategy to annotate any text by:

- Underlining key words and phases
- Circling unfamiliar terms to look up or decode in context
- Writing questions in the margins
- Summarizing passages to prepare for future discussion or analysis activities

These lessons stuck. An alumna from the class of 2006 shared her perspective on the usefulness of this strategy:

As a junior in college I have realized that the most important method of doing homework must truly be talking to the text. I feel that college is all about analyzing and breaking down literature. I do nothing but research, read, and write. I strongly believe that talking to the text was one of the most useful techniques that I got out of EPAA. I read hundreds of pages per week and the only way I can remember, understand, and discuss the context of the reading is by talking to the text, and writing down my thoughts and questions.

Another graduate also expressed gratitude toward her high school teachers for insisting that she practice this strategy:

Talking to the text helped me come prepared to class with questions and comments on my reading. I still use that habit today. I've told some of my friends about that and it's helped them also.

Other explicit teaching focused on developing social skills that would support success during and after high school: how to enter a classroom appropriately, how to ask questions in an academic environment, and how students could advocate for themselves in a professional way. Staff taught students how to *code-switch*, by adapting their speech and behavior to match different situations and settings.

Teachers understood the importance of a curriculum focused on both academic and social skills. One teacher commented: "We're educating students to be prepared for college and to be prepared to be active citizens. So we are educating the person as well as the scholar." Even as they did so, the staff continually respected students' cultures and languages, celebrating students' pride in their communities. The point was not to force students to assimilate into the dominant culture, but rather to give them the needed tools to succeed in it, by reinforcing and building on the skills they already had.

## Scaffolding

Another important strategy the teachers used and continually refined was scaffolding—breaking all assignments and projects down into small, manageable tasks, and teaching each discrete subskill or piece of content. Many traditional high school assignments ask students to complete a complex task like writing an essay, assuming that students already have the basic knowledge and skills to tackle the assignment. At EPAA, faculty quickly learned not to make assumptions about what students knew, because during the first few months their assumptions were shattered. Furthermore, all students could benefit from relearning a skill or subject in order to gain a deeper understanding. Humanities teacher Marysol de la Torre described the importance of scaffolding:

Whether we were planning schoolwide exhibitions or common assessments in our classrooms, we quickly realized as a staff that "scaffolding" needed to be a major part of the EPAA curriculum and our day-to-day practice. We couldn't simply assign students a five-paragraph essay and give them the due date and independent work time to complete the task. Students in our humanities classrooms ranged in terms of literacy levels; one of my classrooms in particular had two students who read at a 2nd-grade reading level and others who read above [their current] grade level.

We scaffolded our daily activities and assignments to meet the needs of every student as much as possible; no one was to be left out. When an essay was assigned, we would provide the building blocks for students to complete the multistep task. We incorporated many prewriting strategies and created graphic organizers throughout the writing process to help students organize their thoughts and learn to write paragraphs that would become a part of a more cohesive piece—an essay. We revisited these strategies and graphic organizers throughout the school year so that students would be familiar with the terminology and language of writing, such as outline, thesis and topic sentences, transitions, analysis, and revision.

Scaffolded instruction gave those students who were new to the topic an opportunity to get on board with the rest of the class. Students who were already familiar with the topic benefited from relearning the content and could serve as experts in the class to help the other students. As a teacher, it's easy to assume that students already have the background knowledge and skills needed to complete what you ask them to do in class, but students need to be guided step-by-step. Only then will students be given an even playing field in the classroom and an opportunity to succeed.

## Differentiation

Teachers also used differentiation to personalize education in their classrooms, designing lessons and adapting activities to respond to students' multiple intelligences and varied abilities.[7] This meant that teachers needed to provide a variety of instructional activities and tasks that matched learners' capabilities with appropriate content and assessment, even during direct instruction. William Dean described the differentiated assessments in his humanities classroom:

Listening to my students indicate how they learned best was another factor I considered seriously, so I responded to data that they themselves created. Using the computers, students took an inventory about their multiple intelligences, and after they analyzed the findings, they had a clearer awareness of their strengths and weaknesses. They were pretty much in agreement with the data. Then I used the data to establish a list of choices for tasks from which the students could select. Some students were more hands-on and kinesthetic than others, while some were more linguistic or visual. As expected, I observed students feeling more comfortable to have a voice in how they were learning, especially when they experienced favorable results because their strengths, interests, and talents were tapped.

While Mr. Dean and other teachers sought to enable students to tap different intelligences to build on their strengths, they never watered down or distorted the goals or the outcomes students were to accomplish. Students did not substitute visual art or poster boards for essays or research papers. They often did begin with their strengths en route to those goals; for example, drawing a storyboard before writing a narrative or working with manipulatives as a means to solve an equation.

Teachers differentiated inputs to support access to content by, for example, allowing students access to different levels of texts or shortening texts for some students as they built up their reading skills. For example, students read versions of Shakespeare's plays with a modern translation on one page and the original language on the opposite page. Students had access to different levels of the history texts and Spanish translations of math textbooks. Here, too, the long-term goal was to encourage more extensive reading and the development of broader content knowledge that ultimately could support comprehension of complex texts. Reading research finds that it is important to provide accessible texts along with explicit teaching of reading strategies, if students are to read independently and develop their reading skills by reading more extensively.[8] For new English learners and previously struggling readers who otherwise would shut down entirely, this approach built their skills more effectively than assigning reading they could not do and would just ignore.

Teachers also differentiated instruction and assessment by assigning distinct tasks to different students or allowing students to complete a modified task. Tasks might be differentiated by students' interests—for example, by allowing students to choose a research topic that had special meaning to them and present their findings in different modalities (orally, in writing, using multimedia technologies, and so forth).

Tasks also might be differentiated by students' needs; for example, new English learners might write in Spanish initially, if they were literate in their native language, and learn to translate their work. Students with reading disabilities might read shorter selections or, in certain contexts, use books on tape. A student with auditory processing difficulties might receive written notes or graphic organizers in class to support listening and comprehending.

These are common accommodations but, we learned, not always known to or considered by high school teachers without additional professional development or coaching to enable them to be used appropriately, not as long-term crutches, but as means to build skills over time.

## Complex Instruction

A critically important, schoolwide pedagogical strategy was Complex Instruction, a particularly sophisticated form of groupwork that has been found in extensive research to raise achievement for all kinds of students, including low- and high-achievers in heterogeneous classrooms and English learners.[9] The majority of EPAA teachers had graduated from STEP and had been trained in Complex Instruction by one of the architects of this technique, professor Rachel Lotan, who had worked closely with Stanford professor Elizabeth Cohen in developing this method.[10] Thus, faculty had a consistent understanding of this strategy, so it functioned similarly in all classrooms. As its creators wrote, the goal of Complex Instruction is as follows:

> To provide academic access and success for *all* students in heterogeneous classrooms . . . [and] to foster the development of higher-order thinking skills through group work activities organized around a central concept or big idea. The tasks are open-ended, requiring students to work interdependently to solve problems. Most importantly, the tasks require a wide array of intellectual abilities so that students from diverse backgrounds and different levels of academic proficiency can make meaningful contributions to the group task. . . .
>
> The teacher trains students to use cooperative norms and specific roles to manage their own groups. The teacher is free to observe groups carefully, to provide specific feedback, and to treat status problems which cause unequal participation among group members. . . . Teachers use status treatments to broaden students' perceptions of what it means to be smart, and to convince students that they each have important intellectual contributions to make to the multiple-ability task.[11]

When teachers see unequal participation among group members resulting from status differences among peers, they bolster the status of infrequent contributors by publicly recognizing specific talents that students exhibit or good ideas or contributions they offer. This can happen in the context of the whole class or during groupwork by offering praise, reinforcing the idea and attributing it to the student, or asking the student to explain his or her idea publicly. Research finds that this proves to be a key practice for equitable outcomes.[12]

There is strong evidence from multiple studies conducted over 2 decades supporting the success of Complex Instruction strategies in promoting student academic achievement in literacy, mathematics, and science, with gains for all students and especially strong gains for initially lower-achieving students and for English learners.[13]

In Complex Instruction, every student's participation is necessary to complete the group task, and every task also has an individual component. Complex Instruction honors the multiple intelligences that all students possess and shows students that "all of us are smarter than one of us." Each member has a role—such as recorder, reporter, materials manager, resource manager, communication facilitator, and harmonizer—and is accountable to the student-led group, resulting in more even participation. Teachers also can conduct quick formative assessments of students' current understanding to inform future direct instruction.

A major component of this approach is the development of "group-worthy tasks" that are sufficiently open-ended and multifaceted to require and benefit from the participation of every member of the group. Tasks that require a variety of skills, such as research, analysis, visual representation, and writing, are well suited to this approach. EPAA teachers used Complex Instruction in all classrooms, developing tasks that required higher-order thinking and analysis. For example, in math, students were challenged to explore and create multiple representations of abstract concepts like adding and subtracting negative numbers using lab gear (small tiles of different shapes and colors). In science, students coded human DNA in biology labs. And in humanities, students analyzed primary documents from various historical eras.

At East Palo Alto Academy, teachers discovered that the use of these strategies, like many others, had to be scaffolded. For example, William and Jeff discovered that their students at first had difficulty working in groups of four or five, juggling their roles and analytic tasks with which they were unfamiliar, as well as the language demands of groupwork for English learners. William described how he approached Complex Instruction by meeting his freshmen where they were, starting with pair work and gradually working toward authentic Complex Instruction:

> What I knew already about having good classroom management to conduct group activities became apparent in my classroom. I established pairs to engage the students to work with each other. I reduced the number of roles and duties so that the pairs could master the task on a smaller scale, without compromising the standards. I demonstrated and modeled what I wanted them to achieve, and I visited each pair, almost as a third member, to move them toward the Complex Instruction model.
>
> I never imposed my thinking about the best way to achieve an excellent performance. So I just asked questions for them to figure out the answers, and I never offered direct answers to their questions when

they felt the need to be rescued from a dilemma or problem that had them stuck. Instead, I repeated how they as a group could solve their problem by communicating to each other, relying on each one's strength, knowledge, skills, and even weaknesses, and recalling our deductive/ inductive reasoning lessons. Regardless of my approach and strategy, many students still attempted to resist tapping into their own thinking. I gradually built up to a more complete version of Complex Instruction as I determined their readiness for it.

Marysol noted that both she and the students had to learn to reduce their dependency on the teacher. As she delegated authority to the group, she had to fight her instincts to jump in and help students solve a problem whenever they were stuck:

> During groupwork, students turn to each other for help and not the teacher. With the proper initiation of roles and norms, students can be trained to take responsibility for their learning and hold themselves accountable. Students must learn to work out conflicts on their own. Next time, I won't physically join the group, I'll drop the activity cards on the desks, answer every question with a question, and say, "I'll be back to see how you're doing." I have to take risks in order to teach that they can too. I must encourage them to turn to each other first. I have to unlearn in order for them to learn.

As students became more proficient with the strategy, the benefits became clear. Seth observed:

> Complex Instruction allows all my students with various skill levels and abilities an entry point. Multiple-abilities tasks that are organized around clear norms and include explicit roles give individual students ownership of the mathematical content. And most importantly, my students engage in and discuss the math with each other as they become independent learners.

Students eventually began to see the merits of learning to work productively in groups. As one student put it:

> Because the teachers encouraged me to get along with people I work with, I [will] be successful. When I started going to school I was independent and wanted to work by myself, but I had to learn how to work with other people in groups. It's a good technique they have in working with groups.

## Teaching Academic Habits for Success

Teachers also realized they needed to teach explicitly the necessary habits for academic engagement and ultimate success. This cannot be overstated: The majority of EPAA freshmen faced challenges fulfilling the most *basic* of expectations—coming to school daily; arriving to class on time with pens, notebooks, and texts; and completing homework. There were various reasons for these challenges. In some cases, students did not want to carry a backpack walking to and from school because they were harassed by neighborhood peers who had already dropped out of high school. For a number of families, financial constraints made it difficult to purchase school supplies. Then there were students who simply did not want to be in school; they wanted to drop out and either get a job or hang out on the streets. Other students who had never had successful experiences in school were stuck in self-fulfilling prophesies of failure and saw no point in academic endeavors. Of course, there were exceptions, like Lena and Esperanza, who came to school every day prepared and ready to learn, but these students were frustrated when their peers were less well organized or less prepared to learn.

The staff saw that simply punishing students for not having their homework done and their tools in hand did not produce greater success. How, then, could teachers begin to build the foundations of academic behavior and reinforce them for success? They came to realize that developing these habits required very consistent structures. As one teacher commented:

> Our kids are much more effective when there are clear structures. [We were] not doing a good enough job of it the first year. . . . The second year [those] who taught the new freshmen were much better about creating structures. You just see the kids react so much more positively to knowing exactly what they are supposed to be doing, where they are supposed to be, and just being clear so you don't get any debate. Over time we are trying to increase the amount of consistent structure that happens in classrooms.

The first step for teachers was to explicitly teach and reinforce desired behaviors. Over time, the faculty adopted schoolwide norms for classrooms, such as posting the daily agenda, materials needed, and homework on the board. Students were taught and retaught to enter a classroom quietly, read the instructions on the board and retrieve the necessary materials before placing their backpacks on the back counter, sit in their assigned seats, and start the warm-up. These norms helped students get right to work with minimal distractions.

Keeping backpacks at the back of the classroom ensured that students were not distracted by makeup, iPods, cell phones, notes, and the like. It also prevented students from hiding out behind their backpacks strategically arranged on their desks. Students also were taught that the teacher dismisses the class, not the bell; indeed, EPAA did not ring bells at the end of class, only at the beginning. Some teachers assigned rotating daily jobs to students, such as handing out materials, answering the classroom phone, running an occasional errand for extra copies or supplies, erasing the board, and stacking or unstacking the chairs.

Teachers also employed another strategy—called "Ticket Out the Door" (TOD)—for training students to produce work during class. Teachers decided on the baseline amount of work necessary to show understanding of the day's objectives; students had to complete this work before leaving class. Teachers posted the daily Ticket Out the Door on the board and held students after class who did not finish their TOD. For some students this was an effective way to motivate them to work productively throughout class. Most students were able to finish their TOD and get to their next class before the 10-minute passing period elapsed. Other students stayed in through brunch or lunch to finish, or a note was sent to their advisor indicating the work to be finished that day in advisory.

A final tool to help students organize their work and their thinking was the class notebook. Each course required students to maintain an organized binder or notebook that included a running table of contents and all their classwork and homework assignments. William described his set of practices in this way:

> When it came to delivering information in the form of directed teaching or having whole-class discussions, I had to provide a way for students to record adequate notes in an organized manner. I observed that they did not know how to discern major and minor points to engage in quality thinking. So I introduced how to maintain graphic organizers and interactive notebooks, while I practiced strategies to extend student thinking: utilizing wait time, asking follow-up questions, instructing them to engage their partner in a pair-share discussion, playing devil's advocate, or asking for a summary to promote active listening.
>
> The students found the notebook and graphic organizers helpful tools for recording information, compartmentalizing facts and ideas, applying rules and principles, synthesizing ideas, and developing opinions and decisions. I conducted discussions and directed teaching much better because the students had organized notes to review for study and mastery. To ensure that they created decent entries from which to study, I checked their notebooks frequently, making comments, asking questions, and indicating good points in the margins. Also, depending on the assessment, students could use their notebooks or organizers as reference tools while completing the assessment. I was interested in their academic behavior as a response to my approach;

it was a measuring stick that I used to facilitate their learning. When students were successfully learning, then I was successfully teaching.

William's comment—"when students were successfully learning, then I was successfully teaching"—captured the philosophy of the school. Until students were successfully learning, the teachers and their partners from the university felt it was their obligation to continue to seek out and invent new strategies to support student success.

Faculty always tried to uncover the reasons or overcome the obstacles that made school difficult for students who did not respond to the strategies teachers had put in place. The school kept a supply of new and donated backpacks, notebooks, pens, and pencils, and would give them away or sell them cheaply. The principal's office always had extra t-shirts, sweatshirts, and pants for students to change into if they violated the dress code. The school also convened Student Study Teams (SSTs) to discuss a struggling student's needs more thoroughly and to formulate a plan of action. A student's parent or guardian, teachers, advisor, and the principal or vice principal attended the SSTs, and action plans might include modifications to instruction received by the student or changes to his or her class schedule. Sometimes students needed a new seating assignment in a class or needed to attend counseling or a tutorial. For the most extreme cases, teachers instituted a behavior contract (see Chapter 3). The advisor was always instrumental in monitoring the student's support plan.

Advisors routinely reinforced the schoolwide expectations for academic habits. For example, advisors conducted daily materials and notebook checks in advisory during the first few months of school to make sure that students were prepared for their classes. In general, EPAA teachers would observe student behavior in detail, correct or redirect students to meet basic academic expectations, and celebrate the eventual successes.

## OUTCOMES FOR STUDENTS AND STAFF

By the end of the first year, the majority of EPAA students were responding well to these strategies, and one student from the class of 2005 commented:

What sticks out for me is the amount of time that the teachers devote to students, and how they are dedicated to making sure that we get our work done. They help you whenever you need it. There is never an excuse not to graduate at EPAA because they do everything that they can for students except for taking the test. . . . You have to do that on your own.

Another said:

> They taught me to do math the right way, and English the right way, to
> do essays; the steps and skills you need . . . [for] essay[s] or any projects.
> . . . My essays are much more detailed. My reading got much better than
> it was before.

Meanwhile, the staff learned that they could expand their individual and
collective repertoires by listening to and watching the students, innovating
and observing the results, sharing with one another what they learned, and
developing common practices that were reinforced across classrooms.

A central core of best practices emerged over the years, what Nicky referred to as EPAA 101. These were practices that teachers needed to learn if
they were to have a productive and eventually successful experience teaching
at East Palo Alto Academy. Nicky would say to teachers, "If you can teach well
at EPAA, you can teach well anywhere." The skills needed to reach students
and design strategic pedagogy, curriculum, and assessments tailored for their
needs were the universal skills of an accomplished teacher and would make
teaching successful at any school.

What did the most successful teachers at EPAA do? Some teachers learned
more quickly than others not to take on the lives of their students at the expense of the instructional process. Even though the EPAA way was to build
strong relationships and personalize students' educational experiences, the
majority of students and families were living with so many complex and often tragic situations that it would be possible for teachers to focus exclusively
on students' nonacademic needs and not have enough time for the work of
college-preparatory teaching and learning. Well-meaning teachers working
with underserved students often feel they need to save them; EPAA teachers
felt it was more important to empower their students. Teachers could give
guidance, but students ultimately needed to develop the knowledge and confidence to resolve their own issues.

Successful teachers each had their own teaching and student-management
approach. Despite these stylistic differences, successful EPAA teachers had more
and more in common as they worked closely together. This helped the students
immensely. The faculty became so skilled at reinforcing one another that it was
a common occurrence for a teacher having an important conversation with a
student to pull in a passing teacher to reinforce the message of the conference,
as if the encounter had been choreographed. What were teachers reinforcing?
The main message was clear: maintain high standards and help students reach
them. Each successful teacher, skilled in his or her particular way, related to this
message and modeled this technique for the rest of the staff.

Jeff often said, "Good classroom management is good curriculum." He
modeled how good lessons engage students productively for the whole period.

Jeff was meticulous about students' understanding, and his lessons were focused on critical and creative thinking. When Jeff mentored other teachers and witnessed a breakdown in classroom management, during his debriefing with the teacher, he always asked, "What did you want your students to know and be able to do at the end of the lesson?" He helped teachers pinpoint the parts of the lesson that contributed to the breakdown in management. Teachers found that students began behaving poorly when an activity had gone on for too long, instructions were unclear, students didn't understand how to do the task, or the task wasn't sufficiently scaffolded.

In a similar vein, Marysol modeled how classroom structure and organization were strong supports for high expectations. Students knew what to expect in her classroom, and colleagues knew they could count on Marysol to follow through with her responsibilities. Her classroom had a focus on process—be clear at all times what students should be doing and how they should be doing it. At first it was difficult for EPAA students to ask for help because many already had bruised academic egos and shied away from situations where they might feel vulnerable. Marysol's structure and organization made students feel safe to respond to the high levels of academic rigor in her classroom, and she was able to push them to high levels of productivity.

Tina modeled how to connect students to the curriculum. She cared about social-emotional issues like the right to speak, be heard, and have one's opinion respected. Her classroom was a place of spirited discussions, and she pressed students to connect themselves to the subject matter and think deeply. Every assignment had to be meaningful and relevant to the students, or else why do it? Tina could push her students because she knew them well. She wanted her students to enjoy learning, and she modeled what it meant to be a lifelong learner by taking numerous night classes for fun while a teacher at EPAA and even writing a novel in her spare time. Tina brought her sense of humor into the classroom and was always joking with her students or pretending to swear at them in her native language, Farsi. Because she cared so deeply about her subject, her passion was contagious, and students more readily connected to her humanities curriculum.

Rebecca modeled unyielding stubbornness and an ability to get staff and students to accomplish what they initially thought was impossible. She used a full-court-press approach and harnessed all resources available to tackle each problem. Because of this dogged persistence and strategic use of resources, Rebecca made sure that all of her advisees applied to college and had adequate funding to attend. Some teachers said, "You have to choose your battles." Rebecca said, "I choose all battles. If we really want our students and staff to succeed, then we must do this. If not us, then who?" If there was any potential for a situation to improve, Rebecca was adamant that the school always do its best work. Her refusal to accept mediocrity inspired other staff and students to aim high.

Seth modeled how to use data and facts to help students and teachers make changes in their behavior. It was common for Seth to pull out a spreadsheet during a conversation with a student or teacher to frame an issue and to provide a dose of reality. Data are undeniable and cut through attempts by teachers and students to argue, "No, it's not like that." Like all staff, Seth kept track of student attendance, participation, and production, but what distinguished Seth was how he used the information to influence and guide students' and teachers' awareness of their own behavior. When novice teachers were at their wits' ends and started to make blanket statements like, "My freshmen are out of control," Seth encouraged them to support their claims with facts and gather data to put the situation in perspective. Often this would help teachers to stop focusing on the negative and recognize the good things that were happening in their classrooms.

William modeled how to listen well to both students and teachers, and as a result they felt safe to confide in him and examine their issues with him. William used a metacognitive approach to problem solving that began with uninterrupted listening and observation. Because William had instilled such trust in students and staff, he could be blunt and completely honest without insult. This powerful combination of receptiveness, respect, and straightforwardness allowed William to successfully mentor teachers and students. His focus on staff's and students' feelings and behavior gave him an instinctual ability to sense unease on campus. This served as an early warning system that allowed Nicky and Jeff to defuse problems before they escalated.

Nicky modeled how to build relationships with all students and teachers, and especially those whom no one else could reach. Nicky used to tell students who said they didn't care about anything, as well as teachers who said that students didn't care, that of course students cared or they wouldn't have bothered to come to school that day. Nicky was skilled at connecting quickly with people, then using the connection to push them to improve. For Nicky, the most important outcome of a conversation was that the student (or teacher) left with a clearer sense of his or her personal strengths and potential. People will do their best work and behave well when they are motivated to do so, and most people are motivated by feeling good, not bad, about themselves. This is why Nicky told teachers to focus on their students' strengths and tell students what they were good at, especially when obstacles arose. After all, people can build only on their strengths, not on their weaknesses.

The most important thing was that teachers' unique abilities and their pedagogical strategies were routinely shared. Based on the models of other successful small schools,[14] EPAA was designed for ongoing teacher learning and collaboration, so that teachers could become increasingly knowledgeable and skilled. The many ways that teachers were supported in their learning are detailed in the next chapter.

## CHAPTER 7

# A Professional Place

> I became a teacher at EPAA because I was inspired by the amazing staff that
> was determined to change the lives of East Palo Alto youth and its community.
> All the teachers were effective and had a gift for noticing—what researchers
> call "withitness"—noticing what exactly was needed to educate, empower, and
> change the lives of EPA teenagers.
>
> —Misla Barco

Learning to teach so that students could learn was an ongoing endeavor at
EPAA. The school hired founding teachers who were well prepared and experienced, and could create curriculum and build new programs. All EPAA
teachers were well schooled in their subject matter, and the majority came
from one of the best teacher preparation programs in the country, the Stanford Teacher Education Program.[1] Nicky and Jeff, both graduates of STEP,
each had over 10 years of experience teaching high school. William, a graduate of Rutgers, had over 30. The school's faculty sponsor, Linda, had been
a secondary school teacher, previously had worked with others to create and
study successful school designs, and was engaged in the national school reform movement. Many teachers hired were from ethnic backgrounds similar
to the students' and were fluent Spanish speakers. But the most important
qualities EPAA teachers possessed were their commitment to their own learning and self-improvement, their passion for secondary education, and their
dedication to teaching underserved students.

## DESIGNING A PROFESSIONAL LEARNING COMMUNITY

First and foremost, teachers were committed to collaborating with and learning from one another. It was important for the staff to bond so that teachers
could support one another throughout the intense experience of meeting the
high expectations EPAA had for all its educators and students. Long before the
term *professional learning community* had been popularized, the school created
such a community to support teachers in meeting students' needs.

## Collaborative Norms

As an example of how the EPAA teacher community operated, during the fourth year of the school, Rebecca had a particularly challenging group of 9th-graders with an unusually intense accumulation of needs. Many had been mainstreamed from middle school special day classes[2] and didn't know how to behave as students in regular classes. Other students struggled with drug abuse or depression, or difficult life circumstances such as a parent dying from cancer.

Because of the collaborative norms that had been established in the school, Rebecca's instinct was not to close the door and struggle alone; instead, she invited other staff in to help her. Jeff and William observed her teaching and helped her refine her pedagogy to meet the needs of this particularly challenging group of students. Another teacher, Cristina Galvan, taught science to the same cohort of students, and she and Rebecca supported each other and shared best practices to help get each other through the year.

Linda came to observe as well. She shadowed one emotionally disturbed student through all of his classes and helped problem-solve with Rebecca, the student's other teachers, his advisor, the resource specialist, and Nicky. They strategized how to more successfully teach this young man while maintaining classroom environments that worked for all students. Rebecca reflected on the support she received:

> One thing that was humbling was that at first I thought, "What's wrong with me? I'm not good enough." Jeff and William helped validate my struggle; it's not just that something was wrong with me. Anyone would struggle in this situation. There wasn't an easy answer I was missing. They helped me see that I was doing a lot of things well, but I needed to adapt my pedagogy for this group of students. William's and Jeff's support enlightened me. They were patient with my progress and came into my classroom throughout the year to help support me. Even though that was such a hard year, it made me become a better teacher and focus on being able to differentiate. It also reaffirmed the importance of teaching culturally relevant curriculum that piqued students' interests in order to get them to engage.

Rebecca's experience was replicated many times over for virtually every teacher, at one time or another. Together, the school leaders purposefully created a culture based on patience and consistent, long-term mentoring. Teachers needed ongoing coaching if they were going to adapt their teaching to high-needs students. When an issue arose, such as how to get students to do more homework, get to class on time, or prepare to take standardized tests, faculty approached it as a school-community issue, not a student or individual teacher issue. Staff did not have the attitude, "What's wrong with our students?" or "What's wrong with that teacher?" but asked instead, "What can we do together to better serve our students and improve their achievement?"

## Addressing Dilemmas

Teachers understood that the answer to this question was not simple or clear-cut. Most issues they faced were *dilemmas*, not problems with simple or obvious solutions. According to Larry Cuban,[3] dilemmas are problems that highlight a conflict between equally important values. For example, EPAA valued giving each student a personalized education, yet also valued having a standard and clear set of expectations for all students. Sometimes the needs of individual students were in conflict with the needs of the whole group. In the case of the student struggling with deep emotional issues mentioned above, developing a plan to serve him within a mainstream class without compromising the academic or behavior standards for the rest of the students was a dilemma; there was not an easy solution. Furthermore, any strategy implemented in response to a dilemma needed to be revisited and adjusted until an acceptable balance between the two values arose. There were not right solutions to dilemmas, only better solutions.

Earlier we saw how one teacher, Rebecca, reached out for help to solve some classroom dilemmas. Getting students to do homework offered another example of how the staff as a whole reached outward and inward for help in solving a schoolwide dilemma: When the teachers noticed a pattern of declining homework completion, they discussed it at length. Teachers saw homework as a vital part of helping students to learn by practicing concepts and skills introduced in class and as a means to transfer and apply knowledge independently. Faculty gathered data from their classroom records to diagnose which groups of students were not consistently doing their homework. Staff talked about what got in the way of students doing homework. Linda sought advice on the homework dilemma from many of her education contacts, important players in the school reform movement and former founding principals of small New York City schools, such as Deborah Meier, Ann Cook, and Olivia Ifill-Lynch.[4] Deborah wrote to Linda about her experience at Central Park East:

> We soon realized that a sizable number of students didn't really know how to do the homework, or at least how to do it well enough to get any satisfaction from it. A smaller number truly didn't have time, and we needed a whole-family conference to tackle the issues of jobs, babysitting, etc. A third group just couldn't or didn't plan, so we tried having a brief meeting at the end of each day to plan for homework. Some students were just expressing their general despair this way.[5]

Meier's comments resonated with EPAA faculty. They worked to create more meaningful assignments. Staff communicated with one another about homework—over email, blogs, and shared calendars. Teachers set up conferences with families of students who were not consistently completing homework and put students on homework contracts with daily progress reports. Most important, staff decided to re-evaluate the use of advisory time. Instead of adding more curriculum to advisory, staff resolved to use the advisory period 3 days a week to focus on homework completion.

At the beginning of each afternoon advisory, many advisors polled their students for the day's homework assignments and had advisees set a goal for what they would complete during the period and write a plan for finishing the remaining work. Staff taught students to record their homework in notebooks and planners, and experimented with Friday tutorial and Saturday school. Ultimately, these weekend sessions were focused primarily on major exhibitions or end-of-semester assessments. Staff also scheduled office hours after school for individual help in subject areas. EPAA's approach was not to force the students to attend these extra weekend and afternoon sessions, but to foster students' intrinsic motivation to show up. Almost every teacher had a "Wall of Fame" in his or her classroom for their advisees and posted notices with positive comments to publicize students' successes. Staff did all this in the name of addressing the dilemma of homework completion and as a way to acculturate students to college work habits.

## CREATING STRUCTURES AND PRACTICES TO SUPPORT PROFESSIONAL LEARNING

There were many aspects of the school that supported the professional learning of all members of the school staff. These included:

- EPAA's designation as a *professional development school* partnering with Stanford University
- Access to internal and external *expertise* for ongoing mentoring, coaching, curriculum development, and problem solving, including support for National Board Certification
- *Collaboration time* scheduled weekly for joint planning and professional development
- Teacher involvement in *shared decisionmaking* and *distributed leadership*
- Compensation and school design features that *valued* teachers' commitment and their efforts to expand their expertise

In what follows, we describe these structures and practices, and then show how they came together to create a strong teaching practice for one of the teachers, Marysol de la Torre, who began at EPAA as a student teacher.

## A Professional Development School

As much as East Palo Alto Academy functioned as a professional learning community internally, it also connected to other schools for learning as part of a wider community of professional development schools (PDSs) organized through STEP at Stanford. The STEP Professional Development School partners worked with the teacher education program to create mutually beneficial contributions to the growth of the teaching profession. Each of the schools served as placement sites for student teachers, while STEP also provided curriculum and school improvement support to the veteran teachers at the schools. Quite often, the schools would be sites for research and development activities as well. Additionally, teachers from PDS schools could participate in Stanford courses for free, engage in research with Stanford professors, and be involved in a variety of teacher leadership initiatives. A number of veteran teachers took advantage of this opportunity by taking curriculum and instruction courses in their field or courses like Principles of Learning for Teaching, Teaching and Learning in Heterogeneous Classrooms, or Adolescent Development, among others.

STEP created a network that brought these PDSs together each month to learn with and from one another. The schools had access to School of Education faculty who held professional development workshops at different schools in the network. The network conducted "Grand Rounds" in which faculties visited one another's schools to observe particularly interesting or successful practices in action and to analyze them together. Faculty from the schools would decide on topics they would like to explore together—like how to design differentiated curriculum—and STEP would support them in taking on these initiatives.

As a PDS site, EPAA had a close relationship with STEP and had as many as a half-dozen student teachers each year. The involvement of student teachers at the site augmented the staffing for the school, providing an enriched ratio of adults to students. Given the full-year model of student teaching used at STEP, these teacher candidates were at the site daily from the first day of school until the last day of school, and brought with them a growing knowledge of cutting-edge pedagogy, as well as unbounded enthusiasm and commitment to contribute to the lives of the students in the school. In return, EPAA's cooperating teachers provided new teachers with valuable on-the-ground training. One cooperating teacher commented:

> Student teachers need models of really high-quality teaching. And I think that happens here. You are not only getting trained by people who are very effective in the classroom; you are also getting trained by people who are teacher leaders and have a sense of ownership over the school. I think that is powerful in creating change because when our student teachers leave and go into these big comprehensive high schools, they have this notion that teachers should be involved in decisionmaking

and teachers should get involved outside of their own classrooms. And I think that is powerful in terms of school reform possibilities.

Of course, EPAA also regarded STEP student teachers as possible future employees, and since the school was growing as it admitted another class of students each year, many accepted positions at the school after they graduated.

## Access to Expertise and Coaching

During these early years and beyond, Stanford faculty worked with school staff on developing curriculum, accessing materials, and developing practice through staff development at the school site. In some cases, like science, professors worked hand-in-hand with teachers to design a multiyear curriculum plan, including specific units and projects. In others, like literacy, English language development, and mathematics, professors and their graduate students advised and taught or coached in the school for periods of time. Some faculty designed and conducted ongoing professional development, often in conjunction with teachers in the school. Some faculty taught courses at Stanford that trained undergraduate and graduate students as tutors and mentors who worked in the school to help students learn to conduct research, read more proficiently, and write personal statements for college.

*Mentoring for Beginners.* Beginning teachers received mentoring as part of the state-funded Beginning Teacher Support and Assessment Program (BTSA). Seasoned veterans on the staff, like Jeff Gilbert and William Dean, supported the new teachers initially with classroom observations and coaching. Because so many of the young teachers came from STEP, often they also continued to reach out to their curriculum and instruction professors for advice on curriculum issues in much the same way that EPAA students reached out to their advisors after graduation.

We found that subject-specific mentoring, especially for curriculum development and content pedagogy, was extremely important for beginners. Although BTSA did not require a match between the subject area of the mentor and that of the novice, the new teachers did much better if they had someone whom they could consult about very specific pedagogical issues in their field. In later years, the school worked with Stanford's Center for the Support of Excellent Teaching to access subject-matter mentors for new teachers who otherwise did not have access to that kind of curriculum support.

*Coaching for Veterans.* Veteran teachers also had access to coaching. One of the requirements of employment at EPAA was that faculty would commit to earning National Board Certification within 5 years of working at the school.

Designed to certify accomplished practice, the Board requires that teachers have at least 3 years of experience before they are eligible to pursue certification. In this endeavor, EPAA teachers initially were assisted by their colleague, William Dean, and by Maria Hyler, a former teacher who had taught with Mr. Dean in his previous school and was now a graduate student at Stanford, as well as the school's resident researcher. Both William and Maria had been certified through the National Board Resource Center at Stanford University, which held monthly meetings to support teachers going through the certification process.

Designed by teachers for teachers, the National Board portfolio is the first national, voluntary assessment to certify accomplished teaching in the United States. It is not only an acknowledgment of teaching excellence, but often has been described by teachers who have completed it as the best professional development they have experienced.[6] The process requires teachers to submit a portfolio of their teaching practice that contains artifacts such as lesson plans and materials, student work samples, and videos of teaching. Along with these artifacts, teachers must submit a written commentary analyzing their planning, instructional, and assessment practices, as well as showcasing reflection and professional decisionmaking. Research-based, subject- and grade-specific standards guide this structured analysis of teaching. Last, content knowledge expertise is assessed through open-response essays administered at a testing center.

During the school's second year, four of ten eligible teachers, including the principal, pursued National Board Certification, and all received the news in the third year that they had been certified, bringing the total number of National Board certified teachers at the school to five. In subsequent years, teachers pursued National Board Certification as they gained enough experience to become eligible and when they felt ready for the challenge. Nicky became board-certified while teaching 9th-grade humanities and serving as principal, to lead by example and develop her own understanding of the process.

Rebecca stepped up in her third year of teaching, assisted by William and Maria, and noted that the experience pushed her practice even further, while setting an example for her students, who had to assemble their own portfolios to graduate. She remembers:

> I met with Maria frequently at Stanford after teaching long days at the high school and joined her thesis writing group, which helped me stay accountable and on track to meet the impending deadline. They pushed my thinking, and my teaching craft improved. My students witnessed me working harder than ever, balancing both teaching and my own learning, and I think they really respected that.

Her colleague, a new young science teacher, Cristina Galvan, watched Rebecca go through the process and helped her assemble the final portfolio, fondly known as "packing the box," that is sent off for scoring. Cristina recalled:

> As I began my own National Board portfolio, that experience resonated deeply, as I had learned two things: First, I needed to be organized from day one of my portfolio creation, and second, at EPAA I knew I would have a support team from my colleagues to help me sort out not only the papers, but my reflective thought process along the way.

The result of EPAA's commitment to accomplished teaching was that there was a shared vision of quality teaching across the school. Teachers knew research-based best practices and were able to engage in collaborative conversations around teaching and learning. NBC also set a standard for professional accountability. EPAA teachers held themselves and one another to a high set of standards of what teachers should know and be able to do in order to teach their students effectively. As one teacher remarked: "I think there is more accountability here for everybody. In other schools, I never felt that way. I felt, oh, I could just do whatever and nobody cares. Here everybody cares." Another noted that this professionalism was a real attraction to stay in the school: "Staff members are really professional. I love how professional the staff is. . . . I like the dedication to all of our kids."

***Learning for Problem Solving.*** That dedication meant that teachers were always looking for ways to address the problems they encountered in order to improve learning for students. Professional development was not designed as a "menu of the week," disconnected from teachers' needs and goals. It was focused directly on the aspects of teaching identified as pressing concerns.

As we've described, one of the biggest initial hurdles East Palo Alto Academy teachers had to face was that the curriculum they had designed for imaginary 9th-graders in the summer before the school opened had to be revised to become relevant and adequately scaffolded for the real 9th-graders who enrolled. Over that first year, the combined expertise of the EPAA teachers and their Stanford colleagues led to a major redesign of the curriculum that proved increasingly successful as it was refined.

The second major hurdle was learning how to support students' social-emotional needs. Teachers initially were not prepared for the level of need they would encounter, not only in terms of students' low skill levels but also in terms of social-emotional challenges. Many students experienced traumas that spilled over in a variety of ways into their school lives. Some students did whatever they could to defend their fragile academic self-esteem, exhibiting apathy or antagonism toward the adults on campus. The more teachers found out about their students, the more they realized why the students behaved as they did. There seemed no end to the students' difficult life circumstances:

not enough money for rent or food, caregiving responsibilities for multiple siblings or sick relatives, post-traumatic stress after witnessing or experiencing violence and crime, chaotic circumstances at home.

Teachers relied heavily on their professional learning community as well as its connection to resources in the larger network to acquire needed skills. Expertise came from both educators inside the school and some from outside the school. New or novice teachers looked to Nicky, Jeff, and the lead teachers for guidance. Even veteran teachers admitted that they felt like first-year teachers because they had never taught in a school that served a community with such intense needs. And because EPAA was committed to not screening out students through selective or complicated admission processes, it was often a tremendous challenge to serve every student who walked through the door seeking a high school education.

The most veteran teachers had the shortest learning curves and were soon discovering and modeling successful practices. At staff meetings, Nicky and Jeff often shared their own challenges and struggles with students so other teachers felt safe doing the same. They and others also shared their breakthroughs. For example, Nicky shared lessons learned from the interactions she had in her class as well as with those students sent to her by advisors. These included figuring out how to get students to open up and tell adults what was really going on; requesting an action, then giving students the space to do it; finding ways to quickly de-escalate situations; having faith in students eventually to respond. This helped other teachers connect the dots to see the bigger picture.

Nicky and Linda brought in specialists from the Stanford faculty and other Bay Area schools to advise teachers on issues of behavior and student support. One specialist spent a week with staff working on school culture. A psychologist taught staff how to identify and manage students' emotional needs. Lucile Packard Children's Hospital provided a health van for complete medical care, and local donors paid for psychologists to run anger management sessions. Eventually EPAA recruited Stanford medical school's child psychiatry team, who supervised interns from the Children's Hospital to offer ongoing services to students individually and in groups. Some years later the school was able to hire a social worker who not only aided students directly but helped teachers learn how to address issues they encountered.

A continuous practice was that if any member of the staff had expertise that others could use, opportunities were made for the sharing of that expertise. Most traditional schools feature an egg-crate design in which teachers or staff members—including those with specialized expertise like counselors, social workers, or special education teachers—minister to the students they are assigned from behind closed doors. At EPAA all of these individuals were considered resources for professional development and coaching, so that their expertise could inform increasingly knowledgeable practice by other staff as

well. This required making time and space for the sharing of that staff expertise, which was a key part of the school's design.

## Time and Space for Collaboration

The school founders created structures so that professional learning could be
an ongoing and central part of each teacher's daily work experiences. Bor-
rowing from the school designs developed by Meier, Cook, and others in New
York City, they found time for regular collaborative planning and professional
development, as well as shared space for teachers.

*Physical Space.* To facilitate collaboration, the staff decided to set aside a
classroom as a staff center where all teachers would have desks. "Room 4"
provided a hub for the teaching and staff culture. Here teachers could vent,
celebrate, eat, socialize, and collaborate. With at least 15 teachers' desks, a
copier, mailboxes, curriculum materials, a microwave, and a refrigerator,
Room 4 was a busy place. While holiday parties and end-of-year celebrations
took place at individual teachers' homes or other off-campus sites, Room 4
quickly came to symbolize the ethos of staff camaraderie.

*Joint Planning Time.* The master schedule was organized so that teachers
were assigned a 90-minute collaboration period twice a week with their planning partner—3 hours each week. Teachers who initially did not have planning partners because the school was too small (for example, the math and
ELD faculty) were assigned coaches from STEP, with whom they met regularly
throughout the year. All teachers also had an individual work period almost
every day, in which they could grade papers, finalize lessons, hold parent conferences, or work on study group tasks.

This use of time—which more closely resembles the schedules of teachers
elsewhere in the world than it does most U.S. teachers'—is made possible by
the use of block scheduling, the assignment of most school staff to teaching
rather than nonteaching work, and a focus on a core curriculum rather than
a highly tracked curriculum with a wide range of courses and electives.[7] In
the early years, except for the school office manager, everyone in the school
taught and served as an advisor, including the principal and the vice principal.
As the school grew, the principal spent less time in the classroom, and some
support staff were hired, but the emphasis on staffing for a school that could
support collaboration was maintained.

Teachers found this collaboration time to be invaluable. As one commented:

We have common prep periods two to three times per week. I always
collaborate . . . never working alone. I didn't have to write my own
lessons, which was helpful for me as a new teacher. I always had

someone else to talk to about what I was going to teach. Curriculum approaches included producing lesson plans [and] what worksheets to use. We would make some if we couldn't find what we were looking for. Other types of collaboration happen sort of on the spot . . . like with hot issues in the classroom, kids not paying attention in class on Fridays, etc. [There is] no structure for this. [We] just ask questions of others at collaboration meetings.

Despite the generous time allotted, most teachers still had their own "homework"—of papers and tests, additional planning, and the requisite grading—all because of the inordinate amount of time it took to create authentic and meaningful curricula differentiated for the various ability levels and to give detailed feedback to students. One teacher reflected:

I feel that the amount of collaboration . . . benefits the students the most. Their teachers are collaborating on philosophical ideas about what's important in the school, what's important for the students— teaching strategies and methods. I think students benefit from that a great deal, partly because they are getting similar messages everywhere they go. But also because we improve so much as we confer with each other. It improves our ability to manage classrooms [and] to design curriculum. . . . This is very challenging to be constantly interacting with other professionals who have other good ideas that challenge your own constantly—and keep you alive and thinking and making changes. It's very beneficial for your personal and professional growth. It's a really good system.

***Professional Development Time.*** In addition to this collaboration time, weekly staff meetings provided a constant space for professional development. Every Wednesday from 1 P.M. to 4 P.M., the staff met while students were either in internship placements or having an early release day. The student schedule allowed for sufficient instructional minutes on other days to meet the state requirements. Often during these meetings, EPAA teachers who were experts in special education, reading strategies, the writing process, or English language development taught their peers how to refine their practice to meet the needs of their heterogeneous classrooms. This time also was used to discuss whatever needed work in the school at various times during the year: planning exhibitions, calibrating scoring on the rubrics, creating homework supports, developing new strategies for conflict resolution or peer mediation.

At various times over the years, teachers asked for and received training from outside experts in areas such as positive behavior supports, secondary literacy, differentiation, and gang awareness. Teachers continued to educate themselves by going to conferences sponsored by organizations such as the Coalition of Essential Schools, the National Writing Project, and the California Science Teachers Association. Faculty read and discussed books together, like the *Tipping Point* by Malcolm Gladwell and *Good to Great* by Jim Collins.[8] Each summer Nicky and teachers organized a 2-week staff retreat, where they revisited the school mission, guiding principles, and Five Habits rubric, and worked on improving systems like advisory or exhibitions.

## Shared Decisionmaking and Distributed Leadership

Many of the founding teachers came from large, traditional high schools where they were masters of curriculum and instruction in their classrooms or within their department, but had limited opportunities to work collaboratively or participate in major decisions that impacted the school. The founding teachers at EPAA did not want to create a school where top-down decisions were made and teachers felt isolated or disempowered. Thus, the Wednesday staff meeting time also was used for shared decisionmaking about important policies and practices in the school. The school was committed to engaging all staff in deliberating about the matters that would affect them, starting from the proviso that the central consideration would be the best interests of the students.

*Collaborative Staff Meetings.* The founding teachers prided themselves on creating a system for meetings that was:

- Highly structured in order to ensure maximum participation of staff, including novice or less vocal teachers
- Efficient, even though there never seemed enough time to address all the pressing issues completely
- Inclusive of all voices, even dissenting ones
- Able to cultivate teacher leadership by having staff rotate through designated roles

While there was a great deal of business to conduct, these meetings were not just about business. They were also about staff unity on both a personal and professional level. Weekly staff meetings began with 10 minutes of *connections*, a ritualized space for staff to share emotionally important news from their classrooms or lives. This was the time for teachers to share breakthroughs or disappointments with students, announce life-cycle events like pregnancies and marriage proposals, or tell stories about personal accomplishments and experiences. At the end of one very difficult staff meeting, Nicky instituted *appreciations*, a time for staff to express gratitude to their colleagues for their help and support. Subsequently, every staff meeting began with connections and ended with appreciations.

EPAA faculty regarded the meetings as part of their weekly professional development and participated in rotating roles that included facilitator, recorder, timekeeper, process-meister, coach, deadline/next agenda, rover, scribe, snacks (food or drinks), and setup/cleanup. Each week a different teacher facilitated the meeting, helping staff to move through all of the agenda items. The recorder took notes that were filed on the school server, and the scribe wrote notes on the board during brainstorming sessions. The timekeeper gave time warnings, negotiated for more time if necessary, and adjusted the remaining agenda items. The timekeeper also opened and closed connections.

During a discussion, the coach would take down names of staff who wished to speak, calling on them in order and ensuring that teachers wouldn't be cut off or drowned out by more vocal peers. The coach also alerted staff when meeting norms were not being followed due to side conversations, the distraction of open laptops, or disregard of time guidelines. The process-meister intervened if the meeting process was not being followed because staff were not responding to the coach, timekeeper, or facilitator, or if any of the roles were not being properly fulfilled. The process-meister also took notes in order to debrief the meeting, highlighting roles or norms that needed improvement. The person with the deadline/next agenda role would then record and email the "to-do" items that emerged from the meeting as well as record topics for upcoming meeting agendas. The teachers assigned to snacks and setup/cleanup made sure that their colleagues were well fed, and that the classroom was put in order before and after the meeting.

The agendas for staff meetings were always emailed in advance, along with any supporting documents for staff to preview. The agendas also followed a set structure. Each meeting began with connections, guest introductions, and a process debrief of the last week's meeting. The bulk of the meeting was divided into two 90-minute sessions, one for discussion and decision-making, the other for professional development and collaboration. Each staff meeting ended with announcements, to-do items, and, finally, appreciations.

EPAA staff valued and upheld staff norms, which were strictly adhered to during the meetings. Staff decided on the norms and revisited them each year. They included individual and group guidelines such as:

- We collectively own problems and we collectively solve them.
- We value all ideas, experiences, and perspectives from all stakeholders.
- We commit to hearing all voices, especially the dissenting voice at staff meetings.
- We value the importance of sticking to time guidelines.

- We recognize that tension is normal.
- We take time to laugh and enjoy one another, and inject appropriate humor. (We don't take ourselves too seriously.)
- I am responsible for speaking up when I do not feel good about a decision before that decision is made.
- I come prepared for discussion—I do my homework.
- I check out assumptions, and I am not afraid to ask questions.
- I assume positive intent as I listen to the message, not the messenger.
- I am honest.
- I foster a willingness to forgive, learn, and move on.
- I am responsible for my attitude.

Staff valued these norms as a way to create a nurturing, caring, and professional work environment that upheld the school's mission so that they could do the best work possible to meet the educational needs of their students.

*Consensus Decisionmaking.* Nicky felt passionately that she wanted to lead a school where teachers made all major decisions together. Thus the founding staff created a highly structured consensus decisionmaking process for teachers that fit within the larger leadership structure of the school and that included the board, steering committee, Stanford faculty sponsor, principal, vice principal, and lead teachers.

In contrast to a traditional decisionmaking hierarchy where the principal has the final say, in consensus decisionmaking, every teacher gets a vote and every vote holds the same weight. The founding faculty were committed to creating a school where teachers felt heard, had ownership over the school decisions, and were publicly accountable to one another, and the consensus model was largely responsible for the positive and productive teacher culture on campus. As one teacher noted:

> Another aspect of the school that I really, really enjoy is the democratic process that they have in place where . . . everything goes through a [consensus] vote. I think that also empowers the teachers and makes you feel part of the whole. It makes you work harder because it's a team.

As an example of how consensus works, consider the process used to create standardized 9th-grade routines and norms so that the new students would quickly internalize the habits for academic success. During a staff meeting, faculty first framed the issue and listed what they wanted to accomplish and avoid by having standardized 9th-grade routines and norms. The academic culture study group then synthesized this information into a proposal and brought it to the staff at a subsequent meeting. All groups of teachers who made proposals asked themselves the following questions:

- What is the issue at hand?
- How does it connect to our values, our guiding principles, and our mission?
- What are the previous conversations that relate to this issue?
- What is the recommendation of the leadership team?
- What is the opinion of the majority of the staff?

The academic culture study group's proposal included a streamlined set of 9th-grade guidelines that would be easy to enforce, such as teachers writing a daily *materials needed* list on the board at the beginning of each class, having students get their materials, place their backpacks and other distractions at the back of the room, and sit in their seats before the bell rang. The staff discussed the proposal during a staff meeting and made some modifications. Staff then decided whether to accept the proposal, using a *fist to five* vote.

When the facilitator called for the vote, teachers silently indicated their opinion by raising one to five fingers. A vote of five expressed that the teacher loved the decision and would support it wholeheartedly. Four fingers represented that the teacher liked the decision and would support it. Three meant that the teacher was indifferent but would support the decision, or agreed in principle but had some doubts. A vote of two indicated that the teacher had serious reservations but would support it. A vote of one finger (always the index finger) announced that the teacher didn't agree at all with the proposal and could not support it. Any vote of one finger stopped the process and sent the presenters back to amend the proposal.

Votes of one were rare, but always taken seriously. After a vote, the facilitator called on the staff who had held up one or two fingers, to give them the opportunity to express their reservations. This meant that any teacher with a strong opinion could hold up the process of making a decision, even if the lead teachers or administration wanted the proposal to pass. Nicky often said that decisions were stronger if they incorporated dissenting or doubtful voices, and this was typically true. If a proposal was rejected, it was usually because the teachers making the proposal hadn't done their homework by getting enough input, or a step in the process had been skipped such as not having the "accomplish/avoid" conversation. The staff used this consensus process to decide everything that affected teachers directly, such as the school mission and guiding principles, calendar and bell schedule, revisions to the Five Community Habits and exhibition rubrics, advisory structure, behavior intervention system, and school rules.

Clearly, making decisions by consensus was much more complex and time-consuming than a majority-rules vote or a top-down decision. Consensus did not mean that teachers loved every decision; it simply meant that they could live with it and overtly support it. Maura Marino, an EPAA staff member, commented:

At other schools it's really easy to look at a problem and complain about it. . . . Here you are responsible for that decision, so if you voted on the bell schedule [and] don't like 95-minute classes, you should have said something about it before, and you need to say something about it now, so it doesn't happen again next year. . . . You have to own that problem and bring it to the staff meeting. . . . Problems are not someone else's issues. You have a stake as to what is going on and this is your school, so anything that is out there is kind of your obligation to solve.

When consensus decisions were made well and the process was well executed, the decisions lasted and were upheld by the staff.

Although most decisions were made by consensus, there were some exceptions. Nicky had the final say on human resource decisions like hiring and retention, but always solicited feedback from faculty. Teacher salaries and benefits were negotiated with the teachers' recommendations in mind. Other decisions, like the number of instructional minutes, the state testing schedule, or the emergency procedures, were mandated by the state. EPAA eventually created a decision matrix that outlined all categories of decisions, which stakeholders would give input or make recommendations, and which would make the final decision. Stakeholders included families and community members, administration, the board of directors, the steering committee, students, and teachers.

Ultimately, a productive consensus decisionmaking model depended on having the right people. As Jim Collins says in *Good to Great*, an organization's success depends on having the right people on the bus sitting in the right seats.[9] This meant that some teachers realized that EPAA and its complex decisionmaking process wasn't for them. The school valued hiring a diverse staff that could represent myriad points of view, and who were professional enough to learn, negotiate, and compromise. Staff had to be vigilant about adhering to the decisionmaking process and following staff norms and roles. Veteran teachers and the leadership team worked hard to acculturate new members to their unique system.

**Study Groups.** In addition to consensus decisionmaking, leadership was distributed in the school in other ways. Early on Nicky realized that there was no way she could manage running most aspects of the school by herself and organize large events like graduation, awards ceremonies, or the 4 weeks of exhibitions every school year.[10] Consequently, she created study groups to guide decisions and manage the logistics of these events, and every teacher was assigned to serve on one. The study groups met occasionally during weekly staff meetings, but accomplished the bulk of their work before school, during lunch, after school, and on weekends. The same culture of revision and redemption in place for students existed for faculty as well. Each study group worked diligently toward continuous improvement, with exhibitions, graduation, and award ceremonies being better planned and executed each year. The study groups were responsible for bringing decisions to the whole staff as needed to change existing policies or practices.

## Valuing Growth in Teaching

There is no doubt that teachers at East Palo Alto Academy worked harder than many teachers in other schools. In turn, EPAA worked hard to provide teachers with competitive salaries, although it was sometimes difficult for the school to compete with the wage levels of neighboring wealthy school districts that were able to maintain elevated salary schedules, thanks to substantial monies from local property taxes.

*Support for Teachers.* Despite this larger context, EPAA made every attempt possible to compensate teachers for taking on additional responsibilities and for engaging in extensive professional development. Teachers pursuing National Board Certification received support from the state for their fees, and if they achieved certification, they received a stipend of $5,000 for each of 4 years if they taught in a high-needs school.[11] When budget cuts caused the state to discontinue these supports, Stanford found resources to cover teachers' fees and maintained a salary stipend.

In the early years when EPAA was operated by a charter management organization, the school did not have a set salary schedule; teachers were hired based on what the market would bear. Mindful of morale and the challenges of working in the EPA context, Nicky tried not to put too much budgetary pressure on her teachers because, as one stated:

> Teachers resent being "nickel and dimed" and told what to do by top-down leadership. They resent it and stop doing all the extras partly because they can't take ownership when they're being told what to do and partly because they're not being recognized for the work they're already doing.

Staff preferences for teaching certain subjects or working with certain teaching partners were taken into consideration when the master schedule was created. Nicky encouraged and supported teachers who wanted to create new classes or innovative programs like Student Leadership and Academic Literacy. In return, Nicky was adamant that teachers not call Jeff and her "the administration." She felt that because of their democratic structures, everyone at East Palo Alto Academy was empowered to create change and no one needed to feel powerless against a distant administration. "Call us Nicky and Jeff," she would say. "It's real people who are doing this. We're in this together."

Later, when the school left the Aspire umbrella (in 2006) to operate under the auspices of Stanford New Schools (SNS), a more rationalized salary schedule was put in place. SNS board members and a committee of faculty created an innovative system that compensated teachers for master's degrees and National Board Certification, as well as for useful skills, such as bilingualism in Spanish, special education knowledge, reading degrees, and additional licenses used in the school. In addition to the traditional stipends for athletic coaching, teachers were compensated for a range of leadership roles, such as serving as lead teachers and study group leaders, as well as for taking on the leadership of a major exhibition. Retention bonuses were added for teachers who had stayed for 5 years.

**Teacher Retention.** Research has long found that schoolwide achievement is strongly influenced by staff continuity,[12] and that teachers' willingness to stay in a school is strongly influenced by having a supportive administration, as well as a strong collegial environment.[13] In addition, teachers who are well prepared and well mentored stay in the profession longer.[14]

As the school grew by a new student cohort each year, leaders worked hard to bolster teacher recruitment and retention, in the face of the difficult teaching challenges, low levels of resources, and the usual moves of beginning teachers to their home communities. In the third year, there were a total of 15 teachers on staff, of whom seven had continued from the original staff of eight, and five were second-year returning teachers. Teacher retention steadily increased over the first 3 years. In 2004–2005, 94% of the full-time staff returned to teach at the school.

When asked why they stayed at EPAA, all of the factors we discussed earlier emerged as important: Teachers often spoke of their genuine love and regard for the community of students and teachers. This is from Cristina, a 7-year EPAA veteran:

> I really love the community. The students are so resilient in the face
> of so many challenges. I learn so much from working with them. I
> also really love the staff—the people I work with are some of the most
> amazing people I have met. They are incredibly dedicated, intelligent,
> and creative.

And from Danielle, Cristina's planning partner, who noted after she had moved away:

> I worked at EPAA for several reasons. One, to work against the social
> injustice that exists in that community—there are many students who

want to learn but lack access to college-bound programs. Two, because of the existence of other like-minded teachers. It's difficult to find a staff that is so united and dedicated to doing whatever it takes to serve students well. And finally, because I loved creating, collaborating, and working with such an amazing staff and student body.

Maura Marino began working at EPAA as an undergraduate senior at Stanford writing her thesis on service learning at EPAA. Here is why she stayed for 4 more years:

For a new teacher, the professional learning community established at East Palo Alto Academy created an incredible environment to learn the art of teaching. Every day, I was surrounded by talented, committed, veteran educators, and we struggled together with our collective challenges. We made a lot of mistakes, but we picked each other up, learned from those mistakes, and moved on in service of providing the best education possible to our students. Our students' resilience was inspiring, and my colleagues' dedication to serving them well pushed me to be my best every day.

## BECOMING A PROFESSIONAL TEACHER: MARYSOL'S STORY

One can better appreciate what these structures mean for teaching by following how they played out in the life of one teacher. Marysol de la Torre had not planned, when she was growing up, on becoming a teacher. However, when she was a high school student in northern California, her counselor had questioned her citizenship and even her right to be a student in honors classes. It was in the counselor's office that Marysol realized how teachers could change the course of an individual's life with only a few words, how they could support a student's aspiration to learn or make that student "feel like dirt."

As one of only three Mexican students in her college-preparatory classes, Marysol was acutely aware of the racialized tracking system at her school. She had taken her sister's advice to be her own advocate and enroll in college-prep classes to be eligible to apply to the University of California. She was accepted into and attended UC Berkeley, where she planned to major in math, until junior year, when she took a course called Race and Ethnicity in Schools with Pedro Noguera, a renowned education professor.

That class changed my life. Everything he was saying reflected my own educational experiences. Everything I knew that needed to be changed in the educational system, he said it. Through the educational system you can fight ignorance and injustice. I thought, "I need to be a teacher. This is for me." The teaching population needs to reflect the student population. I understood the social impact of a group of Mexican American students having a Mexican American teacher. The social impact extends itself dramatically.

The newly turned ethnic studies major spent a semester in the Dominican Republic teaching Spanish, an experience that confirmed her belief that teaching was the right profession for her.

Marysol wanted to stay in California for her teacher training and was drawn to the Stanford Teacher Education Program. "I knew that Linda Darling-Hammond was an influential person in STEP," she said, "so I would be taught directly by the source as opposed to a professor using her book."

## Learning to Teach

Marysol thrived at STEP. She loved the small size of the program and quickly became a STEPpie, as students were called. A few weeks into the program, during the summer of 2002, she was asked to choose her student teaching placement. She was told that if she worked at EPAA, she had to be ready to work harder and would have more responsibilities than other student teachers, yet would still have to meet the same expectation to manage the heavy workload of her STEP classes.

> I remember going to the presentation at EPAA. The classroom was in horrible shape, but hearing Jeff speak about how they were trying to build the school from the ground up inspired me. He was very honest about the challenges and what we were in for. He said, "If you want to be a member of this team, this is what we do, what our vision is, and what we're going for." I thought, this is something I want to be a part of.

Once she was placed at EPAA, Marysol and another STEP student went to lunch at a local *taquería*[15] with Tina, Seth, and Rebecca. At one point, Tina turned to the STEP students and asked, "So which one of you is a social revolutionary?" Marysol thought, "Wow. She just gets straight to it." Tina soon became Marysol's cooperating teacher and together they began to plan their sophomore humanities curriculum in world history and literature.

As a student in Linda's Adolescent Development class (where Maria Hyler was the teaching assistant), Marysol appreciated how Linda stressed the importance of getting to know your students. "You can't serve them unless you know them," Linda often said. All STEP students had to choose an adolescent at their school site whom they wanted to better understand and write a case study describing the student's cognitive, social, and emotional development. This entailed interviewing the student and family, observing the student inside and outside of class, and assessing the student's learning.

When Marysol visited her student's home for a family interview, she gained critical insights about the student and the community that helped her become a more insightful teacher:

> Walking into the house, I saw that 12 people shared three beds in the living room. [My student] was so welcoming and happy that we were visiting her. I realized this is what she comes home to after school, no desk or resources to help her out, and having to take care of all the kids and cousins running around. This is her day-to-day life.

Even though Marysol connected well with adolescents, EPAA students challenged her just as they challenged all the teachers. However, it was clear that Marysol was a quick learner and had a real talent for teaching. With a calm, professional demeanor and striking black hair neatly pulled back from her smiling face, Marysol was unflappable:

> My style was very structured. This is the expectation; this is what you're going to do. I treat you with respect, and you respect me. I was always consistent. It was clear what to expect once students walked into my classroom. A lot of students would get defensive with other teachers, but I never felt that defensiveness from them because I was clear: You need to act like a student, get with the program, and do a, b, and c. I was not changing so the students had to change.
>
> When disciplining a student, if I were to get angry or if they saw me getting angry, that would escalate the situation. [My students] would make fun of me: Say the lesson was not going well, and another student who was chronically misbehaving was trying to walk out the door, and I'm trying to deal with this situation while still teaching my lesson. My students would joke that 5 minutes later I'd be smiling at them again. I always stayed calm.

As part of Marysol's coursework at STEP, she had to videotape her lessons and critique her teaching throughout the year. Although intimidating for many teachers, watching oneself teach is eye-opening, as it clearly highlights what is going well and what is not working.

> Watching the videos and seeing my interactions with students and how they interacted with each other was enlightening. I realized what I was doing worked. I remember one lesson about colonial Indian culture where I created a complex group task. The fashion group had five saris, and they had cards explaining the symbolism and what the colors represented. I remember seeing two students, a male and a female, trying on the saris. They went through answering the questions and

were getting into the learning, and I remember thinking to myself, "This is what it's about."

## Making the Commitment

It soon became clear to Marysol that being a Mexican American teacher sent a powerful message to her students of color and those of similar heritage. One day, Santos, a student in her humanities class, bombarded her with a barrage of questions:

> He asked me, "So you're Mexican, full Mexican? Why didn't you get pregnant in high school? Do you know Spanish? Are you fluent?" I answered his questions and told him and the rest of the students not to buy into these stereotypes.

At the end of her student teaching year, Marysol had a difficult decision to make: Should she accept a full-time position at East Palo Alto Academy, even though it meant living apart from her fiancé and family?

> Before I made my decision to work at EPAA, I talked with Linda extensively. Linda invited me to her house. I knew EPAA was a perfect fit, but I needed to hear it more. As Linda phrased it, "There is a lot of work to be done. This and this needs to happen."
>
> I asked Nicky, "Why do you want me here? Is this a good fit?" The one thing she said was about personal relationships: "When I select staff I always think about how are they going to connect with students and faculty, and you do that naturally."
>
> Why did I finally decide to teach at EPAA? The staff and students: the people there. I had grown close to the sophomores and the staff. I liked the whole team aspect. We didn't necessarily agree with each other all the time but we were in it together. I knew I wouldn't be alone like [my friends] at other schools who didn't have the support and didn't feel part of a community. I never felt that way. I knew that if you want to meet the needs of all students it has to be a team effort because there are too many things to consider, too many variables. I had been involved in many school projects, and I wanted to continue participating and seeing them unfold.

Tina was delighted at this decision:

> Marysol was one of those student teachers you dream of having—smart, talented, passionate. We worked great with each other from day one, and I always felt like we were both learning from one another.

At the end of the year, we decided to loop and move up with our kids. We designed the junior year curriculum, and being that both of us had a passion for teaching American history from a person of color's perspective, we knew we'd be able to design something unique and meaningful for our kids.

## Planning the Curriculum

Tina, credentialed in English, and Marysol, credentialed in social science, worked together to develop the 11th-grade humanities curriculum. Marysol described how the curriculum for their juniors connected to the overall vision of the Humanities Department:

> The essential question that guided our Humanities Department was: *What is the role of the individual?* We wanted students to understand the world and themselves, to talk about their identity and their role in their community. Since our students were from the East Palo Alto community and surrounding areas, there were many negative self-fulfilling prophecies that students believed. Whether it was thinking that a high school diploma was not attainable, thinking the only options were to give up or act out when the content was too difficult, or feeling that school just wasn't worth it, as a department we discussed their perceptions about school and themselves and how our curriculum and teaching could change their thinking.

Before the school year began, Tina and Marysol mapped out an overview of the year, noting which California State Standards would be addressed in each unit. Although they contemplated the idea of teaching history thematically, they ultimately decided to take the traditional chronological approach, thinking that because many of the students came to the school with underdeveloped history skills, this method would be less likely to confuse them and they would more easily be able to analyze how certain events in history led to others.

Once they had chosen the historical periods to focus on, Tina and Marysol selected literature that would fit thematically with each period and created overarching questions that connected to both the text and time period. For example, the first unit focused on the pre-1900s. Two overarching questions guided students through the unit: *What is an American? Is identity chosen or given?* As they studied historical texts about the founding of the United States and the creation of important documents like the Constitution, students also read Piri Thomas's controversial book *Down These Mean Streets,* which led to important and meaningful conversations about identity and race. The combination of various texts allowed students to analyze identity from both a personal and a historical standpoint. In addition, by analyzing history chronologically and connecting it to themes in literature from different time periods, students could analyze how a concept like American identity evolved over time.

The overview of the year's units provided a road map to guide Marysol and Tina in teaching and scaffolding the skills and content students needed to master. But there were ongoing refinements needed that made the shared planning time during the school year essential. Marysol reflected:

> What I loved about our school was our common curriculum planning time. I'd never been at a school that prioritizes this. It makes a world of difference having time set aside for teacher collaboration *during* the school day. The thing with teaching and with burnout is that you're working so much. Common planning time with your colleagues gives you the opportunity to break up the workload, share what you're doing in your classes, and talk about curriculum. So you're planning as you go. In the first year planning 11th-grade humanities, there was no way Tina and I could have accomplished designing units for an entire school year and creating the junior research exhibition without the common planning time.

Before beginning each new unit, Tina and Marysol revisited their original plans and, based on students' experiences in the previous unit, revised them as necessary. With a vision for the unit in place, the teachers made sure to plan lessons well in advance. They checked in on a daily basis and made changes in case they had overplanned or wanted to incorporate new information. This combination of preplanning as well as flexibility for revision allowed Tina and Marysol to create a curriculum that served the needs of their students and changed to reflect their growth throughout the year.

As Marysol and Tina planned, they were mindful to incorporate both traditional assessments (like quizzes and tests) and authentic assessments, like a Great Depression scrapbook that allowed students to express their understanding in a more creative manner. Almost always, students were permitted to revise work, giving them a chance to further build their skills and content knowledge before moving on to new material. Having a variety of assessments both throughout and at the end of each unit allowed teachers to gain a sense of where students' strengths and weaknesses were. This also informed their planning for future units. Tina reflected on the collaborative process:

> As an 11th-grade teaching team, we were extremely helpful to one another. I continued to mentor Marysol on the teaching of literature, while she supported my understanding of the historical content. We met during every prep period; we shared and spoke on the phone almost every night. Furthermore, if one of us had a question during class, we did not hesitate to call the other for guidance. It was clear to our

students that the two of us were working together and that we each brought our own strengths that extended beyond the subject matter itself. Marysol was the organized teacher who put together curriculum binders for future teachers who would ultimately take over our curriculum when we left; I was the one who formatted all our graphic organizers and made them student-friendly. We were a team.

Not only were students taught a junior humanities curriculum that was truly integrated, but they also left the year with the same academic foundation. They had all analyzed the metaphor of fog in *One Flew over the Cuckoo's Nest.* Every student had read Zora Neale Hurston's classic text, *Their Eyes Were Watching God,* and participated in discussions analyzing the novel's richness. Not a single one left junior year without knowing about the Harlem Renaissance or the Navajo Code Talkers. Students had covered a great deal of content that pushed them to think analytically about *both* history and literature. And as a bonus, they had witnessed a model of positive collaboration between teachers to better serve their educational needs. It was obvious for Marysol and Tina that it was worth negotiating their individual ideas to create a cohesive curriculum they could both teach. Tina said:

> There is no doubt in my mind that had I not collaborated with a talented history teacher like Marysol, I would have failed my students in providing a truly integrated humanities curriculum. Had Marysol and I not done sufficient planning, we would not have succeeded in melding together literature and history. It is not enough to have a "go to" person for questions; there must be a true collaboration between teachers of these two fields in order to provide students with the best possible understanding of each.

## Developing Practice

As a new teacher, Marysol taught junior humanities and Writing for College with a Stanford professor doing research at EPAA. She also planned the junior research exhibition with Tina and had her own freshman advisory. Being a first-year teacher is challenging, but Marysol managed all her responsibilities well, knowing, as she put it, "what I signed up for and that I wasn't alone."

She used many of the strategies she learned in STEP and from her peers. Focusing on knowing her students, she made advisory a safe space for students to share, learn, and grow:

> In my advisory, I really worked to establish that personal relationship with parents and students early on. I made it clear to the kids that my role was to be their advocate. I let the personal relationship build

from there. I paid close attention to structure in my advisory. I had clear routines: 3 days were for homework, 1 day focused on college information and other presentations, and Friday was for community building. We participated in icebreakers, took walks, played football.

Like all other EPAA advisors, Marysol held meetings with advisees' parents when necessary and oversaw formal student-led conferences for each of her advisees and their families at least once a semester. On Wednesdays, when students had early release, Marysol attended the 3-hour staff meetings where she served in a role that rotated weekly, like facilitator or timekeeper. She also participated in a study group that worked on special programs such as graduation, exhibitions, or student leadership.

## Carrying the Flame

Although Marysol left EPAA after 3 years and relocated to her hometown in northern California as a newlywed, she returned for her advisees' graduation, where she felt pride that so many of her advisees had graduated despite challenging life circumstances. One Latina came from an abusive family and was living on her own in a homeless shelter during senior year; seeing her survive that year without a home or parental support and still make it was inspiring.

> Another of my advisees had a baby she was raising alone because her boyfriend was murdered in her senior year. Yet, she graduated. She had already enrolled at a local community college and is still there. She said to me, "I am not a loser. I don't want to be some statistic. I am going to raise my baby in a good home and go to college."

Marysol noticed the difference in quality of education between the large, comprehensive school and East Palo Alto Academy, and she made great effort to carry what she learned with her to transform aspects of the traditional high school structure in her district.

> Once I left EPAA I didn't see the common curriculum planning time and the consensus decisionmaking and all these things that EPAA strongly adhered to. When I went to a new school, I thought, "How can you run a school like this?" It was really a blessing to be trained at EPAA because this is not how most schools are run.
>
> Some of the things I experienced at EPAA I'm trying to do at my current site. We piloted an advisory program last year and it's going to become a reality on our campus someday. I am a huge advocate of collaboration. Once a week, a group of six of us meets for only 45 minutes. Now we're trying to negotiate it into our contract to meet

more, and the school is trying to create common planning time for teachers to collaborate.

This part of Marysol's story is also a familiar one. When teachers moved on, they carried many of EPAA's strategies with them. Marysol is now a founding teacher of a small school within the district. Jeff left EPAA to become the principal of a nearby comprehensive high school and helped his staff institute a house system: Each house had its own cohort of students, teachers, and advisors, much like EPAA.

## CONCLUSION

Because of the many opportunities for collaboration and mutual support, successful teachers at EPAA were able to learn from one another. More and more, each embodied and practiced the techniques of the most skilled and veteran staff:

- Being a consummate curriculum planner like Jeff
- Being organized and having clear classroom procedures like Marysol
- Creating relevant lessons that students would passionately connect to like Tina
- Harnessing all possible resources to confront challenges and refusing to accept "no" as an answer like Rebecca
- Analyzing data to inform decisions like Seth
- Carefully observing and listening in order to mentor successfully like William
- Having faith in people by inspiring them to leverage their strengths like Nicky

This is only a partial list of the essential skills the faculty learned from one another. In addition, the staff collaborated on what was taught and how to teach it, made decisions together through consensus, and, through all of this, created a professional learning community with student achievement at its core. The founding faculty built structures to help empower them to make positive changes to the school culture, thereby increasing their own professional commitment and capacities. Together, the students and teachers worked to uncover their best selves in response to a structured and nurturing environment where no one was invisible. In the words of one parent, "The dedication and support that the students receive, the teachers give hope to the students. When someone believes in you like the teachers at EPAA believe in their students, the students are motivated to do better" and to "be the change" they wish to see in the world.

## CHAPTER 8

# Life After High School

> Ever since we started freshman year their goal was to get us to college. Even
> though I had to take a year off, it was like a seed. They planted it. Even though
> I didn't do it right now, I have to do it because that is what they taught you and
> it's in your heart.
>
> —Senior, class of 2005

Beginning with that first graduating class in 2005, and continuing through 10
more graduating classes until the time of this writing in 2014, EPAA graduated
more than 80% of each cohort and saw at least 90% of graduates admitted
to 2- or 4-year colleges each year. In 2005, this was more than double the
college-going rate for all students in the state[1] and close to triple the rates for
low-income students and students of color.

Among these graduates, the 4-year college admission rates ranged from
about 38% of seniors in the first year to more than half of graduates in later
years as the school got its bearings. Those admitted to 2-year colleges often
met the standard for admission to the university system, but chose the less
expensive option closer to home, with the intention of transferring to the
university when they hoped their finances would support the move.[2]

In middle-class settings, it is reasonable to think that the major task of a
high school that aims at postsecondary opportunities for its students is to get
them prepared for college by taking and passing the right courses. At EPAA
and similar schools, the challenges are much greater: Getting students and
their families to be willing to entertain the idea of education beyond high
school; then helping them to imagine it; then enabling them to pursue it—
which means not only completing the required courses but then examining
college options and filling out the requisite applications.

As we describe in this chapter, the challenges do not stop there. After
students get *into* college, they need to figure out how to get *to* college with
enough financial resources to pay their bills, having managed the compet-
ing pressures to stay home and get a job, help with child care, or otherwise support family needs. And after students get to college, they need to
get *through* it, managing a variety of ongoing financial and academic pressures, as well as the sense of marginalization many of them experience on

campuses with relatively few students who came from communities and backgrounds like their own.

There are additional challenges when they come back home with changed opportunities and perspectives during and after their time away. We discuss each of these experiences in this chapter through the eyes of our focal students and others. We also describe the various ways in which the early graduates confronted challenges and made a life for themselves, and how their high school experience shaped those decisions.

## GETTING INTO COLLEGE

East Palo Alto Academy built a sophisticated support structure to help students navigate the complicated college admission process. With two-thirds of EPAA students having no parent with a high school degree,[3] and 90% having no experience of college, the faculty knew that almost everyone would be the first in the family to apply to college. Not only would students need to select appropriate colleges, but they also would need to choose the best high school courses and activities in order to build a competitive resume. The faculty also learned that they would need to supervise the scholarship and financial aid process closely, as well as guide students through the social and emotional transition to college.

Support consisted of a traditional full-time college counselor, a cadre of senior advisors, a series of preparation classes for the SAT and ACT,[4] and several humanities teachers who taught students to write their personal statements and college entrance essays. Some students also took advantage of support from college-preparatory and extracurricular programs, or were assigned mentors provided by Stanford University.

### The College-Planning Program

During these years of ongoing budget cuts in California, there were fewer counselors per student than in any other state. The ratio of counselors to students in many large, comprehensive high schools was about 1 to 500, so triage was the only possible strategy for advisement. Students like those from East Palo Alto rarely saw a counselor in such schools. Students who came to EPAA from large schools would describe how, when schedule changes were needed in the early weeks of school, lines of 100 students or more would form outside the counselor's office in the morning, wending down long corridors until the bell rang, chasing them all to class. Perhaps 10 or 20 students would have achieved a meeting. Others would try to come back during lunch or the next day, over and over again, until many gave up and just sat in courses they might already have taken or shouldn't have been enrolled in. Seeing a counselor about postsecondary advisement was typically reserved for the White and Asian students in the honors or AP tracks. It was out of the question for students in the "basic track" or the "ESL track," which were the homes of nearly all the African American, Latino, and Pacific Islander students.

At EPAA, both the full-time college counselor and students' advisors played a constant role in their academic planning, including course-taking, college applications, and other postsecondary planning. The college counselor provided much-needed support to advisors who were intimately involved in their advisees' senior-year transition from high school to college or, for the few who did not apply to or enroll in college, to a trade school, the military, or a job. The presence of a credentialed, experienced college counselor enabled the school to provide more thorough support and information to students, parents, and teachers, and to assist senior advisors with an extra set of skilled hands. The college counselor responsibilities were multifold:

1. Offering guidance about college selection and monitoring all students' college applications and deadlines
2. Providing counseling for individual seniors
3. Organizing and accompanying students on college campus visits
4. Collaborating with senior advisors
5. Tracking students' progress toward graduation
6. Helping students identify and pursue appropriate scholarship opportunities

The lead teachers later designed a semester-long class titled "Apply to College" with the goal that students explore and work intensely on various aspects of the college decision process—career interest exploration, identification of potential colleges, completion of college applications, and applications for financial aid.

Senior advisors received training from the college counselor as well as outside organizations such as College Summit.[5] The advisors then trained themselves and one another to help students navigate the college admissions process, sharing information and best practices. Advisors helped students research colleges and complete applications, and took students on college visits to schools like UCLA, Santa Clara University, San Jose State, San Francisco State, and, of course, Stanford University.

## The College Support Process

The support went beyond applying to college. Advisors also helped students identify scholarships and, through a combination of lectures, demonstrations, and role-playing, prepared them for college and scholarship interviews.

Advisors enrolled their students in on-campus SAT and ACT preparation courses, taking care to monitor attendance; they also helped students apply for these tests and obtain fee waivers. Some advisors even accompanied their students to these exams, going as far as taking the tests *with* them, a strategy recommended by the Princeton Review Foundation.[6] Advisors stayed at school after hours, helping students fill out the Free Application for Federal Student Aid (FAFSA)[7] and keeping the computer lab open so that students could complete their online forms. They read applications, pored over numerous drafts of essays, and wrote endless letters of recommendation. A reporter from the *San Mateo County Times*[8] described the process this way:

> While her students enjoy winter break, Rebecca Padnos Altamirano will finally get the chance to make their college recommendation letters shine.
>
> At any other high school, perhaps the humanities teacher wouldn't feel personally responsible for the thick file of stamped envelopes, transcripts and resumes. She might not spend three hours on each letter, agonizing over adjectives and striking just the right balance between sob story and inspirational anecdote.
>
> "I'm really nervous," Altamirano said, contrary to her confident smile and easy manner with departing students just moments earlier. "These kids are really pioneers."
>
> Everywhere they turn, EPA High students see colleges. Even their classrooms have a different university painted on each door.
>
> "It gets people thinking about college," said Reggie Robinson, 17, one of Altamirano's 13 advisees and one of four seniors who have gotten acceptance letters so far.
>
> The school encourages students to attend presentations from local college recruiters, visit their campuses and attend summer programs. Every afternoon, the seniors must work with their advisors in small groups on applications and discuss their progress.
>
> As an advisor, Altamirano also finds herself fielding late-night calls and sharing her own college experiences with the class.
>
> "She tries to do anything to get us interested," said Cecilia Vasquez, 17, another college-bound advisee.
>
> Robinson, who has been accepted to the University of California and wants to study marine biology, and Vasquez, who has been accepted to a California State University and wants to study social work, would both be first in their families to get a bachelor's degree.
>
> Their classmate, Sofia Bracamontes, 18, has the option of studying anthropology at a UC school, as well.
>
> All three still hope to hear from eight or nine more schools before making their decision.

"I think everybody here is going to get into at least one school," Bracamontes said. "Some will go to two-year, because it's cheaper, but a bachelor's degree is better than an associate's."

Inside Room 10, or "Wellesley," in honor of Altamirano's alma mater, the walls are covered in colorful posters listing class rules, themes from *The Lord of the Flies* and facts about the Industrial Revolution.

A laptop computer with rough drafts of six recommendation letters sits open on the desk, each Microsoft Word document more poignant than the last. None do her students complete justice, Altamirano frets.

One lives in a tool shed and writes poetry; another calls her at night in hopes of hearing a kind word from an adult before going to sleep. A third has decided to pursue the military route to college, having told Altamirano, "I'm just as likely to get shot on my street as I am fighting in Iraq."

But there are happy stories, too. In Robinson's letter, Altamirano boasts of a confident young man who found the scholarships and raised the money needed to take advantage of study programs in Italy and Washington, D.C.

In a few more weeks, all the letters will be finished, the carefully typed, stapled and packaged applications sent off into the ether. The waiting game will last until April or May.

"Spring will be a nerve-wracking time," Altamirano said, with a rueful chuckle, locking her door for the night.

By the end of senior year, about half of the class of 2005 had submitted applications to 4-year universities, with the rest applying to 2-year colleges. As part of the required senior exhibition, graduation portfolios included a completed college application. Many students had done everything their teachers and advisors had instructed them to do—enrolled in a summer program, gotten involved in extracurricular activities, took the SAT or ACT, completed their required courses, and brought up their grades. Students in the first graduating class received numerous acceptance letters to schools like UC Santa Cruz, UC Berkeley, UCLA, San Jose State, National Hispanic University, Smith College, Santa Clara University, Chaminade University, and the University of Colorado at Boulder. Beaming with pride, students brought these letters to school to show their teachers and advisors.

## GETTING TO COLLEGE

But then the most troubling question surfaced: How would students pay for college? How would a family living below the poverty line afford college tuition ranging from $15,000 a year for in-state colleges to upward of $40,000 a year for private colleges? Once admitted, most EPAA students were hard-pressed to pay the $250 deposit to secure their spot at the college of their choice, and even with a generous financial aid package, many students still could not afford college. Three students from the class of 2005 each received $40,000 President's Scholarships to attend Menlo College, a small liberal arts college just a few miles from East Palo Alto. Despite this generous contribution and their financial aid packages, none of the students could afford the $120,000 tuition price tag for 4 years at this college. Two of them opted for community college and the other for a public university instead.

An excerpt from a December 2008 *New York Times* article[9] highlights key issues with funding college:

> The rising cost of college—even before the recession—threatens to put higher education out of reach for most Americans, according to the annual report from the National Center for Public Policy and Higher Education.
>
> Over all, the report found [that] published college tuition and fees increased 439 percent from 1982 to 2007, adjusted for inflation, while median family income rose 147 percent. Student borrowing has more than doubled in the last decade, and students from lower-income families, on average, get smaller grants from the colleges they attend than students from more affluent families.
>
> The report, "Measuring Up 2008," is one of the few to compare net college costs—that is, a year's tuition, fees, room and board, minus financial aid—against median family income. Those findings are stark. Last year, the net cost at a four-year public university amounted to 28 percent of the median family income, while a four-year private university cost 76 percent of the median family income.
>
> Among the poorest families—those with incomes in the lowest 20 percent—the net cost of a year at a public university was 55 percent of median income, up from 39 percent in 1999–2000. At community colleges, long seen as a safety net, that cost was 49 percent of the poorest families' median income last year, up from 40 percent in 1999–2000.

The message was clear: If EPAA wanted students to attend college, the faculty and university supporters would have to do more than just help them apply and get accepted; they would have to raise funds.

## Funding College

In the first graduating class, almost none of the highest-achieving students could afford to attend the colleges they had gotten into. Pablo was a good example of the challenge. Having completed high school with exceptional grades and leadership contributions, he nearly despaired of attending the out-of-state flagship university he most wanted to attend. Although the university offered him significant aid, the required financial contribution (about $15,000) was nearly twice his mother's annual income of $8,000. A combination of donations and large loans got him to college.

Working with the Stanford School of Education development office and with the tireless fundraising efforts of Dean Deborah Stipek, EPAA created two donor-funded programs. The first, "Success Grants," offered one-time scholarships ranging from $200 to $2,000. Students admitted to community colleges used these monies to cover books, lab fees, bridge programs, and partial tuition. The second program, "Stanford New Schools Scholars," granted renewable scholarships for students admitted to 4-year colleges. The awards ranged from $5,000 to $25,000 and were paid directly to the institution on the behalf of the attending student. Thanks to this program, EPAA was able to award one guaranteed 4-year college scholarship and several one-year renewable scholarships over the course of several years.

Needless to say, the school would have preferred to grant guaranteed 4-year scholarships to all deserving students, but the scholarship fund relied solely on the generosity of the community, which could vary from year to year. Indeed, every year saw a scramble to raise as much money as possible so that more students could continue their education.

To put the challenge in perspective, it is important to remember that there was a time when the United States made a promise to its young people: If they had worked hard and earned the right to be admitted to college, the nation—and in California, the state—would ensure that they could afford to go.

In the 1970s, California's public university system was designed to educate the state's top students at almost no charge: the Master Plan promised that the top 10% would be admitted to the University of California system and the top third to the California State University System, with others able to access community colleges. At that time, the federal government was also generous. In 1979, for example, the maximum federal Pell Grant award covered about 75% of the cost of a 4-year college education.

In those days, the United States was first in the world in college participation. And in 1975, the proportion of White, Black, and Hispanic students enrolled in college was equal—a short-lived achievement that vanished with the cuts to higher education subsidies in the 1980s. By 30 years later, Pell Grants covered only 33% of college costs.[10] Meanwhile, in 2009, as a full-fledged fiscal crisis set in across the nation, state after state announced large cutbacks in higher education. In California alone, the state university system cut 25,000 seats while dramatically raising tuition, even though the number of young people prepared for college and needed for high-technology jobs was increasing.

To raise funds for college when universities were increasing tuition and governments were substantially abandoning the programs that had provided access for low-income students was an enormous job for students and school staff and a huge struggle for philanthropists of goodwill who were pressed on from all sides by the heartbreaking stories of deserving young people.

## Supporting Undocumented Students

We also learned that for students who were undocumented and therefore not eligible for federal or state loans, the school would have to raise funds to cover an even more substantial portion of college tuition. Advisors, students, and the college counselor spent countless hours searching for scholarships that did not require U.S. citizenship, but they found that most covered only a small fraction of the cost.

The teachers had frank discussions with undocumented students like Esperanza about her options, one of which was to attend a less expensive community college for 2 years, then transfer to a 4-year university to complete her bachelor's degree. At the same time they searched desperately for a solution to make Esperanza's dream of attending a 4-year college a reality.

What they really needed was a true-life fairy godmother. It happened that a volunteer at the school not only had the resources but the desire to make a difference. She knew of Esperanza's successes and was impressed with her perseverance and resilience. When informed of Esperanza's acceptances to several 4-year colleges, she agreed to finance Esperanza's college education. When Esperanza heard the news, she burst into tears of joy, hugging her advisor tightly and for so long that it seemed like she would never let go.

Esperanza's donor's generosity inspired other community members to get involved. Esperanza and other undocumented students understood the faith that was placed in them and the responsibility they carried to give back to the community. A few times a year, students sent progress reports to the donors who were paying their tuition and they kept in regular contact with teachers and administrators at the high school. One student's letter, for example, included the following:

> Dear Mr. and Mrs. X,
>
> I am currently a junior at UC Berkeley. Thanks to your contribution I just started my third year as an undergraduate. During my college experience I've learned exceptional things that will help me achieve my future goals. When I was a freshman in high school I thought about college as a dream that was not possible for me to reach. At the beginning of my senior year thanks to my teachers I found out that there were people who really cared about youth education and I started applying to scholarships. I was amazed when I found out the great number of scholarships that focused specifically on supporting minorities. Coming from a predominant Latino/African American area, I thought I was hardly visible. I am very grateful to you and every

other person who contributed to my education. I promise that I will take advantage of all the opportunities that I have and I will follow your footsteps when I have the opportunity to contribute to this cause. This year I had the opportunity to contribute more to my community. I started a program at Berkeley High School to help undocumented students apply for scholarships to go to college. This is an experience that I would not change for anything else. Thank you very much for your great contribution. It is truly appreciated!

Even as the community worked to get more students access to college, new trials emerged. Like Sisyphus pushing the rock uphill, the students and staff learned that the rock was growing larger and the hill steeper when a state law (AB 540) allowing undocumented high school graduates in California to pay in-state tuition was challenged.[11] In 2005, out-of-state students who attended California state schools sued the University of California, alleging that it was unfair for undocumented California residents to pay in-state tuition while legal residents coming from out of state had to pay higher tuition.[12] Although the case was dismissed in 2006, the plaintiffs appealed.

On September 15, 2008, the California appellate justices ruled that the benefits of this statute apply only to U.S. citizens who have attended a California high school for 3 years and not to any undocumented residents, regardless of how long they have attended California schools. The state supreme court overturned this verdict and upheld the statute, but the issue was not finally resolved until the case was appealed to the U.S. Supreme Court. Finally, in 2011, after nearly 6 years of petitions, the U.S. Supreme Court refused to hear an appeal, and the issue was resolved.[13]

Throughout these years, the uncertainties weighed heavily on the EPAA faculty and students. If the statute was overturned, how would they find donors willing to fund upward of $200,000 per student to pay for 4 years of out-of-state tuition for the University of California or California state schools? A lawyer for the Mexican American Legal Defense and Education Fund (MALDEF) summed up the sentiments of EPAA's students, staff, and supporters:

> [This] appellate decision must not close the door to higher education for undocumented immigrant students in California. They are graduates of our public schools and they, and their parents, have paid taxes to the state. California needs them for our future and ignoring their California ties makes us all poorer.[14]

## GETTING THROUGH COLLEGE

There was great excitement when the new graduates arrived at their campuses. Compared with the average middle-class students for whom dorm life was a step down from the comforts of home, EPAA's college-bound grads were entering a new world with amenities that had existed only in their dreams. For some, like Pablo and Jade, it was the first time they had their own bed and a desk.

Nonetheless, despite the natural resilience of most EPAA students, it was difficult for many to navigate the new territory of college—not just the academic landscape, but the social and emotional terrain as well. For many it was the first time they had taken courses with White students. Indeed, Sofia remarked that the first time she ever sat in a class with a White student was when she took the SAT exam in Palo Alto. Regular tasks that might not faze those who are not the first in their family to graduate from high school could become stumbling blocks for EPAA students. Tasks like registering for classes and gaining admittance to oversubscribed ones, understanding financial aid packages, packing for college and moving into the dorms, buying textbooks, getting a tutor, and forming a study group—all of these were potential barriers to continuing and succeeding in college.

Some students who had trouble accessing resources necessary for college turned to their high school advisors for help. Seth recalls learning that Jade, then a sophomore at a university in California, did not have enough money for her books because her scholarship monies had abruptly decreased just before the start of sophomore year. His solution? Donations from EPAA teachers and staff. Another student, Kristine Lewis, gave cash to Rebecca to buy plane tickets for her move to an out-of-state university, since neither Kristine nor her family had a credit card or home Internet access to buy tickets online. Nicky, Rebecca, and Maura helped several students going to a nearby college move into their dorm, sometimes visiting them in person or checking in on them by phone to provide emotional support. Many advisors fielded phone calls, answered emails, and reviewed essays for the graduates who needed continued assistance.

## Transitioning to a New Culture

As has been noted, most students came to East Palo Alto Academy with memories of a substandard elementary and middle school experience and the resultant gaps in their knowledge and academic skills. In only 4 years, EPAA students had to overcome these challenges and master the new college-preparatory curriculum to catch up with their Palo Alto peers already primed for AP classes. There simply wasn't enough time. How could one school make up for years of insufficient preparation and, in many cases, a fragmented support system?

Even EPAA's valedictorian, Lena, was conscious of the differences in her preparation for college compared with her college classmates. She attended a 4-year competitive university in southern California. Despite her stellar success at EPAA, Lena initially had some difficulties in college stemming from her insecurities as a minority student. "Cultural differences often made me feel intimidated in college. I was always worried about how to phrase things—I didn't want to come off as offensive. Maybe if I talk how I usually talk in East Palo Alto—that wouldn't be accepted here."

Lena began her college career with a distinct sense of marginalization when she was finally confronted with peers who grew up with college-educated parents living in affluent communities. In her words:

> I definitely struggled my first year in college in all aspects. Growing up in East Palo Alto, I was not exposed to the predominant ethnicities in [my] college—Whites and Asians. I often felt intimidated, maybe because I thought they were more prepared than me. Being the only Brown student in my classes and hearing them talk, it seemed like my vocabulary wasn't up to par with theirs. EPAA [teachers] did their best to prepare me, but I also now realize that I did not start high school where I should have been. Sure, I could read and write pretty well, but [not] in comparison to someone who went to school in Palo Alto, [who] would most likely do better than me on a standardized test.

But as she had done many times before, Lena gathered her strength, worked through these challenges, and emerged successful. By her third year, she had figured out how to fit in and had even found places where she could advise and support the same peers who initially intimidated her. Because of the Early College credits she had acquired, she graduated in 3 years.

Pablo also struggled with that sense of marginalization and worried he would not be accepted in college. He observed:

> Coming from an under-represented minority community, I thought that I would have a hard time fitting into a college town where my skin color would stand out everywhere I would go and where I would find myself feeling uncomfortable in my own skin. At these times I would remember how my amazing teachers would always tell me to do my best and not be afraid to just be myself. I'm forever grateful and consider them my family.

Throughout his school experience, Pablo had demonstrated an inordinate supply of personal resilience. He demonstrated that resilience when he entered college. Choosing a mathematics major in a rigorous college, he earned a few low grades in the first year, but he learned from his experience and improved his performance in subsequent years. Although he was not earning as many A grades as he would have liked, he was driven to learn as much as he could: "What's most important to me is that I take something away from each class because, 10 years from now, having an A in a class won't matter but what I remember and learned will." Always unique, Pablo combined his math major with a women's studies major. He offered this rationale for his choices:

> Math has always been my hardest subject and being that I'm the first person in my family to go to college I wanted to take this enormous challenge. And while it's extremely hard for me, I enjoy it every day. It feels so good when I get a long, hard problem correct.
>
> Growing up, I never understood why women everywhere were treated like second-class citizens. Some of my friends would even abuse their girlfriends. Frankly, I want to do something about it because if I have children I would hate for them to grow up in a misogynistic world. I think that being a women and gender studies major could help me with this. Plus, I'm a feminist.

As in high school, Pablo quickly became involved in many extracurricular activities, most of which supported the goal of social justice, such as the Academic Excellence Program, an organization focused on welcoming and supporting students of color as well as those with financial needs. Pablo was the president of another organization, Stop Hate On Campus, an organization that funded events geared toward ending racism, sexism, and homophobia. A natural leader, Pablo was a residential advisor in the dorms and was captain of an intramural ultimate Frisbee team. He also served on two student advisory boards, one for the women and gender studies program and the other for the Student Academic Services Center.

After graduation, Pablo hoped to return to the East Palo Alto community in order to serve as a positive role model, someone "who knows what it's like to grow up there and understands their many struggles, someone who will not turn his back on his community. . . . I want to help change East Palo Alto and I think I can do much good through teaching." Pablo aspired to attend the Stanford Teacher Education Program and earn his master's degree and teaching credential in math. Because of EPAA's strong relationship with Stanford University and STEP, students had many opportunities to interact with Stanford tutors and teachers-in-training, seeing firsthand how novice teachers cultivated their craft and helped students in meaningful and important ways. Pablo credited his desire to become a teacher to his high school experience:

> I can honestly say that if I hadn't gone to EPAA, I would have not gone to college. Two of my three older siblings dropped out. I would have probably done the same. If it weren't for the dedication and *love* of all those teachers, I think that I would either be working a minimum wage job or be in prison. They showed me that, just because everyone around me was not going to college, it didn't mean that I couldn't, and that I could do anything as long as I tried my best and did it for the right

reasons. If it weren't for them, I wouldn't want to be a teacher today. This is the biggest gift anyone has ever given me.

Lena also credited her high school experience with both her ability to succeed in college and her desire to become a teacher:

> At EPAA, I was encouraged to speak in class. I was able to participate in the development of the school. All of this helped me to develop relationships that helped me to succeed in college. . . . [Now] I know how to respond to teachers' questions. My presentation skills were better than I would have thought they would have been when I entered college. I thrived in small freshman classes. Professors gave me feedback on how well I answered questions and how I explained myself.
>
> This is why I want to become a teacher. I want to be the person who makes a difference in a child's life; to provide the path to a door that wouldn't normally be open, especially to kids who grow up in neighborhoods like East Palo Alto.

## Straddling Home and College

Straddling the worlds of college and life in East Palo Alto proved a challenge for even the most resilient students. Those who succeeded leaned on strong work habits they developed at EPAA, cultivating relationships with their new professors, even in the largest college classes. Individuals navigated these challenges in different ways. Some chose not to visit East Palo Alto at all during college; others either lived at home or returned for the weekends. Often those choosing the latter strategy had a harder time maintaining their academic focus.

Sone (pronounced Soe-nay) Tatafu was a student, like a number of others, whose route through college was a more torturous one, in large part because of financial pressures and the pulls on him from his family. As a high school student, Sone liked "doing school," and he always seemed genuinely interested in learning. He was happy to be in a small, personalized, intellectually engaging learning community. Sone's advisor, Tina, remembers their first meeting:

> Sone was one of the first recently graduated 8th-graders I interviewed the summer before EPAA opened. I didn't know at that time that the tall, skinny, curly-haired Pacific Islander student who sat in front of me would become one of my advisees with whom I would travel grade to grade. There was no way of knowing that even after he and I both left the school 4 years later, we would still keep in touch—that he would feel comfortable enough to call me whenever he had a problem, or that I

would feel a close enough connection to him that I would share my own news. Out of all my advisees, he is the one I talk with most frequently, the one I worry about the most, and the one I am certain has benefited greatly from being in a small, personalized environment.

While some students rolled their eyes when teachers like Tina asked them to "go deep" and complained that they couldn't analyze any further, Sone was more than willing to push himself to think below the surface. Reflective by nature, he was well suited for East Palo Alto Academy in many ways. Advisory, for example, was a structure that allowed him to connect closely with his advisor and his fellow students. When Tina held her weekly "Pits and Peaks" ritual, Sone did not balk at sitting in a circle and sharing one highlight and challenge of his week. He was not someone who passed or gave a superficial response like "my pit is that I have homework and my peak is that it's almost Friday." Sone shared details about his life and listened closely when others did the same. Unlike some students who saw advisors as nosy people who wanted to know everything about them, Sone appreciated having a space to share what was going on in his life and knowing that his advisor was always there to support him.

Sone benefited from the concrete feedback he got from the Five Habits rubric about his academic progress. It was also a constant reminder of his high skills and his ongoing struggle with procrastination. Knowing that he was a capable writer and analytical thinker gave him hope and the desire to use these skills to tackle his weaknesses.

Sone's peers respected his self-awareness and quiet disposition, and chose him as one of the speakers at the first graduation. He and Kristine, also chosen by her peers, gave a joint speech. In his part of the speech, Sone summarized what he gained from East Palo Alto Academy:

I have definitely learned to acknowledge my accomplishments as a student and as an individual. I have also become widely aware that I have made it, not to the end of high school, but to a new beginning and a new chapter in life, where we can reinvent ourselves, reflect on our past, and learn from it.

Although Sone was academically successful at EPAA and had been admitted to college, the path there, given his own and his family's financial need, was not straightforward. As Tina commented:

Sone taught me a great deal as an educator. I learned that sometimes no matter how much we supported a student academically, there were certain factors over which we had no control. There was a point when we all realized that we had to let students make their own decisions and pursue their own paths. We could help them apply to college, but once they left us, there was no way we could keep them from dropping out to take a job that would pay their bills.

Sone enrolled in a local community college after high school, intending eventually to transfer to a better school. However, not long after he started, he called Tina to explain that he was taking a semester off. He began working at the IKEA in East Palo Alto so that he could earn money and have the flexibility to stay home and take care of his niece. Tina exclaimed:

> I was so angry with his family for taking advantage of him, for thinking it was more important for him to stay home and take care of a child than go to college and take care of his own future. In one of my recent conversations with him, he explained that he, too, was getting tired of being used for this purpose and decided he needed to attend another community college outside of the area. . . . Sone explained to me how he was reading books, trying to keep his mind in shape for when he returned to school. We joked about how he should write some essays to stay in practice, and I told him I would read them and give him feedback.

Sone eventually understood the wisdom of being "the driving force in his life" and, because of his desire and motivation, he eventually returned to college in the fall of 2008. He wrote to his advisor:

> I finally decided to go back to school this fall because I was putting it off too much. I was also tired of working, and I did not want to be stuck working menial jobs. So one day I made a decision to just call it quits. I felt that if I was going back to school I needed to resign in order to stay focused. This job was one of many factors that led me to gradually drop out of college the first time, but the most significant was my life situation. I became the sole caretaker for my nieces being that I did not have a job while I was in school. This year, I have decided that I did not want to deal with this anymore. I felt like I was putting everyone else before me. So this year has been a good year for me because I have learned to be more conscious about my life.
>
> My cousin, who is also a student, helped me register for classes and introduced me to some of her friends who would help me. This quarter, I am studying social psychology. It's awesome! I love the teacher. I am still a little lost with how things work but I'm working on it. I've been seeking advice from the counselor, which reminds me that I have an appointment today.

Sone seemed to have remembered Nicky's maxim for success at EPAA: "Show up, do the work, accept help." Quite often, it was students' ability to reach out for help—either during college or en route to returning—that enabled them to get through the college experience. Sometimes this help came from other students with whom they went to high school. Sofia (who, not surprisingly, eventually became a teacher) described how she took it upon herself to encourage her peers who had stopped out along the way to get back "on track":

> I take great pride in being part of the first graduating class and knowing that many of my peers went on to college. But as time has gone by, I've come to realize that some weren't able to stay on that track.
>
> It's very sad to come home and see that some are already caught in the paycheck-to-paycheck phenomenon that has led them to no more than dead-end jobs. It's even worse when I hear that many felt forced to drop out of school because they needed money—for them, to help the family, or to save up to go back to school. It truly breaks my heart to see many people who I feel have tremendous potential coming to the end of a short road they've taken. It's also hard to talk to them about my life because at this point almost all aspects of it revolve around school. I feel like I am a reminder of where they could be. Yet, as someone who constantly preaches the importance of education, I find myself encouraging them to get back on track because I truly believe that it's never too late. I know that everyone develops at a different pace, which is why I have faith in that more and more will be able to continue their education.

Sone was one of many students who started, then stopped out of, college and later returned, with the encouragement of friends, advisors, and, sometimes, family as well.


## COMING HOME AGAIN

Staying home often made it harder for students to get through college, because they could not focus fully on what they needed to do to succeed academically. Coming home from college was also not always easy for students. For some, it was a return to physically difficult conditions. During the summer, for example, Jade lived with her family of eight in a small basement. She looked forward to going back to school where she would have her own space and where she wouldn't feel like all of the people and belongings were crowding in on her.

For others, the return was emotionally taxing. Like some other EPAA students who went away to college, Pablo found it difficult to come home and see his old friends who were on distinctively different paths. He explained:

> Well, it just saddens me to see my friends, whom I love very much, not doing much of anything for the betterment of their lives. Maybe they're content with that and I'm just being judgmental. I just think that if they put in as much effort as they put into partying, then they might actually change their lives in an amazing way.

Lena agreed and said, "I used to love going home freshman year in college. Now I don't enjoy going home because no one has any motivation."

Tina noted that some EPAA students needed to separate temporarily from East Palo Alto to succeed:

> Advisors supported noncollege kids as well—the ones who reach out. Many of our students seemed to have learned that, in order to succeed, they needed to leave the community of East Palo Alto or Menlo Park and return later to help better their lives and those of their families

The faculty also had to come to terms with the fact that many graduates who started community college did not finish, at least at that time. Tina explained: "We remind each other that having graduated high school is a big step—that in a community where so many students of color drop out before the 12th grade, there is something important about our students making it this far."

Many used their postsecondary experiences to acquire a stable career, creating strength and stability in the EPA community. Some enrolled in community college classes or in programs that granted certificates for technical careers like nursing, phlebotomy, or auto mechanics. While some did not have the life circumstances to support continuing their education, they used their hard-earned skills to make a life for themselves free of poverty. It was a victory to have found a job, their own living space, and the opportunity to earn money to support themselves and assist their families. And along the way, they kept their focus on advancing through hard work and continued education.

Students often returned to EPAA's campus to check in with their teachers and advisor after graduation. One student from the first graduating class, a young Fijian woman whose daily antics had frustrated her advisor, returned to EPAA the year after graduation. Transformed in her blazer and skirt, she came to brag about her new promotion from being a hostess in a restaurant to becoming a member of the accounting department. Another from the class of 2005, a young Latino male, became an auto technician at Ford Motors, earning $25 an hour. Worried about the economic slowdown, he returned to

EPAA for a copy of his transcript. His plan: to return to school to become a credentialed electrician capable of earning $45 an hour.

Although not all were aimed at professions, these graduates were on a more positive and stable path than many of their family members. Magdalena, a class of 2005 graduate, and the only person in her family of five with a high school diploma, began working at a bakery during high school. At that time, the family shared a three-bedroom house with two other families. Since Magdalena was working, she was able to rent her own room, while the rest of her family shared the adjoining bedroom. (The second family lived in the master bedroom and the third rented the garage.) After graduation Magdalena became a senior employee at her bakery and the person in her family who had held the same job for the longest time. Eventually, she moved out, renting a room in another house, an independent woman. For Magdalena, the feeling that she "could do anything" remained her primary motivation; her life trajectory had already moved in a more positive direction.

Malcolm Davis, who had experienced so much social as well as academic growth at EPAA, handled ongoing struggles after graduation with continuing perseverance. After high school, Malcolm enrolled in the San Francisco Academy of Art, but found it prohibitively expensive and so he transferred to a local community college. In 2007, his father passed away from stomach cancer. "It hit me hard," Malcolm said. "I went into a downfall after that and haven't been in a happy place since then."

According to Malcolm, the monetary death benefit they received "wreaked havoc" on his life. Because of the added income, Malcolm no longer qualified for financial aid, and he left college to work full time at a grocery store. Malcolm was no longer eligible for low-cost insurance or housing; subsequently his rent skyrocketed from $500 a month to $1,400. Malcolm said, "The money ruined everything. It was a domino effect, but I recently started to get back on my feet." When he left college, Malcolm worked odd jobs to support himself, while still living at home, and launched his own online graphic design business.

Malcolm is innately curious and has a tendency to bounce from one academic endeavor to another. At one point, he re-enrolled in community college and was later admitted to a California State University in southern California, where he hoped to finish his bachelor's degree in graphic design and advertising. In this process, Malcolm looked to his high school teachers, Mr. Dean and Tina, for letters of recommendation. Malcolm explained that he chose the CSU because of the special education program they offer. Malcolm said, "In high school I didn't really take advantage of the services. I was ashamed. I didn't think that colleges had special education programs." His dream is to design movie posters and run a successful graphic design business.

When asked, 7 years later, to reflect on his high school experience, Malcolm said that working with Simone, his freshman reading teacher, was the most important event in his high school career: "I wouldn't have graduated if it wasn't for her. I dropped out for a month in 9th grade. [Simone] got me back in. She and Nicky and Charlene [the school's clinical psychologist] got me back in. Mr. Dean was also really important."

William Dean remained in contact with Malcolm, emailing back and forth, meeting for lunch, talking on the phone, and reassuring the young man about his future:

> I am not sure about any miraculous or defining moment for Malcolm at EPAA, but I do know that he was at the right school. I do know that he feels this was the right place too. One definite thing, though, he continues to hold learning important in his life, sparked by Simone, then dimmed in the interim, and reignited along the way.

## THE ENDURING IMPACT OF EAST PALO ALTO ACADEMY

EPAA's emphasis on academic skills and college readiness continued to help the class of 2005 graduates as they moved through college and took on challenges in the workplace. Graduates, like the ones below, reported that they are still benefiting from their academic experience at EPAA, whether they went on to a 4-year college or to vocational training:

> When I got into [community] college, it just seemed too easy for me. I was like, "Oh, I learned that in high school." We were going over the same things and I was prepared for it.

> It worked for me. I was planning on going to the military instead of college and now I'm going to college. For people who are going to college, the school captured the environment very well with the exhibitions, and college tours we went to all the time. It really focused on the college part of life. The whole school revolves around that. EPAA was great at . . . telling you what college was going to be like and giving you a taste of it. When I got to college . . . it all seemed very familiar.

> The grading system helped me to think critically, to question, to read on my own. In college, no one is directing me; I have to develop my own opinions.

> All that math is coming back and is helping me out. I'm doing classes in automotive technology, and it's all based on math calculations, doing it right.

I had to pass this math test for my job [as a machine operator]. If I hadn't been in algebra I wouldn't have gotten the job. On the day of my test I called my math teacher [Seth] and asked him a few questions!

My reading got much better than it was before. My writing: my essays are much better, more detailed. In the science class we were dealing with real stuff, more exciting stuff . . . I really liked that.

The teachers did give me the right tools to prepare me in life. Reading and writing, doing the agenda: what's the first thing you have to do, the second thing you have to do; the guidelines that you have to do to get things done.

The school helped me to think more critically about things.

Graduates also said that their education in the habits of personal responsibility prepared them for their adult lives as college students and as workers:

The habits for success helped me with being punctual [and] being prepared for different challenges.

In general, [EPAA] helped me become a better person by allowing me to work with others and by teaching me the meaning of personal responsibility.

They tried to teach open-mindedness . . . [and] personal responsibility. I turned in my work every day. High school made me more responsible. I think because of that school, I go to [class] on time every day.

I could relate to the Five Habits. [Before I went to EPAA] I wasn't really good with communicating . . . or personal responsibility. Seth really pushed me towards being more communicative with teachers and being more social around math projects we had. . . . When I go to Cañada [College], I'm not that quiet in class. [Before] I didn't ask questions, even if I had problems. I would sit there and let it go. I was nervous to speak out, thinking people would think I was dumb for asking about it. Now if I don't understand something, I just ask a question, I don't really get nervous when I have to ask a question.

Many graduates talked about the projects and exhibitions as having been important to their success in college and in life:

I think all the projects we did [prepared us]. We learned to talk a lot and express ourselves.

The exhibitions [were helpful]. I had to present a lot. It was helpful for college. Communication skills helped me to present, when talking to a big crowd of people, especially compared to before [high school].

They encouraged my social skills. It was the most important thing I experienced—a big part of my high school. I deal with customers all the time [in] the way that they taught [me]. We had a lot of presentations where you have to talk to a big group. I have to talk to people all the time. I want the teachers to know that the presentations mattered a lot and I do appreciate them.

And the sense of social responsibility had a strong effect on many. As Pablo put it:

EPAA made me realize that there's more to education than just knowing things, but that we should learn to have the ability of teaching others, to become aware of our surroundings, and how to improve one's life while making the world around you better.

Regardless of whether students continued their formal education after high school graduation, the habits of mind and behavior that they had internalized at EPAA empowered them with a confidence to improve their lives. The graduates are now among the strongest advocates for the school. One said, "Kids that I talk to now who are coming out of junior high, I try to get them to go to EPAA."

In fact, the legacy of the class of 2005, adults who are now graduating from college or working steadily, is what helped to inspire future cohorts of EPAA students. The EPAA graduates who successfully completed high school ready to take on the challenges of independent living and service to society have paved the way for the next generations to do the same. Lena summed up the influence of EPAA graduates as role models for the next generation:

They're still setting the example that a person from East Palo Alto can do it. That's where personal responsibility and social responsibility go hand in hand. You're taking care of yourself personally so you can effect social change.

## CHAPTER 9

# The Continuing Journey

> East Palo Alto Academy high school has taught me the importance of hard work, dedication, and most importantly, commitment. In order to reach any type of goal or accomplishment you have, these are the three main things you need to reach it.
>
> —A graduating senior in 2014

These words by an EPAA graduate apply equally to the lessons of the school itself. As noted in Chapter 1, in June 2014, East Palo Alto Academy celebrated its tenth graduating class, with more than 90% again admitted to college, and the first-ever graduate heading off to become an undergraduate at Stanford University. All 57 seniors received a high school diploma, and very few had left before senior year. The most recent state data showed EPAA with a 4-year cohort graduation rate of 92.3%, with 2.6% still enrolled in a fifth year.[1] This would be a remarkable statistic for any high school. However, it is more striking in a high school that continues to serve among the highest proportions of low-income students and English learners in California: 97% qualify for free or reduced-price lunch; 84% do not speak English as their primary language; and 64% have no parent who has graduated from high school.

By now, more than 500 students have graduated the EPAA way—primed for postsecondary opportunities by the Five Habits, their yearly exhibitions, and the cadre of teachers, family members, advisors, and counselors who have relentlessly supported them every step of the way. Graduates from East Palo Alto Academy have been admitted to colleges and universities across the United States, including Stanford, Brown, Columbia, Smith, Loyola Marymount, University of Chicago, University of Pennsylvania, University of Oregon, University of Colorado, Howard, Tuskegee, Florida A&M, Syracuse, Santa Clara, the Pratt Institute of Design, almost all the campuses of the California State University and University of California, and many more. To enable students to pursue these opportunities, Stanford New Schools has provided more than $2,000,000 in scholarships to its graduates.

As they graduate from college, alumni return to encourage their younger peers. An EPAA alumnus who graduated from UC Berkeley in 2014 had this to say:

When I was a high school student at East Palo Alto Academy, I never envisioned myself attending one of the world's top universities. All I knew was that I wanted to succeed, and I knew that I wanted to make my parents proud by obtaining an education that unfortunately was not accessible to them when they were young. Unbeknownst to me, my dedication to school and to my community was slowly paving the road for my path towards a college education.

Each graduate changes the hope quotient in the community. Equally noteworthy, in the summer of 2014, the school returned to the center of the East Palo Alto community, not far from where Ravenswood High School had once stood, in a shiny new high school building constructed for it by the Sequoia Union High School District. Sized to hold up to 400 students, the new building continues to support the small, personalized education EPAA was designed to offer. County voters also passed a school bond for the district to build a separate new gym for the school. At the ribbon-cutting in August, attended by the Ravenswood and Sequoia superintendents and the full Sequoia school board, as well as students and faculty from EPAA and Stanford, the incoming 9th-graders displayed their first mural—a vivid rendering of the word "CREATIVE" they had painted to describe themselves during their Summer Bridge program (described later).

That word equally described the path the school took to get to this point in time. In a historic moment, the school was coming home to its community and to the district that once had bused students so far away from their homes. Now, most EPAA students can walk to their neighborhood high school. The school has come back under the umbrella of the district as a dependent charter school, supported by the district's central office, with teachers a part of the district teachers association. Stanford University will work collaboratively with the district to maintain the innovative program and the connections to Stanford resources that are still part of the charter.

This new chapter in the school's and the community's history was launched through the creative efforts of the district, union, school, and university. Together, they have imagined and agreed to a new way for a public school district to serve its highest-needs students well. The collaborative arrangement redefines the way the district relates to the community and a unique school it now sponsors, the way the university relates to its neighboring district and community, and the way the collective bargaining agreement allows for new ways of supporting both teachers and students.

This story, however, is not a magical fairy tale. As we have pointed out, there have been many bumps and potholes along the way, and there will be more yet to come. In part, this is a story of perseverance in the face of recurring near-defeats. It is important to tell that part of the story as well, and to pull out the lessons for educational practice and policy.

In this chapter we address these questions: How does a school maintain momentum in the face of changing staff, circumstances, and state and federal policy? What practices have proved most valuable for serving students well? What are the implications of these experiences for educational policy, particularly as it is directed at the education of the growing number of low-income students of color in highly segregated communities? What path would education systems need to take to provide what their most vulnerable young people need to make good on the American dream?

## CONTINUITY AND CHANGE

Change has been a constant during the life of the school. Toward the end of its fifth year, the founding principal, Nicky, left EPAA when her daughter was born. Within the next 2 years, most of the founding teachers also had moved on. In part, this was because of the enormous effort needed to launch the school, and the feeling of closure that advisors felt when the students they had mentored for 4 years finally graduated. Like second-time parents, a number of the teachers commented that they could not imagine loving and investing as much in another cohort as the first one. Some took this moment to return to graduate school or to move to a less intensely demanding school environment or a more affordable area in which to live and buy a house. Certainly, there was an element of burnout from the long days, weeks, months, and years needed to invent and start a school. There were also the normal life-cycle events that take many young teachers out of the classroom: childrearing or to be with fiancés or spouses elsewhere.

These teachers took elements of the school's practices and culture with them and planted them in new places, where they continue to support success. For example, when Marysol moved back to her home community to be close to her family and fiancé, she initially taught in the comprehensive high school, where she advocated for and helped to pilot collaborative planning time. Three years later, she was asked to join the planning team for a new small high school for the district, Inspire School of Arts and Sciences. She noted:

> The planning team was well aware of not only my teaching experience at EPAA, but the upcoming trials and tribulations of building a school from the ground up. Now in our fifth year, we have a solid advisory program, we value collaboration and ongoing professional development as a staff, and we've come a long way as a young school. From the very beginning, I pushed for us to adopt the EPAA staff norms and roles. They've not only enhanced our staff culture and productivity, they've been key in our distributive leadership.

Vice principal Jeff Gilbert was sorely missed at Hillsdale High School, where he previously had taught, and he was recruited back there in 2005–2006 to help transform the school into small learning communities. Jeff returned with the new practices he had learned at EPAA and worked with others to plant them at Hillsdale High, which went on to become one of the top-rated high schools in the country as it made access to a thinking curriculum much more equitably available to its increasingly diverse student body.[2] Writing about the Hillsdale changes, *Washington Post* author Jay Mathews described a number of practices that had their origins at EPAA:

> Students are organized into small advisory groups that meet daily with a staff member trained to help them with any problems. . . . The ninth and 10th grades are divided into three houses that focus on interdisciplinary lessons and ambitious projects such as a re-creation of a World War I battle and a trial of "Lord of the Flies" author William Golding. Students of all achievement levels are mixed in the same classes, sharing in discussions but doing different homework based on their needs and wishes. All seniors must define an essential question, write a thesis of at least eight pages, and defend it before a panel of graders including outside experts. More changes are planned. The idea is to do much more than prepare students for the annual state tests, but the changes have helped raise the school's Academic Performance Index on California's 1000-point scale from 662 in 2002 to 797 this year.[3]

## Maintaining the Vision

At EPAA, however, as in other new schools that change leadership, there was an ongoing tug of war to maintain these practices. In the 10 years after Nicky left, there were four different principals (two of them interims) and a number of other staff who came and went. The principals and staff were dedicated and talented people, each of whom contributed important new dimensions to the school's work. Nonetheless, frequent leadership changes pose a common challenge in schools founded by those who are drawn to a common vision and who build new practices together. While the founders deeply understand and appreciate these practices, newcomers may find them mysterious and start from their own different set of precedents and traditions.

Some staff who came to EPAA imbued with a big high school experience did not intuitively understand the practices of this small, personalized school. Traditional scheduling and management practices could easily erode collaborative planning time and begin to reinstate aspects of tracking, while reducing the importance of advisory, exhibitions, and shared decisionmaking. Some new staff raised questions about these practices, which felt like more work, as well as about block schedules that required more active pedagogies, and about the role of the advisor, which was unfamiliar to many. Some teachers wanted the administration to take on all the discipline, and periodically there was a small cadre who lobbied for more suspensions and expulsions to remove the "troublemakers."

The traditional high school socialization generally is not focused on a whole-child developmental perspective and tends toward the impersonal, because these are the attitudes needed to survive in a big high school where teachers see 150 to 200 students a day. The norms in those settings generally can be summarized as: "I teach my subject; the students get it or they don't; those who pass move on; the others fail and often disappear." Often unspoken is the additional note that "life gets easier when those who are harder to teach drop out." Whereas EPAA was founded with strong commitments to support students' development, the big high school culture is better designed to support selecting and sorting based on whether students can already meet the demands that govern the school.

The pull to return to big-school practices was an inadvertent undercurrent whenever new staff entered, especially in years when there was not a strong enough professional socialization experience in the summer retreat, followed by ongoing coaching and professional development. The core practices were maintained over these years by the committed long-term staff and university partners who referred to their own experiences and the language of the charter to sustain and continually reboot these important elements of student success.

Of the new cohort of teachers who entered between the fifth and ninth years, many have stayed on and have become part of the institutional memory and traditions of the school. They are the second group of founders, and they have both built on and supported the evolution of some of the school's practices. As in any enduring institution, although the climate fluctuated, many of EPAA's defining structures remained intact, including block scheduling, yearly exhibitions, daily student advisories, and Early College. The school's program remained centered around college preparation and meeting the social, academic, and emotional needs of its students. EPAA also added new programs, including mental health and social services supports through a social worker, a wellness curriculum focused on mindfulness, and a more structured approach to restorative justice for building personal and social responsibility across the campus.

In part because of the Western Accreditors of Schools and Colleges (WASC) accreditation cycle in the school's 12th year, which was undertaken by a leadership team that had strong connections to both Stanford and the community, the current staff has rededicated itself to the tenets of the school's original vision and charter. One veteran faculty member explained:

> [EPAA has] good people in place . . . who will become excellent over time. This team has been forced to read the charter . . . and to really

reflect on what it is that we are here to do and why it is so important to maintain a perspective that excellence is what kids can achieve and do deserve.

## Surviving External Challenges

In addition to the internal changes the high school needed to manage, there were external political and other challenges, including the coming and going of an associated elementary school, the pressures to survive an era of test-based accountability, and the challenges of making ends meet during several waves of state budget cuts.

***The Politics of the Elementary School.*** After Ravenswood City School District (RCSD)—an elementary school district—had launched and approved this high school charter, the state realized that a number of elementary school districts were approving such high schools in their communities, particularly when they were not tightly connected to the high school districts their students were to attend after 8th grade. (As explained in Chapter 1, many districts in California are designated as either elementary or high school.)

In most cases, the state was responsible for paying the charter school rate for these high school students (set at a level below the state average per-pupil expenditures), because the students were not part of a high school district, and the elementary district was not responsible for paying for their secondary education. Aiming to slow the spread of this idea, a state law was enacted in 2004 requiring that schools must include the grade levels offered by the district that authorizes the charter. In response, Stanford agreed to operate an elementary school in Ravenswood and created an entity called the Stanford Schools Corporation (SSC), which both launched the elementary school and took over the operations of the high school from Aspire.

In 2005, a new K–12 charter was issued by RCSD to SSC. Between 2005 and 2010, in addition to the high school, SSC operated several elementary grades on a different site, with a different staff and group of Stanford advisors. It was at this time that the high school changed its name from East Palo Alto High School to East Palo Alto Academy, which included both the high school and elementary school.

The little elementary school had a difficult time, with facilities problems each year, along with the usual challenges of a startup. Meanwhile RCSD, which had authorized many charters, began to realize that—in light of state budget cuts—it could not make ends meet for its own schools' and district's needs, given the outflow of funds to charters serving K–8 students who otherwise would have been bringing in enrollment dollars to the district. The district began ending charter authorizations, with the EPAA elementary school being the first of several charters to close. In 2010, RCSD re-authorized the EPAA charter with the understanding that Stanford Schools Corporation would discontinue operation of the elementary grades and seek a charter for the high school from the Sequoia Union High School District within the next 2 years.

A process was initiated to obtain a charter for a new high school to serve the same group of EPA students in grades 9–12, authorized by the Sequoia Union High School District. That new charter was authorized in the spring of 2012. The 2012–2013 school year saw the launch of the new school with a new charter, a new principal, a new chief operating officer, significant changes in administrative and teacher staffing, as well as new educational programming. Among other changes, the high school program created a career pathway in the health sciences that augmented a set of Early College courses with high school courses, such as physiology and diabetes awareness, and established an expanded wellness program (described later).

The state and local charter politics that led to the launch and subsequent closure of the elementary school took an enormous amount of resources and attention from both SSC and the school district, and, as Ravenswood moved students around while subsequently closing several other charters, created a great deal of churn in the district. One of the things we learned in the experience is how much distraction from the work of education can result from the focus on governance and competition in the brave new world of choice.

*Test-Based Accountability.* Part of the challenge of operating any school during these years was the pressure exerted by the federal and state test-based accountability systems, which made decisions each year about which schools to identify and sanction based only on their scores on state tests. These systems created incentives for schools to teach to the multiple-choice tests, at the expense of more in-depth reading, writing, mathematical projects, discussion, and inquiry. They also created incentives to avoid admitting or keeping students with high levels of need who would bring average test scores down.

Although we knew that attention to more authentic, in-depth learning would pay off in the long run, there were pressures from donors and from the state to focus on boosting scores in the short run. To a great extent, this required running two different curricula—one focused on important long-term learning: engaging students in reading novels, biographies, and social science research; conducting labs and investigations; applying math in the real world; and writing research reports, journalistic accounts, and health pamphlets for the community—and the other focused on teaching students to understand the fragmented, artificial format of the tests.

This included far too many hours on deconstructing the testing game (how to read short passages not too deeply, so as to find what the test-maker would identify as the theme; how to recognize "distractors" meant to trick the reader; how to decode word clues in the responses that provided the key to the correct answer; how to eliminate obvious wrong answers and select among the remainder, and so on), so that the students could learn to pick one answer out of five. The test-prep process was made more complex by cultural bias in the tests; that is, assumptions that students have had a White, middle-class set of experiences from which to interpret questions (for example, that a "stock" has to do with the value of a company on Wall Street, not a cow in a herd or the base for a soup). Given how much students had to learn, it was frustrating to have to spend time on such decontextualized tasks that had little to do with skills they would use in the real world and in college, but it became clear that that was necessary to do so, so that they could successfully play the testing game while they were separately learning skills that would matter.

With the school starting at the very bottom of the state distribution in its first year, the faculty raised scores rapidly over the next 5 years by running a dual curriculum to raise real skills and test-taking skills simultaneously. (See Figure 9.1, which shows score trends during the years in which the school was assigned an API score.[4]) When compared with the 100 schools designated by the state as "similar schools"—those with the greatest proportions of high-needs students in the state—EPAA's scores typically ranked above most of them, even though only a small handful came close to having as many low-income students or English learners and none had as many parents with less than a high school education.[5]

**Figure 9.1. EPAA Academic Performance Index Trends**

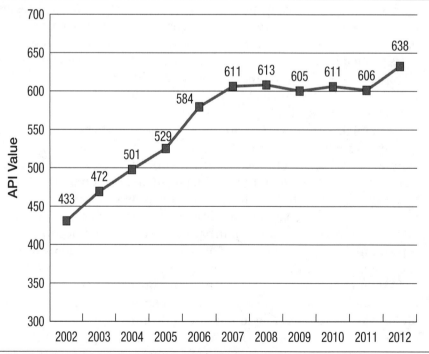

*Note.* Constructed from state API data available at cde.ca.gov.

When the little elementary school began, it, too, started at the bottom, with low scores as its students began to acquire the skills they needed, which caused the school's combined elementary and secondary scores to level off for a few years. Ironically, in August 2010, when the elementary school's fourth year of API scores came in, they had increased by more than 100 points over the previous year (on an 800-point API scale); however, the school had been discontinued 2 months earlier, over the objections of more than 100 parents who crowded the boardroom to vouch for the quality of the education they felt their children were receiving. It was too late for the scores to count, or for educators to build on the lessons of what had worked to improve students' performance.

Even when the school met all of the state expectations for annual improvements in API scores, it could not meet the expectations of the federal NCLB "adequate yearly progress" requirements, because of the "Catch 22" provisions pertaining to English learners, as described in Chapter 2. Schools were expected to increase the percentage of students in each subgroup deemed proficient each year by a steep margin set to hit 100% proficiency by 2014. However, when an English learner became proficient, he or she was taken *out* of the English learner subgroup, leaving in the group only those who had not yet reached proficiency. Thus, it was impossible for the group as a whole ever to make substantial progress toward 100% proficiency by 2014, even if all of the English learner students in a school eventually hit the proficiency mark as individuals. As a consequence, the schools designated as "in need of improvement" and, later, as "failing" under NCLB were those that served the most English learners.

One of the more ironic moments in the school's history was when federal officials visited the school to applaud its safe campus, high graduation rates, and success in preparing students for college, unaware that by their own rules the school was only a step away from being declared failing. Despite its successes in changing students' lives, the school could easily have been shut down because of nonsensical regulations that ignored all of these outcomes and labeled schools serving large numbers of English learners as failing. Today, virtually all of California's schools have failed to meet AYP, since it is indeed impossible to have 100% of students in all subgroups meet a proficiency bar, but those identified first for this "honor" were the schools serving the highest-needs students. And while EPAA escaped the fate of some that were subject to drill-and-kill "improvement" specialists, or were reconstituted or closed, it was not immune to the annual pressures to show gains in scores.

During these years, we watched many charter schools as well as some district-run schools push out the most severely struggling students. EPAA took on students who had been expelled from or counseled out of other charters as well as students who had failed in the big comprehensive high schools and arrived, credit deficient, in 10th or 11th grade. About one-third of its students came in after the start of 9th grade from other schools. Whereas charters over-all underrepresent ELs and special education students, EPAA overrepresented both groups and became known to parents in the community for pulling kids through who otherwise might not have made it.

*The State Fiscal Meltdown.* While EPAA took on the neediest students in the area, it suffered, like other schools, from the state's fiscal meltdown. Already in dire straits by 2000 due to the effect of Proposition 13, California school budgets took greater hits as the decade progressed. When Arnold Schwarzenegger became governor in 2003 and canceled newly passed licensing fees and other revenue sources, he triggered an economic downturn that deepened over subsequent years. Per-pupil funds for public K–12 education, already well below the levels of most other states' systems, declined by more than $2,000 per pupil on average, and still more than that in low-income communities that could not pass additional levies or raise large contributions from parents and other private sources.

Schools in these communities canceled music, art, and physical education classes; closed libraries; fired librarians and school nurses; raised class sizes; reduced curriculum offerings and the number of school days; and capped salaries. EPAA was able to raise funds from donors for some needs and was able to rely on Stanford resources for things like health care for its students, but it was never able to afford a music program, a physical education teacher, a librarian, or a school nurse. It could not build a real library, afford athletic fields (aside from the nearby public park), or create up-to-date science labs. It could not support needed financial aid for all of the students who were admitted to college but could not afford to go. In these grim years, field trips and college trips were also canceled, along with anything that could be considered an "extra."

All of the school's resources went into supporting class sizes and advisories that were as small as could be managed on the dwindling funds, so while some high schools increased class sizes to 40, EPAA managed classes of no more than 30 students and advisories of under 20. Salaries were frozen for a number of years (although supplemented with additional stipends by a federal School Improvement Grant). It was the teachers' judgment that their greatest chance for success was to continue to maintain a personalized environment to the greatest extent possible.

## A NEW DAY IN CALIFORNIA

It is important to note that these conditions have finally changed in California. Under the leadership of Governor Jerry Brown, elected in 2010, a new set of revenue sources for public education was established through Proposition 30, and a progressive new funding formula, allocating resources based on student needs, was passed in 2012. The new Local Control Funding Formula, launched in the 2013–2014 school year, eliminated most categorical programs and created a weighted student-funding approach that adds 20% to the state dollars for low-income students, English learners, and children in foster care; it increases that extra weighting in districts with high concentrations of such children. The funds are being phased in over an 8-year period.

Accountability also has changed. Local communities are engaged in budgeting the funds and setting educational goals through their Local Control Accountability Plans. In these plans districts must show how they are targeting students in need while also addressing eight state educational priorities regarding student learning opportunities and a range of outcomes. Test scores are only a small part of the story: Schools and districts also will focus on graduation rates, supporting students to take college-ready and career-ready sequences of study, and may include local assessments—such as performance tasks or portfolios—along with traditional measures.

The state has eliminated the old California Standards Tests as it has adopted Common Core State Standards and the Smarter Balanced assessments in English language arts and mathematics, which focus more on higher-order thinking skills. The State Board has signaled that it will no longer use an Academic Performance Index to rank schools, but will develop a dashboard of multiple measures that provides transparency around indicators addressing both state and local priorities. And contrary to the zero tolerance policies that were set in law and that led to widespread school exclusion, especially for students of color, the state is now reporting suspension and expulsion rates with an expectation that schools will reduce those strategies in favor of restorative justice practices that keep students in school and support social-emotional learning for personal and social responsibility.

Finally, in October 2011, California's AB131, the Dream Act, was signed into law, allowing undocumented students who had spent 3 years in a California high school and graduated to apply for California state financial aid for college.

In this brave new world, the practices of schools like East Palo Alto Academy will be better supported and more likely to be refined and emulated than when the school—and others like it—existed in a hostile policy environment.

## ESSENTIAL PRACTICES

Throughout all of these changes, an important continuity is that the school has never wavered from its mission to serve the youth of East Palo Alto by enabling them to learn 21st-century skills, to be prepared for college and careers, and to graduate and attend college at high rates. EPAA has always used a completely open admissions process and has adamantly resisted any kind of competitive process. As a public charter school, EPAA has always been open to all students, without admission requirements or tuition charges. Students are admitted by lottery when applications exceed the capacity of the school site.

The East Palo Alto Academy Year End Report for 2013–2014 described the keys to the school's continued success:

> EPAA uses a combination of programs and approaches, refined over more than a decade of practice, always remembering that each student brings a unique set of strengths and interests. The foundation of the EPAA experience includes these building blocks: college counseling that begins in ninth grade; dynamic social-emotional interventions; high levels of personal attention through small class sizes and Advisory; and instructional practice informed by Stanford research across multiple disciplines.
>
> EPAA offers social-emotional support through four avenues: a dedicated social worker who meets individually with students and leads support groups; weekly individual counseling with the Lucile Packard Children's Hospital mental health team of interns; self-regulation and mindfulness coaching for both students and teachers. . . . This year, 186 students—more than half of the student population—were referred for mental health services by a teacher or staff member, with 62 students engaged in ongoing counseling services.

After more than a dozen years of roll-up-the-sleeves work, five key elements have proved essential to the school's sustainability and success:

- A college-focused curriculum with academic supports
- Authentic, high-engagement instruction coupled with performance-based assessment
- Social-emotional learning and supports
- Personalization and a well-developed advisory system
- Collaborative professional engagement

Below we describe what these look like.

## A College-Focused Curriculum with Academic Supports

Since EPAA's inception, each incoming 9th-grade class has demonstrated reading and mathematics skills around the 4th- or 5th-grade level on average, with a range from kindergarten to the 12th-grade level. Many recent immigrants have had little schooling in their country of origin and have no English when they first arrive in high school. And transfer students are often behind academically, both in their skill levels and high school credits.

Wherever students begin in their learning, EPAA has supported them to complete high school and to connect to college entrance and viable careers.

The college-going emphasis may seem counterintuitive, given the school's commitment to admit the full range of students from a high-needs community. However, paired with a commitment to a highly engaging curriculum and a belief that development and learning can be accelerated with the right supports, the college-going focus becomes a motivator, rather than an insurmountable barrier for most students. There are a number of elements needed to attain this goal, however.

*Curriculum Supports.* From their first day in the school, all students are enrolled in a curriculum that can enable them to achieve college readiness. Supports for succeeding at college-preparatory courses are many. All freshmen take a double-block course in English language arts, and most also take a course in academic literacy that helps them further develop basic reading and writing skills. All teachers, after a 2-year professional development program of common readings, professional learning, and coaching in literacy provided by a well-known literacy expert, are prepared to use common literacy development practices across the curriculum. A department-wide effort in English developed a 4-year vertical writing program that includes common rubrics for use across the curriculum.

Alongside algebra in 9th grade, students with skill gaps also take a Foundations math class, which combines targeted teaching to the areas their initial individual assessments suggest are important for them, combining skillful teaching with the use of an online learning tool that allows them to work at their own pace practicing skills in specific areas. Foundations students also may learn content for their algebra class ahead of time, thus permitting them to be ready in class and more confident about the learning process.

The school focuses its policies on supporting the students' ultimate success in learning, not on ranking, selecting, and sorting based on first attempts. Thus, one key principle is the opportunity for revision and mastery. Almost all major assignments are designed to ensure that students will receive feedback and revise their work. Multiple drafts of written work are expected, and generally students also can study further and retake tests to improve their performance. The overall grading policy reinforces this philosophy: If a student does not reach a passing level of work completion and quality in a given course, the student receives an Incomplete in the class initially, until work is revised to a level where it meets a passing standard. If the needed work is not made up within 1 year, the Incomplete reverts to a grade of No Credit. However, at any time through the end of high school, a student can revise and resubmit major assignments from previously taken classes to raise a grade or to bring up a No Credit to a passing grade. The new grade replaces the previous grade, rather than being averaged in. It is the ultimate learning that counts.

A summer school program open to all students each year allows them to retake classes with which they have struggled, redo specific assignments to improve their grades and thereby their college eligibility, or take challenging Early College courses. Students experience high rates of success because of the low class load, time to relearn skills, and personalized attention. All of EPAA's incoming 9th-graders are invited to participate in a Summer Bridge program, which gives students a 1-week introduction to the culture and norms of EPAA and helps build connections among entering freshmen before the start of the school year. Summer Bridge instruction builds community; acclimates incoming freshmen to the school's resources and staff; reinforces the positive school culture; and engages students in beautifying the facility through mural art and other projects, so that students develop a sense of pride in their campus.

***Instructional Supports.*** Because many students enter high school lacking the academic skills necessary to master the content, teachers use a variety of strategies to engage them and accelerate their learning. These include groupwork using the strategies of Complex Instruction,[6] which actively engage all students in learning challenging content together, using specific group roles, and tapping multiple intelligences through relevant and complex tasks. Kagan's Cooperative Learning Structures[7] also are used to encourage participation in a wide variety of ways—from tossing a ball around the room to encourage participation, to having students share ideas with others in one-on-one timed interviews.

Students also communicate with one another on a daily basis through activities such as Think Pair Shares and whole-group discussions, which are scaffolded. For instance, students are provided with agree/disagree statements about a certain topic, such as human nature, and they have to choose an option of strongly agreeing, agreeing, disagreeing, or strongly disagreeing. Students write a couple of sentences using the sentence starter, "I _____ with this statement because . . . " and are asked to give examples.

By structuring language use and communication, these strategies are key in engaging and supporting English language learners. Teachers also use a "sheltered" approach to instruction, including the Sheltered Instruction Observation Protocol (SIOP). This includes the use of visuals to present content and notes; a strong emphasis on the incorporation of reading, writing, speaking, and listening; and strategies for building background knowledge (including the connection between student experiences and the material being taught). All students also are taught how to engage in Socratic seminars, data analysis, and document-based questions that challenge them to think critically and creatively about a research question.

Technology is used to support learning in a number of ways. For example, through the use of teacher-recorded videos, students can watch and, as needed, re-watch a video of their teacher's explanations and translate their understanding into graphic organizers and other demonstrations of their mastery. In addition to enabling a one-to-one ratio of students to computers, technology is used to enliven instruction. Teachers use ActivBoards in classrooms to support an interactive environment. Students can annotate items at the front of the room, vote on answers and ideas, see trends in perspective, and so much more. In math classes, students use graphing calculators across the curriculum, as well as graphing software to show their work. Students also build their software skills in a variety of ways and settings, including regular word processing, as well as website development and presentations using PowerPoint and Keynote.

Students are taught how to cite web-based evidence using resources such as EZBIB.com and Citationmachine.net. In addition, students use computers and the Internet to reflect on their own strengths and room for improvement as learners and to evaluate courses. In World History, the teacher administers a student questionnaire each semester, using SurveyMonkey, asking students to evaluate their own progress as well as the teacher's. Incorporating these activities gives students the chance to self-monitor and reflect on their strengths and areas of growth as learners. Teachers have developed their own websites to keep students and their families informed. Additionally, parents have access to their students' grades and specific assignments in PowerSchool, the online grading system.

Jigsaw teaching strategies (in which students are each asked to learn one part of a body of content and then teach one another in small groups) support students in taking ownership of their learning. When a student becomes an expert in an area of learning, he or she actively engages in the learning process and becomes accountable for learning. In biology, for example, students split up into different expert groups, in which they research evidence for evolution from the perspective of embryology, anatomy, paleontology, and geography. Later, they share their evidence with their jigsaw groups, in which they discuss and determine which area of science provides them with the most convincing evidence.

Similarly, in Government, students are assigned differentiated readings centered on a research question. Each student reads a different document and is taught how to collect evidence that supports the answer to the question by using a quote chart to scaffold claims and evidence. In math classes, students participate in the "Circle Activity" or "Snake Activity." When reviewing for an upcoming unit exam, students begin the activity in pairs. These "home pairs" become experts on their given problem. Then students rotate to practice all types of problems that will be seen on the unit assessment. In addition to being an effective review strategy, this structure builds a sense of personal and social responsibility.

***Early College.*** The Early College program, which provides college courses to students while they are still in high school, demonstrates to students that they *can* succeed in college-level coursework, while expanding the offerings possible in a small school—including a well-developed health services pathway. Virtually all seniors take at least one college class before graduating, and nearly half of all EPAA students are enrolled in one or more college classes in any given year. A member of the school faculty plus AmeriCorps volunteers support students in keeping up with their classes and learning college course-taking strategies.

Partnerships with a wide array of nonprofit organizations offer additional support for students, such as the Foundation for a College Education, College Track, One EPA, and the Boys and Girls Club of the Peninsula. Students may receive mentoring, additional opportunities to explore colleges, and application and financial aid support, among other services.

## Authentic Curriculum and Performance-Based Assessment

As part of its new wave of reform, California adopted the Common Core State Standards (CCSS) in English language arts and mathematics, and the Next Generation Science Standards in science, which EPAA is now involved in implementing. Many practices consistent with the new standards have long been in place in the school. For example, engagement in reading, writing, listening, speaking, and research has been part of the English language arts curriculum, while many of the mathematical practices expressed in the CCSS, such as problem solving and modeling, have been central to mathematics teaching. The Math Department adopted the College Preparatory Mathematics (CPM) curriculum because it fosters learning by combining project-based inductive reasoning with more traditional deductive reasoning. Inquiry-oriented science was always part of the EPAA curriculum as well, although it had been abandoned in many other schools.

*Curriculum.* Curriculum planning to deepen this work involves the development of curriculum maps and/or unit plans to create yearlong courses of study that emphasize the interconnectedness of topics within and across classes. Teachers approach curriculum through the lens of student discovery and project-based learning. Professional development around project-based learning has helped teachers develop lessons that scaffold for complex thinking so students can construct new knowledge and convey it in multiple media. Using backwards planning to design curriculum, teachers generate essential questions from the standards that help students apply learning to the real world. Based on the goals established, teachers think about the types of performance assessments they would like to use.

In the English Department, teachers use a variety of resources and strategies to engage students in writing, analyzing, and reflecting. The culminating assessment of the nonfiction unit asks students to produce a pamphlet on a public health topic that requires students to research, evaluate source credibility, and use persuasive techniques. In their research, students look for information that will appeal to their audience's emotions (pathos) and logic (logos) while evaluating the source's credibility (ethos). After the pamphlets are published, students distribute them in their communities (at community events, in supermarket parking lots, etc.). Finally, students write business letters to send to key stakeholders along with copies of their pamphlets. In many cases, students receive responses from the organizations and people to whom they write. Many students received letters from the Mayor of East Palo Alto in which she thanked them and commended them on their ideas for enhancing health through after-school programs, drug rehabilitation services, and fitness events in the community.

Because EPAA graduates must be able to communicate through the arts, technology, and multiple languages, teachers give students practice in these forms early on. For example, freshmen engage in a variety of performances, including presentation of a Shakespearean scene. Students write poetry to present to their families and community members at Freshmen Poetry Night. As a final component of this project, they reflect on their writing, engaging in the practice of identifying audience and purpose in writing.

Performances also are integrated throughout the year in arts classes, which serve 9th through 12th grade, including poetry, group skits, solo presentations, monologues, and speech performances. The Spanish Department emphasizes authentic learning through a series of projects, often connected to culturally relevant events and performances that are organized by students for the broader community: *Cinco de Mayo* performances, a cultural mini-fair in recognition of Hispanic Heritage Awareness Day, *El Día de las Madres* celebration in May, and *El Día de los Muertos* in November.

In history, the approach is to teach students to think like a historian. The curriculum is designed around the idea of multiple perspectives. In 10th grade, for example, students complete a research project on the Holocaust by doing research on the United States Holocaust Memorial Museum website and writing a research paper on a related topic. Students also create a character journal for Elie Wiesel's memoir *Night* and integrate their learning in both history and English classes. In addition, students take part in WebQuests, where they are assigned websites to navigate from which they collect information to answer a historical research question. As part of the process, students are exposed to different multimedia sources related to the topic.

The Mural, Music, and Arts Program (MMAP), a nonprofit program in East Palo Alto, offers a wide range of courses and programs to EPAA students during the instructional day and after school, as well as over the summer. These include working with students to design and paint a set of large graffiti-style murals on the campus, with the goal of deterring gang graffiti and inspiring positive creativity in students. The school saw a drastic reduction in the amount of gang-related graffiti on campus as a result.

In addition, MMAP introduced Silk-Screening with a Goal (SWAG). SWAG, an urban term that is associated with having confidence and swagger, engaged students in designing sweatshirts and t-shirts that reflected positive imagery and EPAA "Bulldog" pride, so named because of the school's mascot. SWAG has become an integral part of Summer Bridge. The rising 9th-graders design bulldog and class sweatshirts and t-shirts, with MMAP's support, to build unity and spirit within each new incoming class. Through small group-work activities, art projects, and team-building exercises, students explore culture, identity, and creativity through artistic means. Their expression culminates in the creation of apparel, performance art (e.g., spoken-word poetry), a colorful acrylic mural, the inspiring graffiti mural mentioned above, and an inclusive unveiling celebration, which stimulates a strong feeling of pride on the campus and in the community.

***Exhibitions.*** The exhibitions required for graduation have been adapted over time to become increasingly relevant and authentic. For example, teachers adapted the 9th-grade algebra exhibition to incorporate more real-life situations such as problems involving velocity, money and interest, and construction. After completing their work on a problem they have selected, students create a PowerPoint presentation that displays multiple representations of the original problem, highlighting the slope and y-intercepts in each of them to show how they are all related.

In the geometry exhibition, "Flip This House," students first design their own house, with specifications on floor size, wall height, and ceiling type. Using those dimensions, they need to then find the most cost-efficient way to decorate the home, based on area for flooring, surface area for painting, and volume for air-conditioning units, choosing among multiple options. They also have the option to draw or build a model of their house.

In biology, students select a topic, formulate a question of interest, and then undertake a scientific investigation to figure out the answer. After they write up their findings into a report, they create a poster that displays the question, inquiry, evidence, and conclusions, which they present to a panel of judges.

Juniors select and research a social movement, summarizing the historical context, interpreting the causes and effects, and formulating a critical perspective regarding the success or failure of the movement, based on their research. EPAA students are partnered with an undergraduate Stanford student who helps them research primary and secondary sources using resources at the university, such as the Greene Library. The college students serve as mentors throughout the writing, editing, and revision process of the exhibition.

The senior exhibition also was revised, as a research and service-learning project, to allow students to take their learning into the real world. Each student researches the history of a social issue, including its causes and current issues, while working at an organization that addresses the issue, to gain relevant and authentic perspective on the issue in the world today. The papers the students write are informed by both secondary research and their personal investigation into the issue and its potential resolution.

Every grade-level exhibition, scored with the Five Habits rubric (see Chapter 5), additionally requires a student self-evaluation. Students are asked to reflect on what they have learned and also on the metacognitive processes accompanying their learning. This opportunity provides a powerful way for students to reflect on their learning and plan ahead. In addition, EPAA teachers use student self-evaluations as a critical feedback loop to gain clarity about meeting their curricular goals in every class.

## Social-Emotional Learning and Support

EPAA has always included social-emotional learning in its curriculum, through explicit teaching and assessment of personal and social responsibility in the Five Habits, through the emphasis on productive groupwork as an instructional strategy, and through the skills that are acquired in project-based learning. One of the Stanford faculty put it this way:

> You can see [social-emotional learning] when a group of students come together to solve a hard problem, to figure out how to do research, how to do inquiry, how to investigate, how to put ideas together, how to figure out which ideas have the most grounding, how to present what they've done . . . these students need to do a lot of socially intelligent work. They have to figure out how to relate to one another, how to divide tasks, how to solve problems, how to run into dead ends, then pick up the pieces, reorient, and go in a new direction. All of that develops young people's abilities to be socially capable, emotionally capable, and, in the long run, also intellectually capable. This kind of project-based work forms the backbone of how we've designed the learning environment at East Palo Alto Academy.

Over the years, work on social-emotional learning and support has become more comprehensive. Residents of East Palo Alto experience all of the mental health needs associated with the stresses of community poverty, unemployment, crime, gang violence, and lack of social services, as well as limited family resources.

The acute needs presented by students—for counseling and treatment for emotional disturbances, depression, post-trauma stresses (many have experienced violence both in their home countries and in their new community), substance abuse prevention and treatment—have been addressed through a free health van available once every 2 weeks; a social worker who offers group and individual counseling, as well as services to families; and mental health services from Stanford's Lucile Packard Hospital. Approximately 64% of students at EPAA are referred for mental health services. Many participate in support groups geared to issues related to grief, recent immigration, impulse control, and teens' experiences as young parents.

In an effort to create a "trauma-sensitive" school environment, EPAA has sought to build a program of social-emotional learning to augment the mental health services needed for acute situations. In addition to the focus on teaching personal and social responsibility, curriculum in advisory has helped students learn to recognize, talk about, and manage their emotions, and to develop skills for conflict resolution. Teachers have received special training in classroom management that supports a trauma-sensitive environment.

More recently, the school has added self-regulation coaching for both students and teachers, implemented in advisory classes and some special electives, made possible by a multidimensional Mindfulness program. Students describe this work as very helpful in their lives:

> Maybe it will not necessarily solve your problems, but it will give you strength and the open mind you need to deal with everything you are going through. This class has helped me deal with my problems.

> This class is really helpful for me. The things that we do in this class help me in so many different ways. I've learned how to control my anger and not let it affect me; I've learned how to listen to my breaths.

> At first I didn't think meditating EVERYDAY would be fun, but it really got me through things! I have a very bad temper and mindfulness class has helped me to check myself more! I will take what I have learned from this class, and continue to make it a part of my everyday life. I enjoy doing breathing exercises and have even taught others!

The concern for social-emotional learning also is reflected in the school's approach to student discipline. In addition to the opportunities encouraged through the FICA process for students to reflect on situations and find ways to make amends (see Chapter 3), the school has developed a restorative justice program. When two students are having a conflict, a staff member trained in restorative justice meets with them and serves as a mediator. Each student has the opportunity to air his or her grievances, while the staff member repeats back to the students what they expressed in order to clarify their concerns. Then a dialogue ensues, moderated by the staff member, until the students agree on a reasonable resolution. This empowers the students not only to feel heard, but to develop a new conflict resolution strategy that they may use with other peers and perhaps even with their family.

Altogether, these strategies not only have resulted in a calm, safe, and emotionally supportive campus environment, but they also have given students tools to use to be centered, interpersonally effective, and resourceful in seeking needed support throughout their lives.

## Personalization

A small school makes it easier to know what individual students need, but much more is required to meet those needs. A cornerstone at EPAA has always been the advisory program, described in Chapter 3. Each advisor meets daily with his or her group of 15 to 18 students, getting to know the work habits, aspirations, and concerns of individual students, as well as their families. Within the advisory, the teachers create a family, teach social-emotional skills, and advocate for their students if they encounter problems at home or at school. The advisors track weekly progress in getting homework and major assignments completed, along with annual progress toward meeting college requirements. Working with the college counselor, advisors guide students individually toward a postgraduation plan that best suits each student's goals, aptitudes, and achievements.

A key role of the advisor is to be a positive link to families, helping to get a common set of understandings and supports operating at home and at school for each student. A key element of this work is the student-led conference between parents or guardians and the advisor, which occurs at least twice a year. Students set personal, academic, and school-to-career goals; measure the degree to which goals were met; and report their progress in a conference with their own parent or guardian and advisor each semester. This process allows students to take personal ownership of their academic accomplishments and develop metacognitive skills about their own learning. On a smaller scale, some advisors also have students set weekly goals for themselves, which may be revisited at the next weekly check-in.

The student-led conferences create glue between student, parent, and advisor. The meetings take place in the first 6–8 weeks of each semester, and the student "leads" the meeting. In this meeting, the student reflects on one class assignment in which he or she has succeeded. Helpful sentence starters are provided for the students, such as:

- I would like to begin by telling you about one of my classes. The class I'm going to talk about is . . .
- I think that the most important ideas, concepts, and skills we have learned in this class are . . .

- Two things that I now understand deeply because of this class are . . .
- In this class we have worked on many assignments and projects. One that I'm proud of is . . .
- In this assignment we were asked to . . .
- I am proud of this assignment because . . .
- This assignment shows evidence that I am learning and achieving quality work because . . .
- Although I'm learning, I know that there are still places where I can grow. One thing I want to improve in all of my classes is . . .
- I will help myself to improve in this area by . . .
- I would like to ask you (parent/guardian) to help me improve in this area by . . .
- I would like to ask my teachers to help me improve in this area by . . .

Additionally, the student, teacher, and parent/guardian fill out and then sign an "action plan" form, which includes two columns for strengths and challenges, and a third column for the action plan to address challenges and promote success. This in-depth reflection and accountability process empowers students, who gain increasing self-awareness on both a personal and an academic level. Parents feel equally empowered and informed of their student's academic status, and joined in partnership with teachers. In this way, the basis for personalized learning is established and can be pursued through all of the other avenues the school offers.

## Collaborative Professional Engagement

Since its inception, East Palo Alto Academy has been a Stanford University partner school, participating in educational research and providing student teaching opportunities for the Stanford Teacher Education Program and collaboration between university faculty and high school faculty. Stanford offers substantial resources and expertise to the school, ranging from learning opportunities for students and teachers to guidance on curriculum construction, pedagogical strategies, and teaching materials.

The school faculty is deeply involved in school decisionmaking and works collaboratively in both grade-level teams—which attend to the needs of students who are shared—and department teams—which attend to curriculum planning and the design and orchestration of exhibitions and other performance assessments that reflect disciplinary goals. In recent years, teachers have engaged in peer observation to further learn from one another. Building shared planning time and weekly decisionmaking time into the schedule, along with multiple opportunities for joint learning and collaboration, is one way that a collegial culture has been maintained. It is the engine that propels the work forward in the face of daily challenges. As Irene Castillon, one of the more recent STEP graduates to teach at EPAA, described it:

> EPAA does not feel like my workplace, it feels like home. Having grown up in East Los Angeles, the student profile of the students that attend EPAA very much mirrors the population of the high school I attended. However, unlike the high school I attended, EPAA sets high expectations for all students, [and] everyone on staff believes in fostering the potential of every student regardless of race, class, or gender. While I wish that there were an EPAA when I was growing up, I am immensely grateful that I have the opportunity to be part of a community as an educator and as a lifelong learner. My experience working at EPAA has solidified that teaching is truly a reciprocal process where lessons can be learned from my colleagues, my administrators, and my greatest teachers—my students.

Ultimately, where educators can freely learn from one another and their students in an environment that fosters growth rather than fear, there true education can flourish.

## POLICY IMPLICATIONS

Designing schools that serve low-income students of color well is not impossible. EPAA is certainly not the first or only such school. In fact, it learned from the pioneering efforts of others, especially those started in New York City as part of the Coalition of Essential Schools and the Annenberg Challenge, and networks that have since spread from these, like the New York Performance Standards Consortium, the Center for Collaborative Education, the Boston Pilot Schools, and the International High Schools Network.

However, to create such schools on a much wider scale, we must construct a policy environment that routinely encourages successful practices with respect to school design, educator investments, curriculum and assessment, and funding.

### School Design

EPAA and the models it built upon benefited from policies that encouraged the creation of new small high schools designed to offer the personalization and instructional supports needed for successful learning. Both the small schools grants once offered by the federal government and the Early College grants once offered by the Gates Foundation supported many schools' costs associated with planning a new design, recruiting and developing staff, securing facilities and equipment, and growing to a level that supports scale economies. Creating new approaches to school organization requires the kind of venture capital that allows start-up companies to reinvent both technologies and ways of doing business. Unfortunately, both of those sources of funding, which stimulated many successful reforms, were discontinued.

New district-run schools, as well as charters, sometimes take advantage of their start-up phase to think anew about how to organize education to become more effective. However, this is not a given, and even those that want to move beyond the century-old factory model need considerable support in learning how to do so from those who have begun to invent new approaches. The goal is not only to support a vanguard group of uniquely situated schools, but to enable all schools eventually to adopt practices that will be more successful for all of their students. Significant ongoing financial support for creating and sustaining new-model schools will be needed if the designs that support student success are to continue to be developed and spread. State and federal governments also should create a means for documenting and sharing effective school organizational and instructional practices through clearinghouses and networks that allow schools to learn from one another.

A challenge in scaling up more effective school designs is that the century-old model of school organization that has shaped most high schools is now reinforced by a geological dig of regulations that do not always produce the most effective forms of education. Most states' regulatory framework for high schools—as enacted through curriculum and testing rules; assumptions made by categorical funding streams about how staffing, programs, and materials are managed; and approaches to professional development—has not yet shifted to accommodate or encourage the design choices made by these new schools. Thus, new schools also may need assistance from school boards, union leaders, and other policymakers to change state and local rules rooted in old traditions governing staffing, work organization, and funding policies that create unintentional barriers.

One critical aspect of the governance problem is the extent to which the education system relies on bureaucratic or professional forms of accountability—that is, the extent to which the state attempts to create regulations that prescribe and manage what schools do, or, alternatively, strives to develop knowledgeable educators who can be trusted to make responsible decisions about practice. The ongoing tug of war between bureaucratic control and autonomy cannot ultimately be resolved without investments in school capacity and professional knowledge and skill. The autonomies regarding hiring, professional development, curriculum, and assessment that innovative schools rely on to construct more powerful learning environments are not likely to be granted to most schools unless there is a high degree of confidence on the part of the public that defensible decisions will be made. In all professions, this confidence rests on the knowledge, skills, and commitments professionals bring to their work.

Investments in schools' capacities and changes in the current regulatory and funding structure for education will need to include, at a minimum:

- Teacher preparation and development to enable the kinds of pedagogical strategies and advisement responsibilities teachers have taken on in these new models
- School leader recruitment and development to help principals learn how to design and manage organizations in which instructional leadership, organizational design, and change management skills are critically important
- Support for a system of curriculum, assessment, and instruction that encourages the development of 21st-century skills and enables a curriculum that is intellectually rigorous as well as socially and practically relevant
- Funding streams that are adequate to meet students' needs and sufficiently flexible to enable strategic investments in innovative approaches at the school level

## Educator Investments

EPAA has succeeded in part because of its ability to recruit and develop strong teachers. However, there is a substantial shortage of teachers who are armed with the kinds of skills needed for the sophisticated pedagogies used in schools like this one and who are available to teach in urban districts. In high-achieving countries, the costs of teacher preparation are assumed by the government, so that all can afford high-quality training. Often teachers repay this investment by pledging to teach in public schools for a certain number of years. This long-term investment pays off when all teachers have the skills needed for success, and when schools benefit from a stable, committed teaching force. In the U.S. policy context, where teachers typically must go into debt to enter a field that will pay less than other college graduates earn, there is high variability in the amount and quality of preparation they receive, and those teaching in high-poverty communities typically have received the least training. While EPAA could tap the nearby Stanford program, it also struggled to recruit in shortage fields. New incentives are needed to change these widespread conditions.

Once teachers are working in schools, they need ongoing high-quality opportunities for continual learning focused on addressing concrete problems of practice in the content areas they teach and with the specific students they serve. While some states have initiated, at various times, programs to address these concerns, the programs often have come and gone with budget shifts, creating a yo-yo diet of initiatives rather than a steady set of policy supports for developing high-quality teaching in all schools. To address these needs, federal and state governments should:

- *Provide service scholarships for high-quality preservice preparation for candidates who will teach in high-needs schools.* This should include, at a minimum, creating or expanding service scholarships and forgivable loans for individuals who prepare to teach in low-income schools, with special incentives for high-needs teachers with language skills and content backgrounds in short supply.
- *Incentivize improvements in teacher education* to build a foundation in the skills that teachers most need in order to provide rigorous, relevant, and responsive education to diverse students, including new English learners and those with learning differences. This includes the knowledge and skills for teaching an authentic, hands-on curriculum that is engaging and relevant. Program funding should incentivize new designs, such as the strong yearlong clinical preparation offered by universities partnered with professional development schools, like that offered by STEP, and those engaged in residencies with high-needs districts.[8]
- *Provide adequate, stable support for high-quality professional development and collaboration time for educators.* As all high-achieving nations do, our federal and state governments should fund learning opportunities in aspects of teaching that teachers need in order to be effective. This includes increasing support for the sustained, curriculum-focused professional learning institutes, as well as coaching supports that help teachers put ideas into practice. Support also should include time for teachers to learn and plan together, as is common in other nations but rare in the United States. Schools should have the flexibility to determine how to use this time throughout the year.

In addition to having adequately prepared teachers, schools also need well-prepared principals who can be strong instructional leaders who understand how to support good instructional practice. Principals also need to know how to plan professional development, redesign school organizations, and manage a change process. In addition, they need to know how to organize staffing and teacher time to reduce class size, create teams, incorporate advisory systems, and provide time for collaboration and professional learning opportunities. To develop such leaders, research[9] suggests that states and districts should:

- *Proactively recruit dynamic future leaders into the principal pipeline* by subsidizing high-quality preparation, including paid internships under the guidance of expert principals who effectively lead schools serving students of color well, for candidates who have strong instructional and leadership capacities and who reflect today's students.
- *Provide support for systematically improving principal preparation programs,* specifically organizing clinical experiences and content that prepare principals to lead in schools that are organized in new, more productive ways to serve diverse students well.

## Curriculum and Assessment Policies

Schools like EPAA develop rigorous, engaging, and relevant curriculum that prepares their students for the hands-on, minds-on learning they will need to succeed in college and in 21st-century careers. The schools' forward-looking curricula rely both on redefining traditional high school requirements—grounded in the century-old conception of preparation articulated by the Committee of Ten in 1892—and on using challenging performance-based assessments that demand applications of knowledge, provide students and staff with timely feedback about students' progress and success, and support revision to meet standards of quality. When they are collectively scored—as is the case with portfolios or performance tasks presented at exhibitions juried by teachers and external judges—the assessments also construct shared ideas about what constitutes good work and conversations about how to improve curriculum and teaching.

The performance assessments used by schools like EPAA resemble those used in high-achieving nations like Finland, Hong Kong, Singapore, Canada, and Australia, which use local assessments that require students to conduct research and scientific investigations, solve complex real-world problems, and defend their ideas orally and in writing.[10] By asking students to show what they know through direct applications of knowledge, and by embedding these assessments in the process of teaching and learning, these nations' assessment systems—like those of the schools in this study—promote serious intellectual work. While EPAA, and schools like it, must attend to the demands of state accountability systems, they do not find that current multiple-choice tests promote the kind of 21st-century learning that enables students to find and use resources, analyze and synthesize information, produce and explain ideas, apply knowledge to novel situations, use new technologies, and work productively with others.

If more schools are to create strong curriculum that is oriented to their students' and society's future, as well as assessments that prepare students for the genuine expectations of college and workplaces of the 21st century, state and local policies will need to evolve to support these efforts. States should take the following steps:

- *Rethink traditional curriculum requirements to more fully acknowledge modern conceptions of learning and curriculum, including interdisciplinary and applied learning that incorporates new technologies.*
- *Redesign assessment systems to better evaluate and encourage applications of knowledge and skill in performance assessments at the state and local levels, including appropriate assessments for English language learners.* In addition to allowing students to demonstrate their knowledge in more open-ended, authentic ways, these assessments should be used for information and improvement, not for sanctions or penalties, which distort school practice and the interpretations of results.

## Funding Policies

The ability of schools like EPAA to provide a rigorous, relevant, and responsive education to low-income students of color requires them to raise additional funds beyond those the state provides. This is particularly necessary in a high-cost-of-living state that spends far less than the national average on its schools. Such schools spend these funds on resources that are necessary to provide a high-quality education—hiring additional core staff, funding professional development costs, and purchasing the kinds of books and materials they need. In California, as in many other states, schools serving low-income children have received less in the way of resources than other, more affluent districts, as inequities in spending have grown for more than 2 decades.

Not only do many schools serving low-income students lack sufficient funds to provide what their students need, but they also lack flexibility in using the funds that they do have to direct the resources so as to best serve their students. This is typically due to many states' fragmented funding streams associated with dozens of categorical programs that are often not well enough funded to provide additional services, but require complicated tracking and monitoring. This overly prescribed funding gets in the way of schools carrying out their vision and undermines the provision of meaningful supports for students. It also can create a set of diffuse, unglued programs that detract from a core instructional focus. To better address the needs of currently underserved students, states and the federal government should (as California recently has):

- *Increase funding for schools and make it more equitable by establishing weighted student funding formulas* in which funds follow the child, and additional funding is allocated for students with the greatest needs, thus ensuring that funds are distributed more equitably.

- ***Create less fragmented funding streams.*** With the exception of major categorical programs intended to address specific population needs (e.g., special education, English language learner funding), governments should reduce the number of small categorical programs and roll monies into core funding through the weighted student formula, so that schools have more flexibility to align funding to their instructional missions in ways that are more efficient and, ultimately, effective.

## CONCLUSION

This story offers one vivid example of how a high school can interrupt the status quo by providing opportunities for low-income students of color to become critical thinkers and leaders for the future. Unless policy systems change, however, such schools will remain anomalies, rather than harbingers of the future. Creating a system that supports the learning of all students is not impossible. It will take clarity of vision and purposeful, consistent action to create a web of supportive, mutually reinforcing elements. In particular, dismantling the institutionalized inequities that feed the racial, socioeconomic, and linguistic achievement gap will require substantive policy changes in recruiting, inducting, and supporting teachers and principals; expanding our conceptions of curriculum and assessment; rethinking funding strategies; and opening access to higher education. These kinds of changes could create a context in which schools like EPAA may become the norm rather than the exception, and all students, regardless of race, income, or zip code, achieve the right to learn.

# Five Community Habits Rubric

**HABIT 1: PERSONAL RESPONSIBILITY**

| | Exceeding the Standard | Meeting the Standard | Approaching the Standard | Emerging Competency | No Evidence |
|---|---|---|---|---|---|
| **Be Punctual**<br>Attendance<br>Tardies | Student is present, on time and is fully prepared to begin. | Student is present and comes on time. | Prior accommodations are made when tardy or absent. | Student is late but is able to complete required tasks. | |
| **Prepare**<br>Homework | Student is prepared beyond the requirements of the assignment and is ready to overcome unexpected challenges. | Student comes prepared by meeting all requirements and completing all aspects of the assignment. | Student comes prepared by completing basic requirements. | Student shows some preparation. | |
| **Produce and Participate**<br>Classwork<br>Class Participation | Student completes work, stretching the student's ability and going beyond requirements in quality and participation. | Student completes work that represents the student's potential.<br><br>Student participates independently to advance learning. | Student completes work that approaches the student's potential.<br><br>Student participates when required. | Student completes minimal work.<br><br>Student participates when required and asked. | |

**HABIT 2: SOCIAL RESPONSIBILITY**

| | Exceeding the Standard | Meeting the Standard | Approaching the Standard | Emerging Competency | No Evidence |
|---|---|---|---|---|---|
| **Collaborate** Groupwork | Student follows group roles and norms throughout task, and plays a key leadership role in advancing group goals. | Student follows group roles and norms throughout task in order to advance group goals. | Student follows group roles and norms throughout task; doing so with more quality could advance group goals. | Student attempts to follow group roles and norms, and would be more successful if effort consistently supported group goals. | |
| **Interact** Classroom Behavior | Student acts and speaks respectfully even when faced with conflict. Personal and school property is treated appropriately, with safety in mind. Student moderates conflict and plays a key leadership role in moving class in a positive direction. | Student acts and speaks respectfully. Personal and school property is treated appropriately, with safety in mind. Student is a positive member of the classroom and avoids conflict. | Student acts and speaks respectfully or self-corrects when behavior, language, or use of property is inappropriate. Student is a bystander when conflict occurs, neither adding to nor detracting from the classroom environment. | Student attempts to act and speak respectfully and corrects his/her inappropriate behavior, language, and/or use of property when reminded. Student uses these experiences to improve his/her actions and/or language. | |
| **Build Community** Community Interactions | Student helps generate a positive view of school and creates healthy relationships with the community. | Student represents school in a positive way with appropriate behavior and use of language and property. | Student acts in a way that neither harms nor helps the relationship between the school and the community. | Student takes action to modify behavior when inappropriate in order to better represent the school. | |
| **Take Responsibility for Actions** Personal Honesty | Student takes responsibility for own actions, both good and bad, and recognizes the implications of actions. | Student takes responsibility for own actions, both good and bad. | Student takes partial responsibility for own actions. | Student denies responsibility for own actions, in particular actions that lead to negative outcomes. | |

## HABIT 3: CRITICAL AND CREATIVE THINKING

| | Exceeding the Standard | Meeting the Standard | Approaching the Standard | Emerging Competency | No Evidence |
|---|---|---|---|---|---|
| **Ask** Pose Problems | Student understands the problem and poses precise questions that clarify and simplify the problem. | Student defines the problem and poses questions that help clarify the problem. | Student defines some parts of the problem and poses questions that address the problem. | Student needs to define the problem or pose questions that address the problem. | |
| **Predict** Hypothesize Estimate Infer | Student uses imagination, experiences, and observations to make a logical and creative prediction. | Student uses available experiences and observations to make a logical prediction. | Student uses limited experiences and observations to make a partial prediction. | Student offers an illogical prediction. | |
| **Investigate** Gather and Organize Evidence | Student gathers detailed information from a wide variety of valid sources, organizes it into relevant categories, and accurately decides what information is most useful as evidence. | Student gathers information from a variety of valid sources, organizes it clearly, and decides what information is most useful as evidence. | Student gathers some information from a variety of sources and generally organizes it but without attention to the quality of the evidence. | Student needs to gather more information from a variety of sources, and/or organize it, and/or decide what information is most useful as evidence. | |
| **Answer** Analyze Synthesize Justify Imagine Create | Student creates significant new arguments, ideas, and theories based on a thorough analysis of the evidence. | Student creates new arguments, ideas, and theories based on a thorough analysis of the evidence. | Student creates new arguments, ideas, and theories based on an analysis of the evidence. | Student creates few new arguments, ideas, and theories based on a shallow analysis of the evidence. | |
| **Reflect** Logs Journals Dialogues | Student reflects independently and often, identifying areas of strength and weakness, and using the reflections to grow as a learner. | Student engages in self-reflection independently to identify areas of strength and weakness. | Student engages in self-reflection when required and identifies areas of strength and weakness. | Student completes reflections in a limited manner when required. | |

## HABIT 3: CRITICAL AND CREATIVE THINKING (continued)

| | Exceeding the Standard | Meeting the Standard | Approaching the Standard | Emerging Competency | No Evidence |
|---|---|---|---|---|---|
| **Connect** Make Connections and Implications Answer "So what?" | Student makes deep connections between his work and himself, his community, AND the world. | Student makes deep connections between her work and either herself, OR the world. | Student makes surface connections between his work and either himself, his community, or the world. | Student needs to make connections between her work and either herself, her community, or the world. | |
| **Revise** Seek Other Perspectives Revise work | Student independently seeks alternative perspectives and makes multiple revisions to clarify and advance thinking. | Student seeks alternative perspectives and makes revisions to ideas that clarify thinking. | Student seeks alternative perspectives and makes some revisions to ideas. | Student needs to seek alternative perspectives and/or make more revision to ideas. | |

## HABIT 4: APPLICATION OF KNOWLEDGE IN SUBJECT AREA
*TO BE CREATED BY EACH SUBJECT AREA*
Hold Content and Skills Constant

| | Exceeding the Standard | Meeting the Standard | Approaching the Standard | Emerging Competency | No Evidence |
|---|---|---|---|---|---|
| **Understand Content** Curriculum Standards (what to know) | Student shows extensive knowledge of all key concepts and content and is able to apply concepts to an unanticipated task or context. | Student shows complete understanding of most or all key concepts and content and is able to apply key concepts in a specific manner. | Student shows some understanding of many key concepts and much of the content. | Student shows limited understanding of key concepts and content. | |
| **Demonstrate Content Area Skills** Skills Specific to the Discipline (what to do) | Student demonstrates an independent and sophisticated mastery of all required skills, going beyond the requirements of the assignment and integrating other content area skills. | Student demonstrates proficient mastery of all required skills and works independently to accomplish the assignment. | Student demonstrates beginning mastery of skills and works independently to accomplish the assignment. | Student demonstrates beginning mastery of skills when guided by the teacher to accomplish the assignment. | |

## HABIT 5: COMMUNICATION

| | Exceeding the Standard | Meeting the Standard | Approaching the Standard | Emerging Competency | No Evidence |
|---|---|---|---|---|---|
| **Communicate Key Idea** | Student communicates main idea clearly. Main idea is provocative. | Student communicates main idea clearly. | Student communicates main idea. | Student needs to develop and clarify main idea. | |
| **Organize Thoughts** | Student has organized thoughts clearly and all parts flow. | Student has organized thoughts clearly and developed all required parts. | Student needs to reorganize thoughts for clarity and/or add missing parts. | Student needs to organize thoughts for clarity. | |
| **Present Ideas in Writing** | Student work has no grammatical/spelling errors. | Student work has few grammatical/spelling errors. | Student work is understandable despite grammatical/spelling errors. | Student work is difficult to understand due to grammatical/spelling errors. | |
| **Present Ideas Orally** | Student's eloquence and passion come across with his/her eye contact, body language, and voice. | Student uses appropriate eye contact, body language, and voice throughout presentation. | Student at times uses appropriate eye contact, body language, and/or voice. | Student needs to use appropriate eye contact, body language, and/or voice. | |
| **Present Ideas Visually** | Student presents key ideas in vivid, clear, and unique manner. | Student presents key ideas in vivid, clear manner. | Student presents key ideas. | Student needs to clarify the key ideas to present and determine how best to present those ideas. | |

# FICA Template

**Name:** _____

**Date:** _____

## FACTS

Details of what happened. Who was involved? What happened? What was YOUR role?

_____

_____

_____

_____

_____

_____

_____

## IMPACT

Who did your actions affect?

_____

_____

_____

_____

_____

_____

_____

## CONTEXT

What's the big picture? What is your history with the person(s) involved? Was this your first incident in this class?

_____

_____

_____

_____

_____

_____

_____

## ACTION

What will you do to resolve the problem? How will you make up any missing work? How will you behave differently in the future?

_____

_____

_____

_____

_____

_____

_____

# Summative Evaluation Rubric for Civil Rights Unit Final Essay

Name: _____ Title of Essay: _____

**Mark all criteria completed:** ___ Essay Outline

___ Essay (Rough Draft and Final Draft)

___ Bibliography

## HABIT 1: PERSONAL RESPONSIBILITY

|  | Exceeding the Standard | Meeting the Standard | Approaching the Standard | Emerging Competency | No Evidence |
|---|---|---|---|---|---|
| **6Be Prepared** <br> Turn in essay on time and complete all criteria | Student is prepared beyond the requirements of the assignment and is ready to overcome unexpected challenges. | Student comes prepared by meeting all requirements and completing all aspects of the assignment. | Student comes prepared by completing basic requirements. | Student shows some preparation. |  |
| **Be Productive and Participate** <br> Write multiple drafts of essay; attend office hours | Student completes work, stretching the student's ability and going beyond requirements in quality and participation. | Student completes work that represents the student's potential. <br><br> Student participates independently to advance learning. | Student completes work that approaches the student's potential. <br><br> Student participates when required. | Student completes minimal work. <br><br> Student participates when required and asked. |  |
| **Self-Reflect** <br> Complete the self-evaluation | Student engages in independent and frequent self-reflection, identifying areas of strength and weakness, and using the reflections to grow as a learner. | Student engages in self-reflection independently to identify areas of strength and weakness. | Student engages in self-reflection when required and identifies areas of strength and weakness. | Student completes reflections in a limited manner when required. |  |

**HABIT 3: CRITICAL AND CREATIVE THINKING**

| | Exceeding the Standard | Meeting the Standard | Approaching the Standard | Emerging Competency | No Evidence |
|---|---|---|---|---|---|
| **Investigate** Gather and organize evidence | Student gathers detailed information from a wide variety of valid sources, organizes it into relevant categories, and accurately decides what information is most useful as evidence. | Student gathers information from a variety of valid sources, organizes it clearly, and decides what information is most useful as evidence. | Student gathers some information from a variety of sources and generally organizes it but without attention to the quality of the evidence. | Student needs to gather more information from a variety of sources, and/or organize it, and/or decide what information is most useful as evidence. | |
| **Create** Use evidence to support a strong argument | Student creates significant new arguments, ideas, and theories based on a thorough analysis of the evidence. | Student creates new arguments, ideas, and theories based on a thorough analysis of the evidence. | Student creates new arguments, ideas, and theories based on an analysis of the evidence. | Student creates few new arguments, ideas, and theories based on a shallow analysis of the evidence. | |
| **Connect** Make connections and implications Answer "So what?" | Student makes deep connections between his work and himself, his community, AND the world. | Student makes deep connections between her work and either herself, her community, OR the world. | Student makes surface connections between his work and either himself, his community, or the world. | Student needs to make connections between her work and either herself, her community, or the world. | |

Summative Evaluation Rubric for Civil Rights Unit Final Essay

## HABIT 4: APPLICATION OF KNOWLEDGE

| | Exceeding the Standard | Meeting the Standard | Approaching the Standard | Emerging Competency | No Evidence |
|---|---|---|---|---|---|
| **Understand Content** — Civil Rights historical knowledge | Student shows extensive knowledge of all key concepts and is able to apply concepts to an unanticipated task or context. | Student shows complete understanding of most or all key concepts and is able to apply key concepts in a specific manner. | Student shows some understanding of many key concepts. | Student shows limited understanding of key concepts. | |
| **Demonstrate Content Area Skills** — Cite historical sources | Student demonstrates an independent and sophisticated mastery of all required skills, going beyond the requirements of the assignment and integrating other content area skills. | Student demonstrates proficient mastery of all required skills and works independently to accomplish the assignment. | Student demonstrates beginning mastery of skills and works independently to accomplish the assignment. | Student demonstrates beginning mastery of skills when guided by the teacher to accomplish the assignment. | |

## HABIT 5: COMMUNICATION

| | Exceeding the Standard | Meeting the Standard | Approaching the Standard | Emerging Competency | No Evidence |
|---|---|---|---|---|---|
| **Communicate Main Idea** — Write a strong thesis and topic sentences | Student communicates main idea clearly. Main idea is provocative. | Student communicates main idea clearly. | Student communicates main idea. | Student needs to develop and clarify main idea. | |
| **Organize Thoughts** — Follow persuasive essay structure | Student has organized thoughts clearly and all parts flow. | Student has organized thoughts clearly and developed all required parts. | Student needs to reorganize thoughts for clarity and/or add missing parts. | Student needs to organize thoughts for clarity. | |
| **Use Language to Support Understanding** | Student work has no grammatical/spelling errors. | Student work has few grammatical/spelling errors. | Student work is understandable despite grammatical/spelling errors. | Student work is difficult to understand due to grammatical/spelling errors. | |

# East Palo Alto High School Student Guide

*Redefining the three Rs:*
*Respecting differences,*
*recognizing strengths,*
*and realizing dreams*

**Aspire Public Schools**

### STUDENT GUIDE FOR 2002–2003

OUR MISSION: As a united community, we will engage, educate and empower all students for academic and personal success.

### GUIDING PRINCIPLES FOR EAST PALO ALTO HIGH SCHOOL

- Learning occurs within the context of activities that produce something authentic and valuable.

### Students

- Teachers focus on personalized learning that taps students' passions, develops their interests, supports their learning and builds on their potential.
- All students participate in heterogeneous grouping in all classes.
- Our integrated, project-based curriculum focuses on authentic activities and based on school-wide standards.
- School-wide standards (The 5 Habits) prepare students for college and social activism. Standards are rigorous, meaningful, focused on depth rather than breadth and guide curriculum and assessment.
- Student performance relative to school-wide standards is measured using authentic assessments.
- Every student has a significant relationship with an adult, allowing for individual attention and different styles of learning.

## Teachers

- Teaching is supported through necessary resources and professional development.
- As a school we accept the responsibility for assessing each student's learning needs and providing the necessary individual support.
- We participate in a culture of collaboration, self and group reflection, and self and peer evaluation.
- We are committed to upholding a democratic and shared decision-making process involving staff, students, parents and other community members.

## Community

- We believe that education is a long-term commitment that must include the community in a reciprocal relationship.
- Learning occurs beyond the school setting. We welcome parents, mentors, employers, and other community members who wish to participate in student learning.
- The various cultures of the community are respected and examined. This process of understanding other cultures helps shape the social and academic culture of the school.

## GRADUATION REQUIREMENTS

To be eligible to graduate from East Palo Alto High School, students must:

1. Complete and pass all the required classes below
2. Complete and successfully exhibit all 9 tasks in the student portfolio
3. Pass the California State High School Exit Exam

| Year One Required Classes | Year Two Required Classes |
|---|---|
| Humanities (Psychology, Sociology, Cultural History) | Humanities (World History and World Literature) |
| Integrated Math I | Integrated Math II |
| Biology/Chemistry I | Biology/Chemistry II |
| Spanish | Spanish |
| Elective | Elective |
| Lab | Lab |
| Advisory | Advisory |
| Community Based Learning | Community Based Learning |

**Additional Courses:**

Independent Studies

On-Line Learning

Community College Classes

Sports, Clubs and Extracurricular Activities

| Year Three Required Classes | Year Four Required Classes |
|---|---|
| Humanities (History and Literature of the Americas) | Humanities (Government, Economics and Literature) |
| Integrated Math III | Senior Seminars |
| Physics | Portfolio Work |
| Elective | Advisory |
| Lab | Internship |
| Advisory | |
| Internship | |

**Additional Courses:**

Advanced Courses in Math, Science and Spanish

Independent Studies

On-Line Learning

Community College Classes

Sports, Clubs and Extracurricular Activities

## THE GRADUATION PORTFOLIO

- Students will work closely with their Advisor to create a portfolio of work that represents their knowledge and skills. Students will present each of the portfolio pieces to a grading panel that will consist of teachers, students, and community members. Completion of the portfolio will serve as evidence for graduation.
- Each of the following TASKS needs to be included in a student's graduation portfolio.
- Each of the COMPONENTS must be included in at least one task.
- Students may complete projects in other languages; however, students should move toward demonstration of proficiency in English.

| TASKS | COMPONENTS |
|---|---|
| Autobiography | a. Technology |
| • 9th Grade: Personal Autobiography | b. Proficiency in a language other than English |
| • 10th Grade: Creative or Applied Arts | |
| • 11th Grade: Post-Graduate Plan | |
| • 12th Grade: Resume and Reflection | |
| Pure or Applied Math | |
| Social Studies Research Project | |
| Science Experiment | |
| Writing Portfolio | |
| Senior Project | |

### Schedule to Complete and Exhibit Tasks

| | Freshman Year | Sophomore Year | Junior Year | Senior Year |
|---|---|---|---|---|
| *Task to be completed during class this year* | *Autobiography:* Personal Autobiography | *Autobiography:* Creative or Applied Arts | *Autobiography:* Post-Graduate Plan | *Autobiography:* Resume and Reflection |
| | | Math | Social Studies Research Project | Senior Project |
| | | | Writing Portfolio | Science Exhibition |

*Note.* During the exhibition of the Autobiography Resume and Reflection, the graduation review panel for the student will review the entire portfolio and grant or deny graduation.

## EAST PALO ALTO HIGH SCHOOL'S 5 COMMUNITY HABITS

### Personal Responsibility

- Be Punctual
- Be Prepared
- Be Productive and Participate
- Self-Reflect

### Social Responsibility

- Collaborate Effectively
- Interact Respectfully
- Build Bridges

### Critical and Creative Thinking

- Ask
- Predict
- Investigate

- Create
- Discuss
- Connect

### Application of Knowledge

- Understand Content
- Demonstrate Content Area Skills
- Answer Questions

### Communication

- Communicate Main Ideas
- Organize Thoughts
- Use Language to Support Understanding
- Present Orally

## ADVISORY

### What is advisory?

One of our guiding principles is that at least one adult will know each student well. During the first year, students will be placed in small groups with two advisors per group acting as a team to initiate learning and conversations. The role of advisory is to keep track of and facilitate student growth. Students will earn course credits for advisory and will be assessed on a pass/fail basis.

### What is the purpose of advisory?

The purpose of advisory is to ensure that each student at our school will:

- . . . be known well by at least one adult at the school.
- . . . be supported to identify his or her strengths, passions, interests and future goals.
- . . . be connected, along with their family, to necessary resources in the community.
- . . . be supported and assisted with completion of graduation and portfolio requirements.
- . . . be assisted to select his or her service learning opportunities, work internships and early college coursework.
- . . . have his or her community connections, such as work, clubs and hobbies, welcomed and known.
- . . . have a Personalized Learning Plan, including course selection and scheduling, that is developed and designed with his or her advisors and family.
- . . . have his or her progress monitored and success supported systematically, with intense scrutiny of academic performance by his /her advisor.

- . . . have a forum for student voice and a safe and comfortable space in which to address issues of concern to the student, school and society.

## What is the role of an advisor?

- Facilitate advisory meetings and monitor the academic and personal progress of a small group of students.
- Keep in contact with students' families via family visits, student-led conferences, and calls to home.
- Assist students in identifying their strengths, passions, interests and future goals.
- Recognize students' needs for outside resources and connect their families to appropriate organizations in the community.
- Help students develop study skills, test taking strategies and habits of mind that are consistent with school culture.
- Support and assist students with completion of graduation and portfolio requirements.
- Help students select service learning opportunities, work internships and early college coursework, as well as plan for college and future careers.
- Know and welcome students' community connections, such as work, clubs and hobbies.
- Develop a Personalized Learning Plan for each student with his/her family and handle any and all course scheduling requests.
- Provide a forum for student voice and a safe and comfortable space in which to address issues of concern to the student, school and society.
- Be an advocate for students.

## What is the curriculum of advisory?

The following topics may be covered in advisory:

- Work habits/study skills
- Test preparation
- Groupwork skills
- Discussion/participation skills
- College preparation
- Career development
- Portfolio work
- Race/gender/class issues
- Cultural awareness and knowledge
- Conflict resolution/peer mediation
- Health (drugs, alcohol, fitness, nutrition, eating disorders)
- Image/self identity issues
- Sex education
- Current events (local, national, international, personal and school)

# East Palo Alto High School Daily Schedule 2003–2004

| | MONDAY | TUESDAY | WEDNESDAY | THURSDAY | FRIDAY |
|---|---|---|---|---|---|
| 8:00–9:30AM Block 1 | A | B | 8:00–8:55AM W1 Wednesday Block 1 | A | B |
| | | | 9:00–9:55AM W2 Wednesday Block 2 | | |
| 9:40–11:10AM Block 2 | C | D | | C | D |
| | | | 10:00–10:55AM W3 Wednesday Block 3 | | |
| | | | Brunch 10:55–11:15AM | | |
| 11:10–11:50AM Lunch | | | 11:15AM–12:10PM W4 Wednesday Block 4 | 11:10–11:50AM Lunch | |
| 11:50AM–1:20PM Block 3 | E | F | | E | F |
| | | | 12:15–12:45PM AD Advisory | | |
| | | | 12:50PM School Ends | | |
| 1:25–2:25PM Challenge Period | CP | CP | 1:30–4:30PM Staff Meeting | CP | CP |
| 2:30–3:30PM Advisory/ Tutorial | AD Tutorial | AD Tutorial | | AD Tutorial | AD Advisory |
| 3:40–4:45PM Bulldog Period | BP | BP | | BP | BP |

# Notes

## Chapter 1

1. The school originally was named East Palo Alto High School. As described in this book, the school was renamed East Palo Alto Academy when it added an elementary school some years later. For consistency, we have called the school East Palo Alto Academy throughout this book.

2. Kente stoles are made of kente cloth from Ghana. Historically, it was the cloth of kings worn for important occasions. In the United States, kente stoles are draped around the neck and worn by many African American students during graduation ceremonies.

3. In the Polynesian community, leis made of candy, money, and flowers are draped around the necks of graduating students. It is not uncommon to see students with more than a dozen leis piled high around their necks.

4. A study released in 2000 by the Haas Center for Community Service at Stanford tracked 8th-graders from Ravenswood City School District entering the local comprehensive high school district. Four years later, 36% of these students had graduated on time from the high school district.

5. U.S. Census data, 2000.

6. Anning (1998).

7. East Palo Alto Academy's mission is to serve the same neighborhoods as its chartering district and is open to all of East Palo Alto residents as well as residents of Menlo Park neighborhoods east of Interstate 101. If there are spaces available, students from outside this area can attend East Palo Alto Academy. For each year in which the number of applicants exceeds the number of spaces available, admission is determined by lottery. Priority in the lottery is given to residents of East Palo Alto and east Menlo Park, and to siblings of current students.

8. Blockbusting was a practice used by real estate agents and developers in the United States to encourage White property owners to sell their homes by giving the impression that minority groups (such as African Americans) were moving into their previously racially segregated neighborhood. See Keating (1994).

9. Henry M. Gunn High School in Palo Alto typically is ranked in the top 100 schools in the nation according to both *Newsweek* and *U.S. News and World Report*. Both Gunn and Palo Alto High School traditionally are ranked in the top 100 schools in California.

10. Center for a New Generation was created by Stanford provost Condoleezza Rice to bring music and other after-school enrichment opportunities to East Palo Alto youth.

11. For one account of the founding of the school, see Vanides (2001).

12. See Hart & Burr (1996).

13. J. D. Berry (2001).

14. Ravenswood City School District, a K–8 school district, approved the initial charter for EPAA, then named East Palo Alto High School. When the charter law changed in 2005 and elementary districts could no longer charter high schools, Ravenswood's board approved a new K–12 charter for EPAA and plans were made to open a sister elementary school.

15. East Palo Alto Academy is located in Menlo Park, one-fourth of a mile from the East Palo Alto border. In 2008, San Mateo County voters passed a school bond for the Sequoia Union High School District to fund the construction of a new high school building for East Palo Alto Academy in East Palo Alto.

16. Darling-Hammond (1997).

17. Meier (1995).

18. EPAA moved to 2-year advisory loops (9–10 and 11–12) in 2014.

19. Alvarez (1994).

20. All of the students' names are pseudonyms.

21. Ladson-Billings (2007).

## Chapter 2

1. A *coyote* is a person who helps immigrants cross the border illegally. Families pay up to U.S. $5,000 per person for the chance to get to America.

2. Mauer & King (2007).

3. Durand (2014).

4. The only streets that cross Highway 101 and San Francisquito creek to connect Palo Alto and East Palo Alto are University Avenue and Embarcadero Road, along with the rarely traveled Newell Road, which crosses a tiny, old one-lane bridge.

5. "East Palo Alto Welcomes Opening of New California Bank" (2002).

6. Albach (2007).

7. California Retail Survey, 1995–2000.

8. See www.muralmusicarts.org.

9. Much research indicates that these motivators are stronger for expert teachers than merit pay bonuses or other individualistic, material incentives. See Darling-Hammond (2013).

10. For the first year, Adrian Kirk served as co-principal and taught Spanish for Native Speakers. After the first year, Nicky remained as sole principal when Adrian left to lead another Aspire school.

11. Merrow (2004).

12. EdSource (2001), p. 1.

13. Rogers, Terriquez, Valladares, & Oakes (2006), p. 10.

14. Orfield & Lee (2006).

15. The national average funding level was $10,469 per pupil in 2006–2007 (Baker, Sciarra, & Farrie, 2010).

16. Darling-Hammond (2003); Oakes (2003).

17. Rogers, Bertrand, Freelon, & Fanelli (2011).

18. Richburg & Surdin (2008).

19. Kowal (2011).

20. California budget for higher education, 2014–15 (www.ebudget.ca.gov/BudgetSummary/HigherEducation.pdf).

21. California Department of Education Data and Statistics (www.cde.ca.gov/ds).

22. Darling-Hammond (2004).

23. The alternative NCES calculation (averaged freshman graduation rate) dropped from 73% to 71% (Rumberger & Taylor, 2013).

24. www.usa.com/east-palo-alto-ca.htm.

25. Grattet & Hayes (2013).

## Chapter 3

1. Darling-Hammond, Milliken, & Ross (2006).

2. A *quinceañera* is a celebration of a girl's "sweet fifteen" birthday.

3. Rosenberg (2003).

## Chapter 4

1. Student ambassadors were a group of students who were organized to greet and educate guests—both visitors interested in the school and prospective students—about the school.

2. As determined by the Measures of Academic Progress (MAP) test given at the beginning of the 9th-grade year.

3. For more discussion of the importance of emotional intelligence, see Goleman (1995).

4. For more information on 21st-century skills, see Wagner (2008).

5. Ali (2008).

6. Students' participation in this program was spearheaded by Tina Ehsanipour and Marysol de la Torre, who helped raise funds and led the school's journey, building curriculum around the civil rights lessons it offered. For more information, see sojournproject.org.

7. For more information, see www.babec.org/node/19.

8. Powell, Farrar, & Cohen (1999).

9. Alexander, Entwisle, & Olson (2007).

10. Stanford University's Upward Bound was a federally funded program for low-income or first-generation, college-bound students that provided an intensive residential summer experience at Stanford University, including college-preparatory classes and tutoring. The tutoring program continued throughout the academic year. Stanford Upward Bound subsequently changed its name to the Stanford College Preparation Program and became an NGO (nongovernmental organization) that served only EPAA students. Unfortunately, changes in federal regulatory requirements that staff viewed as ethically questionable led to Stanford canceling the program.

11. Woodrow Wilson Early College Newsletter (August/September 2008, www.woodrow.org/about/past-programs/#ECHS).

12. Berger, Adelman, & Cole (2010).

13. "AmeriCorps is a program of the Corporation for National and Community Service, an independent federal agency whose mission is to improve lives, strengthen communities, and foster civic engagement through service and volunteering. Each

year, AmeriCorps offers 75,000 opportunities for adults of all ages and backgrounds to serve through a network of partnerships with local and national nonprofit groups" (www. energycorps.ncat.org/americorps.php).

14. Woodrow Wilson Early College Newsletter (August/September 2008, www. woodrow.org/earlycollege).

15. In 2006, passing the CAHSEE in English and mathematics became a requirement for all California high school students. The CAHSEE was abolished in October 2015 with diplomas awarded retroactively to those who had previously been prevented from graduating because of their performance on the test.

## Chapter 5

1. Black & Wiliam (1998); Hattie (2009).

2. Perkins (1993).

3. For more information about the New York Performance Standards Consortium, see performanceassessment.org/.

4. Cisneros, 1991.

5. See, for example, Gardner (1993).

6. This theory is outlined in Maslow (1954).

7. Sheltered English instruction consists of delivering the same content to English learners as students in nonsheltered classes receive. Curriculum is more scaffolded and focuses on English vocabulary development and contextual understanding.

8. For more information, see www.charlesarmstrong.org.

## Chapter 6

1. For a summary, see Oakes (2005).

2. Wiggins & McTighe (2005).

3. Marzano (2003).

4. Delpit (1995).

5. Delpit (1987).

6. Delpit (1997, pp. 126–127).

7. See Gardner (1993); Tomlinson (2001).

8. Fountas & Pinnell (2006).

9. Cohen & Lotan (2014).

10. Cohen & Lotan (1994).

11. cgi.stanford.edu/group/pci/cgi-bin/site.cgi

12. Cohen & Lotan (1997).

13. For a summary, see Cohen & Lotan (2014).

14. See, for example, Darling-Hammond (2002); Darling-Hammond et al. (2006).

## Chapter 7

1. STEP was named as one of the top four secondary teacher preparation programs in the country by Arthur Levine (2006) and was ranked number 3 by *U.S. News & World Report* in 2008. Stanford's School of Education has been ranked number 1 many times by *U.S. News & World Report*, including in 2008.

2. Special day classes are settings for special education students that are segregated from other classes and that generally offer a very different curriculum and set of activities.

3. Cuban (2001).

4. For a summary of what they learned, see Darling-Hammond & Ifill-Lynch (2006).

5. Personal communication from D. Meier to L. Darling-Hammond.

6. Haynes (1995); National Board for Professional Teaching Standards (2001).

7. Darling-Hammond (2002).

8. Gladwell (2000); Collins (2001).

9. Collins (2001).

10. EPAA had limited administration and nonteaching staff made up of the principal, vice principal, an office manager and her assistant, and a custodian.

11. Humphrey, Koppich, & Hough (2005).

12. Ronfeldt, Loeb, & Wyckoff (2013).

13. B. Berry (2009).

14. Ingersoll & Kralik (2004); Smith & Ingersoll, 2004.

15. A *taquería* is a Mexican restaurant specializing in tacos made from small corn tortillas piled high with meat and salsa.

## Chapter 8

1. According to the National Center for Higher Education, the proportion of California high school graduates enrolling immediately in 2- or 4-year colleges anywhere in the country was 43.7% in 2004. Although that had increased to 61.7% by 2010 (the most recent year available), EPAA still exceeds that rate by a large margin. See NCHEMS Information Center at www.higheredinfo.org.

2. It is worth noting that although 2-year college is available to all high school graduates in California, the process of applying, getting admitted, and passing placement tests is so substantial that many high school graduates do not make good on their intentions to enroll. EPAA students completed this process.

3. For 67% of EPAA students from 2001–2005, neither parent had graduated from high school. Over the years this percentage has ranged from 60 to 70% in each cohort.

4. The SAT and ACT are both college entrance exams given across the nation. All students applying to most U.S. colleges and universities need to take one of these exams.

5. For more information, see www.collegesummit.org.

6. One year Nicky went with students to take the test and was proud that she improved her high school score by 20 points.

7. The FAFSA is required of all college-going students who apply for federal financial aid.

8. Neroulias (2004).

9. Lewin (2008).

10. "Boost Value of Pell Grants" (2006).

11. AB 540 is a California law that provides a waiver of the out-of-state tuition fees at California's public colleges and universities for any student—regardless of immigration status—who has completed 3 years at a California high school and has attained a high school diploma. In 2010, California passed the Dream Act, allowing for undocumented students who attend University of California and California State Universities to be eligible for state funding in the form of state grants and educational loans.

12. *Martinez et al. v. UC Board of Regents et al.*

13. Bidwell (2011).

14. schoolssocietyandequity.blogspot.com/2008/09/hispanic-immigrant-college-students.html

## Chapter 9

1. dq.cde.ca.gov/dataquest/CohortRates/GradRates.aspx?Agg=S&Topic=Graduates &TheYear=2012-13&cds=41690620126722&RC=School&Subgroup=Ethnic/Racial.

2. For an account of the changes at Hillsdale, see Darling-Hammond & Friedlaender (2006). See also hhs.schoolloop.com/inthenews.

3. Mathews (2011).

4. Like all new schools, EPAA did not receive an API score when it was rechartered as a new high school under the aegis of the Sequoia Union High School District (following discontinuation of the elementary school). California discontinued API scores after 2013.

5. An analysis of the "similar" high schools matched to EPAA by the California Department of Education (those in the state with the lowest socioeconomic status index) found that of those 100 schools, 90% had fewer than half as many English learners and nearly all had a far lower share of low-income students. All of the "similar" schools had a higher parent education index than EPAA.

6. Cohen & Lotan (2014).

7. Kagan, Kagan, & Kagan (2007).

8. For examples, see Darling-Hammond et al. (2006) and Darling-Hammond (2011).

9. For examples of productive principal preparation models and policy supports, see Darling-Hammond, Meyerson, LaPointe, & Orr (2009).

10. For more detail, see Darling-Hammond & Adamson (2014).

# References

Albach, B. (2007, August 17). Growth causes stores worries: Redevelopment in EPA area may relocate business. *Palo Alto Daily News*. Retrieved from unified--communications.tmcnet.com/content.aspx?article=/news/2007/08/17/2870325.htm

Alexander, K. L., Entwisle, D. R., & Olson, L. S. (2007). Lasting consequences of the summer learning gap. *American Sociological Review, 72*, 167–180.

Ali, L. (2008, May 18). The revolutionaries of San Mateo: Hillsdale High. *Newsweek*. Retrieved from www.newsweek.com/san-mateos-hillsdale-high-why-small-schools-work-90251

Alvarez, J. (1994). *In the time of the butterflies*. Chapel Hill, NC: Algonquin Books.

Anning, V. (1998, January/February). Reversal of misfortune. *Stanford Magazine*. Retrieved from www.stanfordalumni.org/news/magazine/1998/janfeb/articles/epa.html

Baker, B. D., Sciarra, D. G., & Farrie, D. (2010). *Is school funding fair? A national report card*. Newark, NJ: Education Law Center.

Berger, A., Adelman, N., & Cole, S. (2010). The early college high school initiative: An overview of five evaluation years. *Peabody Journal of Education, 85*(3), 333–347. doi: 10.1080/0161956X.2010.491697

Berry, B. (2009). *Keeping the promise: Recruiting, retaining, and growing effective teachers for high-needs schools*. Raleigh, NC: Center for Teaching Quality.

Berry, J. D. (2001). High school coming back to Ravenswood. *Palo Alto Weekly*. Retrieved from www.paloaltoonline.com/weekly/morgue/news/2001_Feb_21.CHARTER.html

Bidwell, A. (2011, June 6). Supreme Court upholds in-state tuition for undocumented students. *The Daily Californian*. Retrieved from www.dailycal.org/2011/06/06/supreme-court-upholds-in-state-tuition-for-undocumented-students/

Black, P., & Wiliam, D. (1998). Assessment and classroom learning. *Assessment and Education: Principles, Policy and Practice, 5*(1), 7–75.

Boost value of Pell grants. (2006). *The Ledger.com*. Retrieved from www.theledger.com/article/20061218/NEWS/612180334

Cisneros, S. (1991). *The house on Mango Street*. New York, NY: Vintage Books.

Cohen, E. G., & Lotan, R. (1994). *Designing groupwork: Strategies for the heterogeneous classroom*. New York, NY: Teachers College Press.

Cohen, E. G., & Lotan R. (1997). *Working for equity in heterogeneous classrooms: Sociological theory in action*. New York, NY: Teachers College Press.

Cohen, E. G., & Lotan, R. (2014). *Designing groupwork: Strategies for the heterogeneous classroom* (3rd ed.). New York, NY: Teachers College Press.

Collins, J. (2001). *Good to great: Why some companies make the leap . . . and others don't*. New York, NY: HarperCollins.

Cuban, L. (2001). *How can I fix it? Finding solutions and managing dilemmas: An educator's road map.* New York, NY: Teachers College Press.

Darling-Hammond, L. (1997). *The right to learn: A blueprint for creating schools that work.* San Francisco, CA: Jossey-Bass.

Darling-Hammond, L. (2002). *Redesigning schools: What matters and what works.* Stanford, CA: School Redesign Network, Stanford University.

Darling-Hammond, L. (2003). Access to quality teaching: An analysis of inequality in California's public schools. *Santa Clara Law Review, 43,* 101–239.

Darling-Hammond, L. (2004). From "separate but equal" to "No Child Left Behind": The collision of new standards and old inequalities. In D. Meier & G. Wood (Eds.), *Many children left behind* (pp. 3–32). Boston, MA: Beacon Press.

Darling-Hammond, L. (2006). *Powerful teacher education. Lessons from exemplary programs.* San Francisco, CA: Jossey-Bass.

Darling-Hammond, L. (2011). Effective teaching as a civil right: How building instructional capacity can help close the achievement gap. *Voices in Urban Education, 31,* 44–58. Retrieved from vue.annenberginstitute.org/sites/default/files/issues/VUE31.pdf

Darling-Hammond, L. (2013). *Getting teacher evaluation right: What really matters for effectiveness and improvement.* New York, NY: Teachers College Press.

Darling-Hammond, L., & Adamson, F. (2014). *Beyond the bubble test: How performance assessments support 21st century learning.* San Francisco, CA: Jossey-Bass.

Darling-Hammond, L., & Friedlaender, D. (2006). *Windows on conversions: Hillsdale High School case study.* Stanford, CA: School Redesign Network, Stanford University. Retrieved from edpolicy.stanford.edu/publications/products/783

Darling-Hammond, L., & Ifill-Lynch, O. (2006, February). If they'd only do their work! *Educational Leadership, 63,*(5), 8–13.

Darling-Hammond, L., Meyerson, D., LaPointe, M., & Orr, M. T. (2009). *Preparing principals for a changing world: Lessons from exemplary leadership development programs.* San Francisco, CA: Jossey-Bass.

Darling-Hammond, L., Milliken, M., & Ross, P. (2006). High school size, organization and content: What matters for student success? *Brookings Papers on Education Policy.* Washington, DC: The Brookings Institution.

Delpit, L. (1995). *Other people's children: White teachers, students of color, and other cultural conflicts in the classroom.* New York, NY: New Press.

Delpit, L. (1987). Skills and other dilemmas of a progressive black educator. *Equity and Choice, 3*(2), 9–14.

Delpit, L. (1993). The silenced dialogue: Power and pedagogy in educating other people's children. In L. Weis & M. Find (Eds.), *Beyond silenced voices: Class, race, and gender in United States schools* (pp. 119–142). New York, NY: Oxford University Press.

Durand, M. (2014, January 13). San Mateo County had 15 homicides last year: Most murders took place in East Palo Alto. *San Mateo Daily Journal.* Retrieved from www.smdailyjournal.com/articles/lnews/2014-01-13/san-mateo-county-had-15-homicides-last-year-most-murders-took-place-in-east-palo-alto/1776425116409.html

East Palo Alto welcomes opening of new California Bank & Trust branch. (2002, April 4). BNET Business Network. www.thefreelibrary.com/East+Palo+Alto+Welcomes+Opening+of+New+California+Bank+%26+Trust+Branch.-a084403355

EdSource. (2001, October). *How California ranks: A comparison of education expenditures.* Palo Alto, CA: Author.

Fountas, I., & Pinnell, G. S. (2006). *Leveled books (K–8): Matching texts to readers for effective teaching*. Portsmouth, NH: Heinemann.

Gardner, H. (1993). *Frames of mind: The theory of multiple intelligences*. New York, NY: Basic Books.

Gladwell, M. (2000). *The tipping point: How little things can make a big difference*. Boston, MA: Little, Brown.

Goleman, D. (1995). *Emotional intelligence: Why it can matter more than IQ*. New York, NY: Bantam Books.

Grattet, R., & Hayes, J. (2013, June). California's changing prison population. San Francisco, CA: Public Policy Institute of California. Retrieved from www.ppic.org/main/publication_show.asp?i=702

Hart, G., & Burr, S. (1996, September). The story of California's charter school legislation. *Phi Delta Kappan, 78*(1), 37–40.

Hattie, J. (2009). *Visible learning: A synthesis of over 800 meta-analyses relating to achievement*. New York, NY: Routledge.

Haynes, D. D. (1995). One teacher's experience with National Board assessment. *Educational Leadership, 52*(8), 58–60.

Humphrey, D. C., Koppich, J. E., & Hough, H. J. (2005). *Sharing the wealth: National Board certified teachers and the students who need them most*. *Education Policy Analysis Archives, 13*(18). doi: dx.doi.org/10.14507/epaa.v13n18.2005

Hyler, M. E. (2007). *Membership and marginalization: How school structures make a difference* (Unpublished doctoral dissertation). Stanford University, Stanford, CA.

Ingersoll, R., & Kralik, J. M. (2004). *The impact of mentoring on teacher retention: What the research says*. Denver, CO: Education Commission of the States.

Kagan, L., Kagan, M., & Kagan, S. (2007). *Cooperative learning structures for teambuilding*. Heatherton, Australia: Hawker Brownlow Education.

Keating, W. D. (1994). *The suburban racial dilemma: Housing and neighborhoods*. Philadelphia, PA: Temple University Press.

Kowal, T. (2011, June 6). The role of the prison guards union in California's troubled prison system. Retrieved from ordinary-gentlemen.com/timkowal/2011/06/the-role-of-the-prison-guards-union-in-californias-troubled-prison-system/

Ladson-Billings, G. (2007). Now they're wet: Hurricane Katrina as a metaphor for social and educational neglect. In S. P. Robinson & M. C. Brown II (Eds.), *The children that Hurricane Katrina left behind: Schooling context, professional preparation, and community politics* (pp. 14– 20). New York, NY: Peter Lang.

Levine, A. (2006). Educating school teachers. Woodrow Wilson National Fellowship Foundation. Retrieved from www.edschools.org/teacher_report.htm

Lewin, T. (2008, December 3). College may become unaffordable for most in U.S. *New York Times*. Retrieved from nytimes.com/2008/12/03/education/03college.html

Marzano, R. J. (2003). *What works in schools: Translating research into action*. Alexandria, VA: Association for Supervision & Curriculum.

Maslow, A. (1954). *Motivation and personality*. New York, NY: Harper.

Mathews, J. (2011). Alma mater's improvements knock me sideways. *Washington Post*. www.washingtonpost.com/local/education/alma-maters-improvements-knock-me-sideways/2011/11/03/gIQAcuRKtM_story.html

Mauer, M., & King, R. S. (2007). Uneven justice: State rates of incarceration by race and ethnicity. Washington, DC: Sentencing Project. Retrieved from www.sentencingproject.org/doc/publications/rd_stateratesofincbyraceandethnicity.pdf

Meier, D. (1995). *The power of their ideas: Lessons from a small school in Harlem*. Boston, MA: Beacon Press.

Merrow, J. (2004). *First to worst.* A film from Learning Matters. Retrieved from learningmatters.tv/blog/documentaries/watch-first-to-worst/651/

National Board for Professional Teaching Standards. (2001). *The impact of National Board certification on teachers: A survey of National Board certified teachers and assessors.* Arlington, VA: Author.

Neroulias, N. (2004, December 21). EPA High prepares first graduating class for college. *San Mateo County Times.*

Oakes, J. (2003). Education inadequacy, inequality, and failed state policy: A synthesis of expert reports prepared for *Williams v. State of California.* Retrieved from www.decentschools.org/expert_reports/oakes_report.pdf

Oakes, J. (2005). *Keeping track: How schools structure inequality* (2nd ed.). New Haven, CT: Yale University Press.

Orfield, G., & Lee, C. (2006). *Racial transformation and the changing nature of segregation.* Harvard, MA: Civil Rights Project at Harvard University.

Perkins, D. (1993). Teaching for understanding. *American Educator, 17*(3), 8, 28–35.

Rogers, J., Bertrand, M., Freelon, R., & Fanelli, S. (2011). *Free fall: Educational opportunities in 2011.* Los Angeles: UCLA Institute for Democracy, Education, and Access.

Powell, A. G., Farrar, E., & Cohen, D. K. (1999). *The shopping mall high school: Winners and losers in the educational marketplace.* Boston, MA: Houghton Mifflin.

Richburg, K. & Surdin, A. (2008, May 5). Fiscal pressures lead some states to release inmates early. *Washington Post.* Retrieved from www.washingtonpost.com/wp-dyn/content/article/2008/05/04/AR2008050402054.html

Rogers, J., Terriquez, V., Valladares, S., & Oakes, J. (2006). *California educational opportunity report—Roadblocks to college.* Los Angeles, CA: UC All Campus Consortium on Research for Diversity.

Ronfeldt, M., Loeb, S., & Wyckoff, J. (2013). How teacher turnover harms student achievement. *American Educational Research Journal, 50*(1), 4–36. doi:10.3102/0002831212463813

Rosenberg, M. B. (2003). *Nonviolent communication: A language of life* (2nd ed.). Encinitas, CA: Puddledancer Press.

Rumberger, R. W., & Taylor, L. (2013, August). *Updated trends in California's graduation rates through 2012* (Gevirtz Graduate School of Education Statistical Brief 16). Retrieved from www.cdrp.ucsb.edu/pubs_statbriefs.htm

Smith, T. M., & Ingersoll, R. M. (2004). What are the effects of induction and mentoring on beginning teacher turnover? *American Educational Research Journal, 41*(3), 681–714.

Tomlinson, C. A. (2001). *How to differentiate instruction in mixed-ability classrooms.* Arlington, VA: Association for Supervision & Curriculum Development.

Vanides, J. (2001). The birth of a school. Retrieved from ldt.stanford.edu/~jvanides/ED229B/EPAHS/people.htm

Wagner, T. (2008). *The global achievement gap: Why even our best schools don't teach the new survival skills our children need—and what we can do about it.* New York, NY: Basic Books.

Wiggins, G., & McTighe, J. (2005). *Understanding by design* (Expanded 2nd ed.). New York, NY: Prentice Hall.

Woodrow Wilson Early College Newsletter. (August/September 2008). Retrieved from www.woodrow.org/earlycollege

# Index

# About the Authors

*Linda Darling-Hammond* is Charles E. Ducommun Professor of Education emeritus at Stanford University, where she founded the School Redesign Network and the Stanford Center for Opportunity Policy in Education (SCOPE), and was faculty director of the Stanford Teacher Education Program (STEP). She is also president of the recently launched Learning Policy Institute, which translates research into policy and practice to support equitable and empowering learning for all youth. In these roles, she has worked with countless schools and districts on studying, developing, and scaling up new systems of practice to improve teaching and learning; and has advised many state and national leaders on creating policies to support school and teaching quality, personalized and authentic learning opportunities, student and teacher assessment practices, and educational equity. Darling-Hammond began her career as a public high school teacher, and she has cofounded a preschool and day care center as well as East Palo Alto Academy. As executive director of the National Commission on Teaching and America's Future, she led the development of the 1996 report *What Matters Most: Teaching for America's Future*, which was named one of the most influential policy reports affecting U.S. education in that decade. In 2006, Darling-Hammond was named one of the nation's ten most influential people affecting educational policy; in 2008, she served as the leader of President Barack Obama's education policy transition team. Darling-Hammond is past president of the American Educational Research Association, a two-term member of the National Board for Professional Teaching Standards, and a member of the American Association of Arts and Sciences, as well as the National Academy of Education. Among her more than 400 publications is *The Flat World and Education: How America's Commitment to Equity Will Determine Our Future*, which received the 2012 Grawemeyer Award.

*Nicky Ramos-Beban*, PhD, is a life-long educator, spending more than a decade right out of college teaching English at large, comprehensive high schools and mentoring new teachers before co-founding East Palo Alto Academy with a team of talented peers and advisors. Nicky earned her doctorate in curriculum and teacher education from Stanford University with a research focus on principal leadership and relational trust. Currently, Nicky works at the Santa Clara County Office of Education as assistant director of alternative education, helping to oversee schools for students ages 12 through 24 who have been expelled or incarcerated, or are re-entering the school system to finish their diploma and gain career skills. Nicky was an instructor in the Stanford Teacher Education Program for a decade and currently teaches classroom management in the Lurie College of Education at San Jose State University. Nicky is also a part-time writer; most recently, she wrote the cover story for *Magic* magazine's September 2015 issue.

*Rebecca Padnos Altamirano* is an educator and social entrepreneur. As one of the founders of East Palo Alto Academy, she served as both teacher and administrator, building academic programs and partnerships, including the Early College Program. After working at EPAA for seven years, she applied the school startup lessons to a new partnership, Tangelo, a software development company that helps build new ventures in markets that matter. She leads product development teams delivering mobile applications focusing on health and well-being, education, recycling, and connecting people and cultures. Rebecca earned a master's degree from Stanford School of Education and graduated from Wellesley College. As a Thomas J. Watson Fellow, she traveled throughout South America for one year studying weaving of the Andes Mountains, where she met her future husband. They live together in Menlo Park, California, with their three children.

*Maria E. Hyler* is a senior researcher and policy analyst with the Learning Policy Institute in Washington, D.C. Prior to assuming this position she was an assistant professor of teacher preparation and professional development in the Department of Teaching and Learning, Policy and Leadership at the University of Maryland, College Park. She completed her doctoral studies at Stanford University in curriculum and instruction, during which time she supported the work of East Palo Alto Academy in a variety of ways. Prior to moving to California she completed a dual degree in English and Africana studies at Wellesley College and then her MEd with teaching credential at Harvard Graduate School of Education. Maria taught 10th- and 11th-graders in Belmont, California, where she achieved National Board Certification in Adolescent Young Adult English Language Arts prior to leaving the classroom to pursue her doctoral studies. Her scholarship and teaching interests include school structures that support student achievement, best practices for preparing teachers to teach diverse student populations, and preparing equity-centered teacher educators. Maria has shared her knowledge of teaching and professional development locally and internationally through various workshops, panels, and presentations.